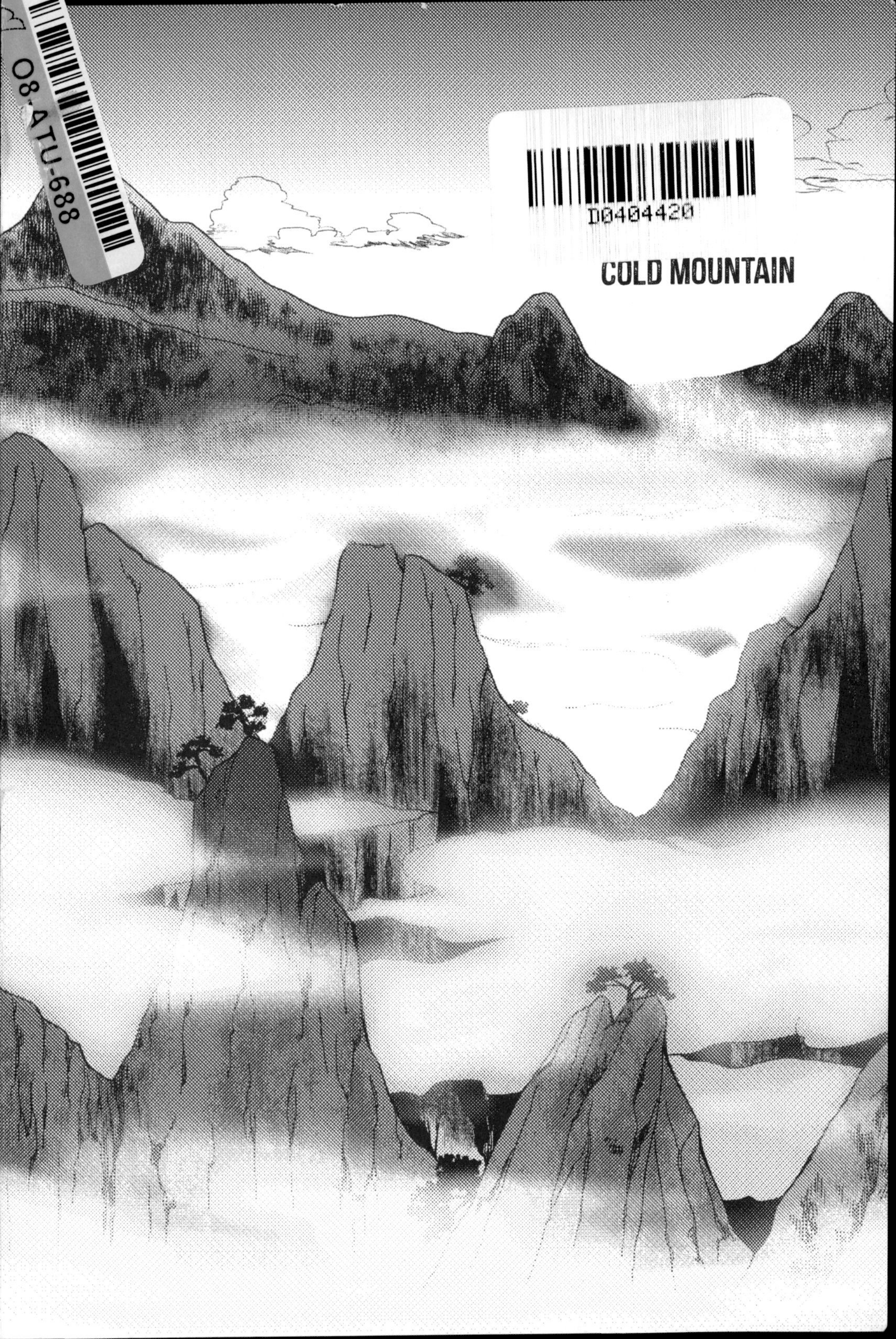

COLD MOUNTAIN

Based on *Cold Mountain Poems* by Han Shan,
translated by J. P. Seaton

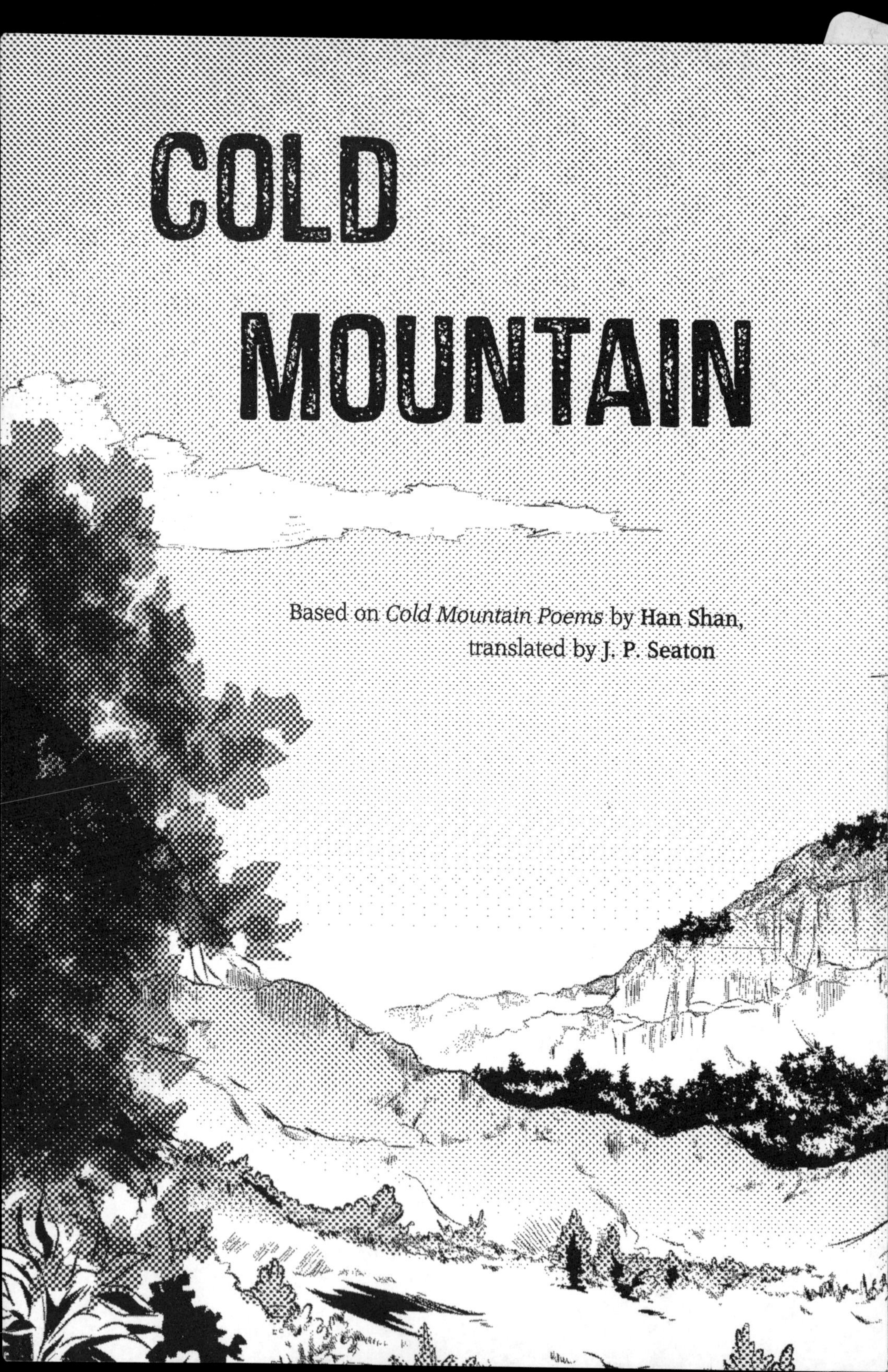

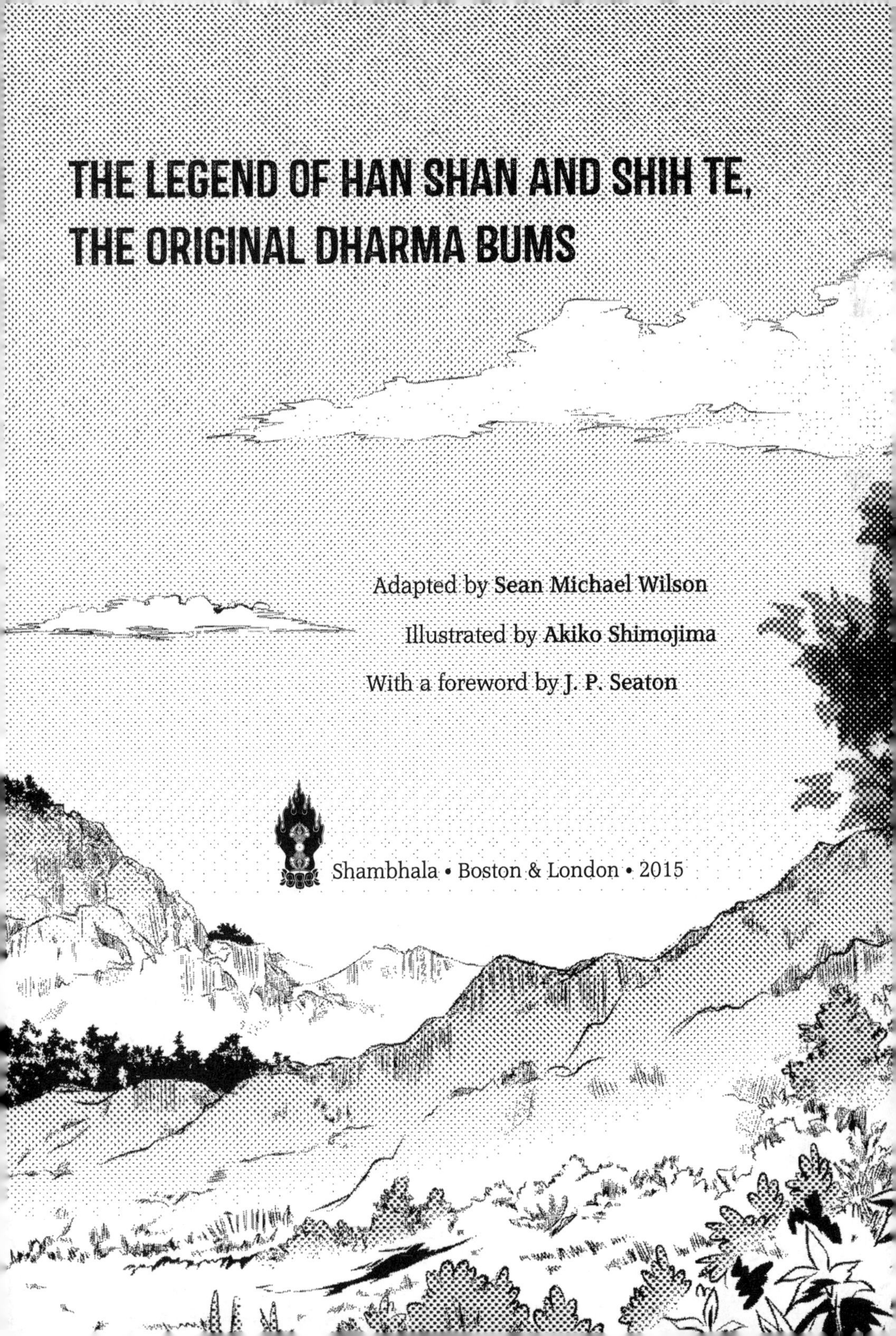

THE LEGEND OF HAN SHAN AND SHIH TE, THE ORIGINAL DHARMA BUMS

Adapted by **Sean Michael Wilson**

Illustrated by **Akiko Shimojima**

With a foreword by **J. P. Seaton**

Shambhala • Boston & London • 2015

Shambhala Publications, Inc.
Horticultural Hall
300 Massachusetts Avenue
Boston, Massachusetts 02115
www.shambhala.com

©2015 by Sean Michael Wilson
Illustrations ©2015 by Akiko Shimojima
Foreword ©2015 by J. P. Seaton

9 8 7 6 5 4 3 2 1

First Edition
Printed in the United States of America

∞This edition is printed on acid-free paper that meets the
American National Standards Institute Z39.48 Standard.
♻Shambhala Publications makes every effort to print on recycled paper.
For more information please visit www.shambhala.com.

Distributed in the United States by Penguin Random House LLC
and in Canada by Random House of Canada Ltd

Library of Congress Cataloging-in-Publication Data

Wilson, Sean Michael.
Cold Mountain: the legend of Han Shan and Shih Te, the original Dharma Bums /
based on Cold Mountain Poems by Han Shan, translated by J. P Seaton; adapted by
Sean Michael Wilson; illustrated by Akiko Shimojima; with a foreword by J. P. Seaton.
    pages   cm
ISBN 978-1-61180-179-8 (pbk.)
1. Hanshan, active 627–649—Comic books, strips, etc. 2. Shide, active 627–649—Comic
books, strips, etc. 3. Poets, Chinese—Tang dynasty, 618–907—Biography—Comic books,
strips, etc. 4. Chinese poetry—Tang dynasty, 618–907—Translations into English.
5. Zen poetry, Chinese—Translations into English. 6. Graphic novels.
I. Hanshan, active 627–649. II. Shide, active 627–649. III. Seaton, Jerome P.,
translator. IV. Shimojima, Akiko, illustrator. V. Title.
PL2321.W55 2015
895.11'309—dc23
2014028377

Foreword

Han Shan made his first big entrance on the stage of American culture in 1959 in Gary Snyder's first book, *Riprap and Cold Mountain Poems*, about the same time that Snyder himself appeared as mountain man Japhy Ryder in Jack Kerouac's novel *The Dharma Bums*. The rough good humor and the lively colloquial flavor of the Chinese poet fit Snyder's poetry perfectly, and Han Shan, like Snyder himself, went on to become an emblem of a lot of young people who thought of themselves as members of the Beat Generation (but *not* as Beatniks), then as hip (but not hippie), and finally as environmentalists or deep ecologists, and maybe Buddhist, maybe Zen.

The "real" Han Shan and his tag-along adopted street kid, Shih Te, were already a couple of thousand years old when they got to America. They were born Chinese mystics, dwellers on Cold Mountain (it's what *Han Shan* means in Chinese). In the beginning they were many men, sitting nearly naked in meditation on the cliffs at Cold Mountain (a small peak in the T'ien-t'ai Mountains).

From the beginning, many of these sitters—those who would become Han Shan and Shih Te—wrote poems to encourage those who would come after them (or become them in other lives). Sometimes their encouragement took the form of challenges that sound like pretty hefty mockery: It's a trick Zen teachers still use, one Han Shan and Shih Te may have helped to invent. In fact, by the time it had come to stand out as its own school of Buddhism, Zen had laid exclusive claim to Han Shan and Shih Te, collecting the best of the poems to be found written on or carved into the faces of the cliffs of Cold Mountain. In the bargain the two were granted official status as the Bodhisattvas, Manjushri and Samantabhadra, Buddhist saints, men who had foregone the "prize" of entering Nirvana upon achieving Enlightenment, to devote themselves for all eternity to helping the last and lowest of us (you maybe, or me?) to work ourselves free. From nameless spiritual seekers to saints, in just a few lifetimes: such is the power of spiritual commitment, poetry, and the folk process . . . the latter maybe the most important of them all.

Now, Han Shan and Shih Te have come to America again, from the pen of graphic novelist Sean Michael Wilson and illustrator Akiko Shimojima. The two unlikely looking Bodhisattvas RE-ENTER a place they've been before. These reincarnations, set to live in a world of computers and global climate change, have a lighter and a sharper feel than the several Han Shans who have come to visit us since Snyder's Beats—better suited to a folk tradition that now includes a generation that has been raised on manga and anime.

I'm delighted that they speak some lines taken from my own translations. But I see them fresh and new in Sean's work. Han Shan reminds me that he's been a feature of Japanese culture as well as Chinese for more than a thousand years already. Shih Te? Well, he's still just an orphan kid, new at being an ascetic monk. But he is, certainly, a Bodhisattva. You can offer your prayers to him, if that's what you want to do. I'll just laugh along with him.

J. P. Seaton
June 2014

COLD MOUNTAIN

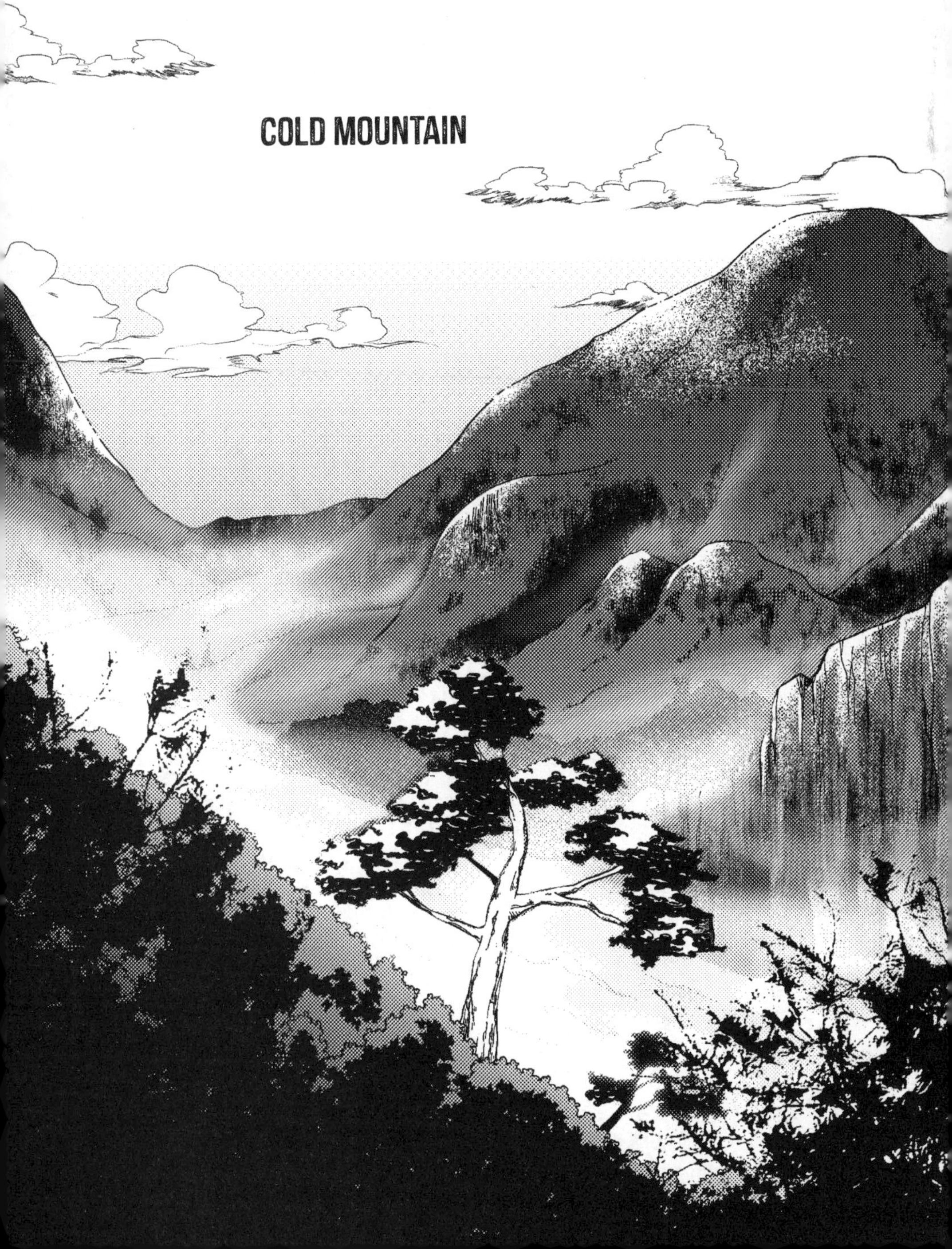

PART 1

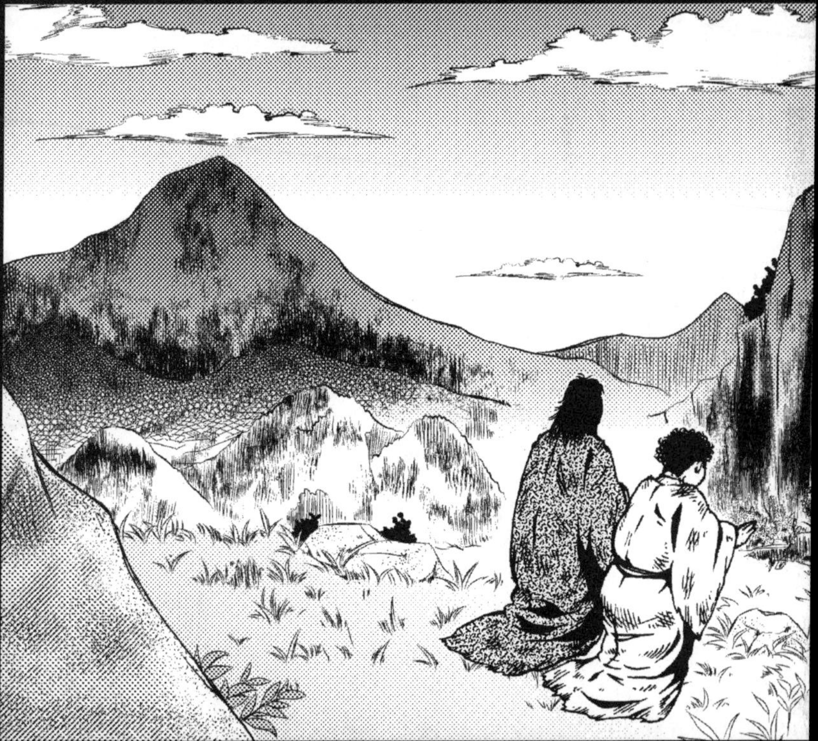

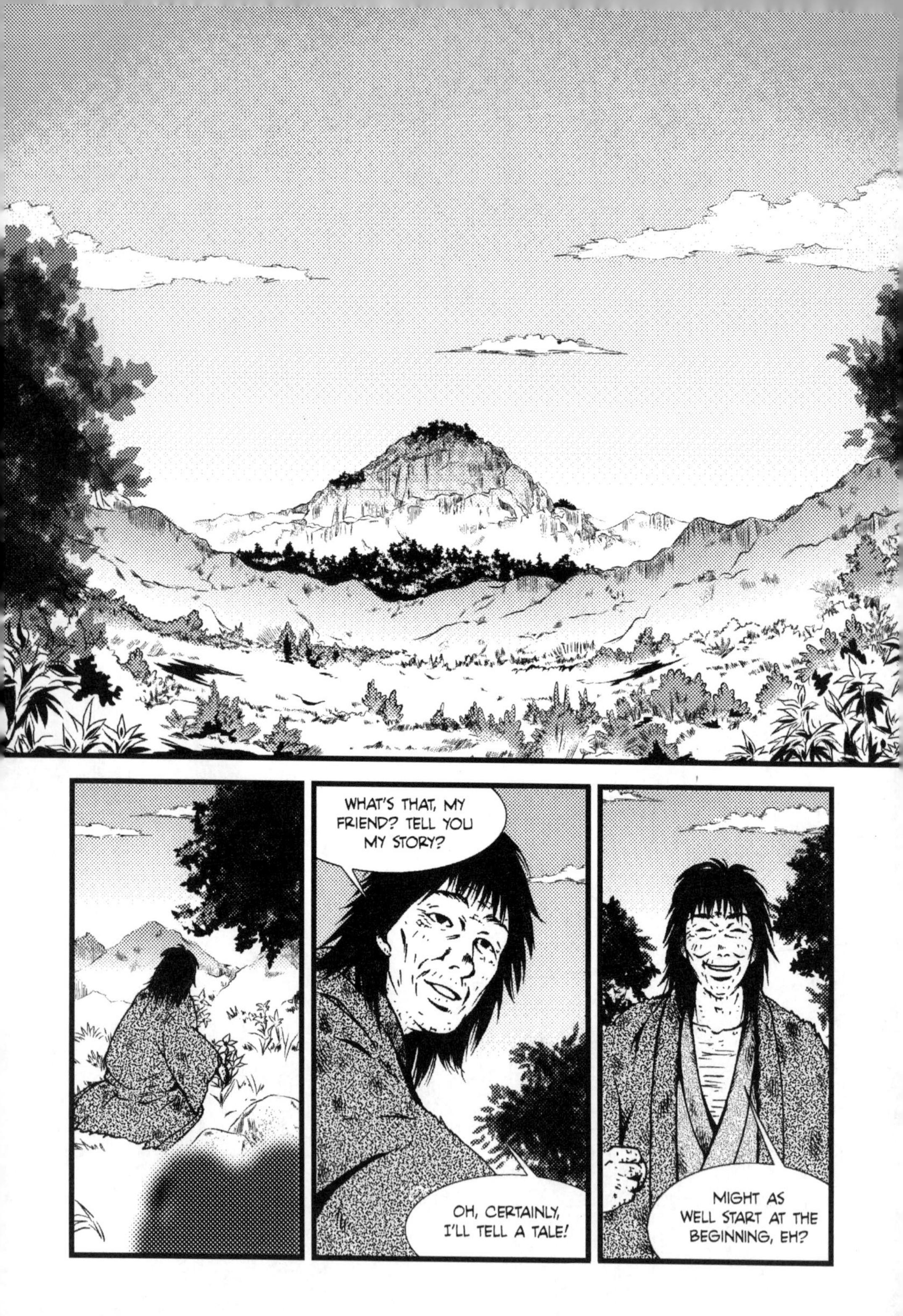
WHAT'S THAT, MY FRIEND? TELL YOU MY STORY?
OH, CERTAINLY, I'LL TELL A TALE!
MIGHT AS WELL START AT THE BEGINNING, EH?

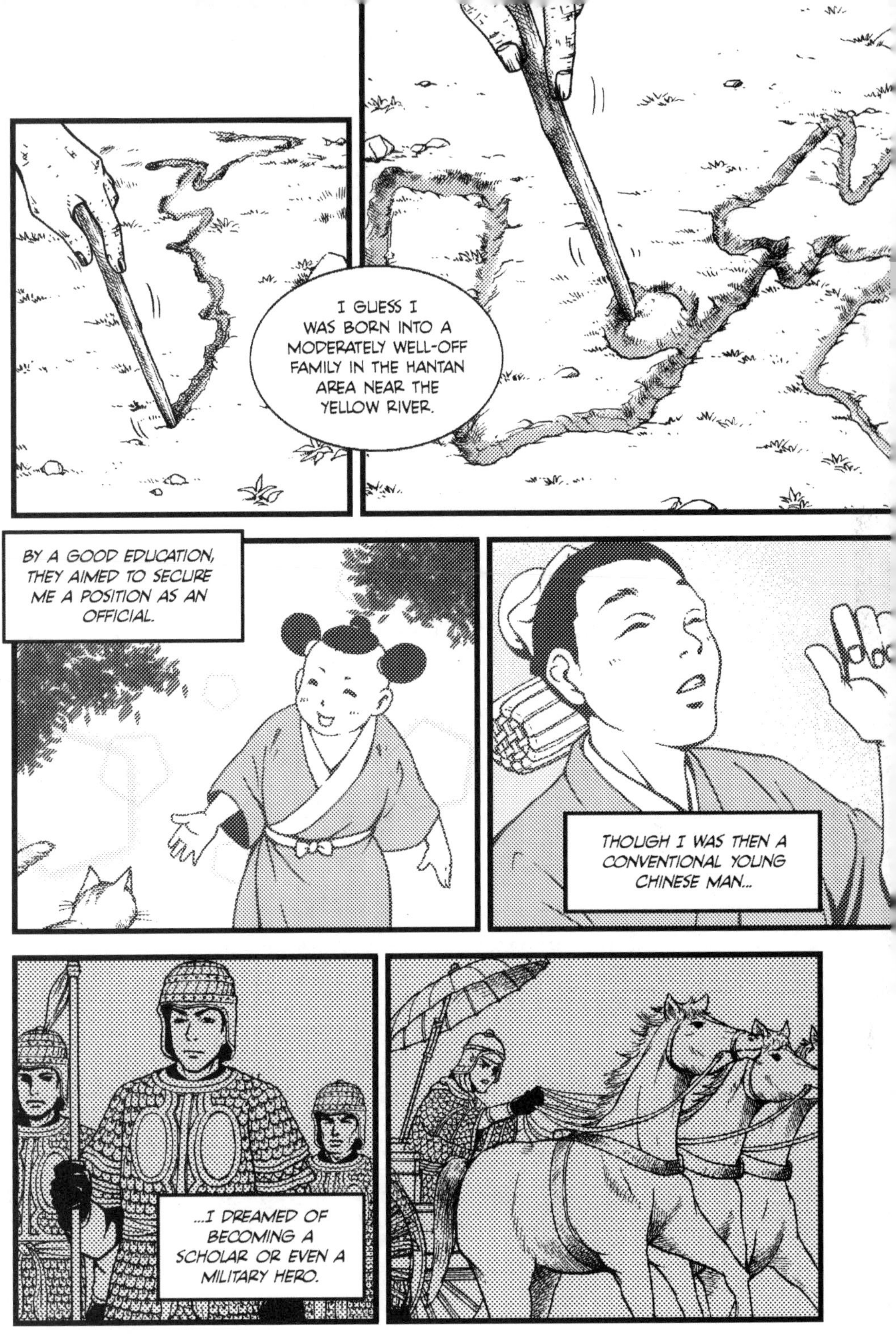
I GUESS I WAS BORN INTO A MODERATELY WELL-OFF FAMILY IN THE HANTAN AREA NEAR THE YELLOW RIVER.
BY A GOOD EDUCATION, THEY AIMED TO SECURE ME A POSITION AS AN OFFICIAL.
THOUGH I WAS THEN A CONVENTIONAL YOUNG CHINESE MAN...
...I DREAMED OF BECOMING A SCHOLAR OR EVEN A MILITARY HERO.

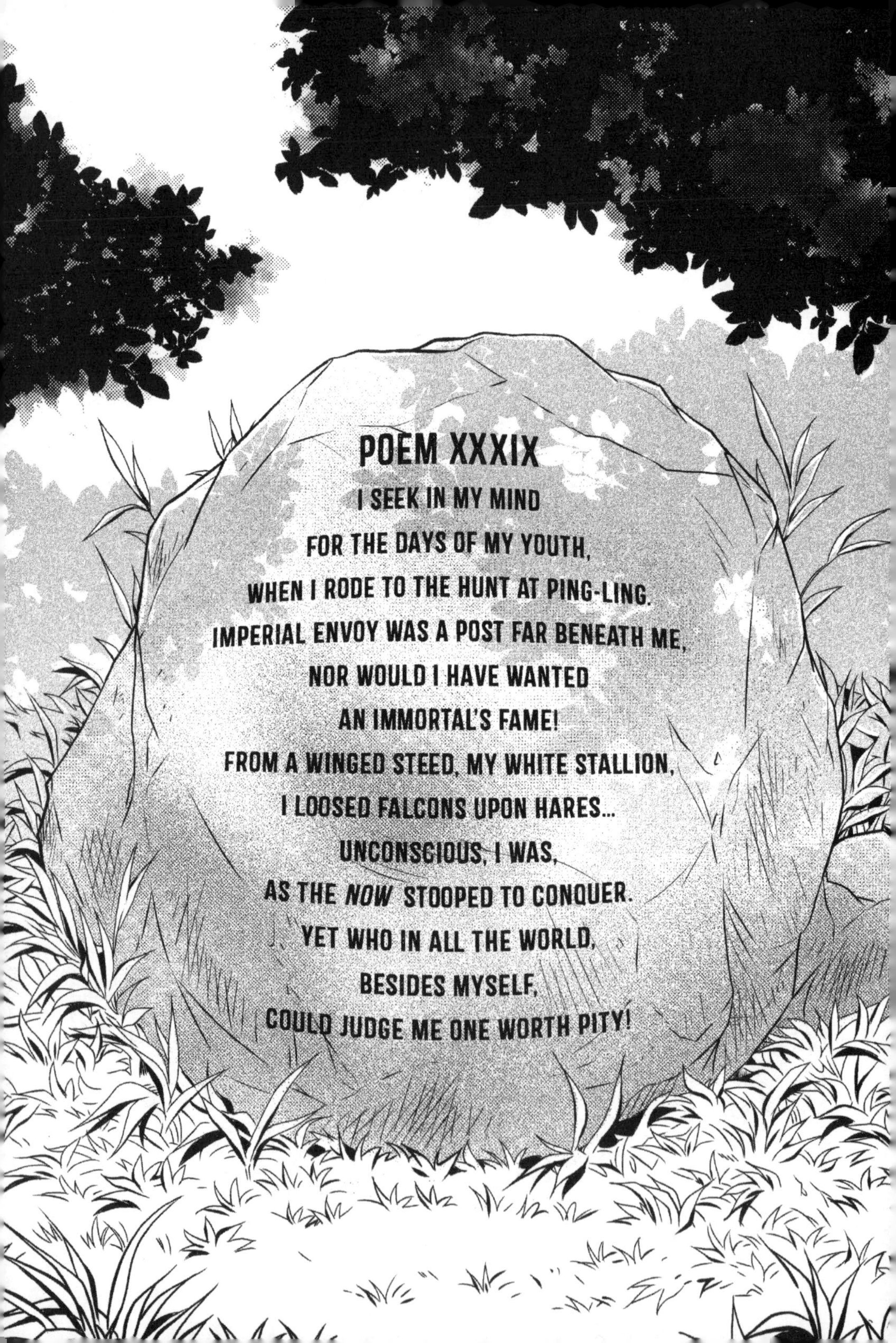
POEM XXXIX
I SEEK IN MY MIND
FOR THE DAYS OF MY YOUTH,
WHEN I RODE TO THE HUNT AT PING-LING.
IMPERIAL ENVOY WAS A POST FAR BENEATH ME,
NOR WOULD I HAVE WANTED
AN IMMORTAL'S FAME!
FROM A WINGED STEED, MY WHITE STALLION,
I LOOSED FALCONS UPON HARES...
UNCONSCIOUS, I WAS,
AS THE *NOW* STOOPED TO CONQUER.
YET WHO IN ALL THE WORLD,
BESIDES MYSELF,
COULD JUDGE ME ONE WORTH PITY!

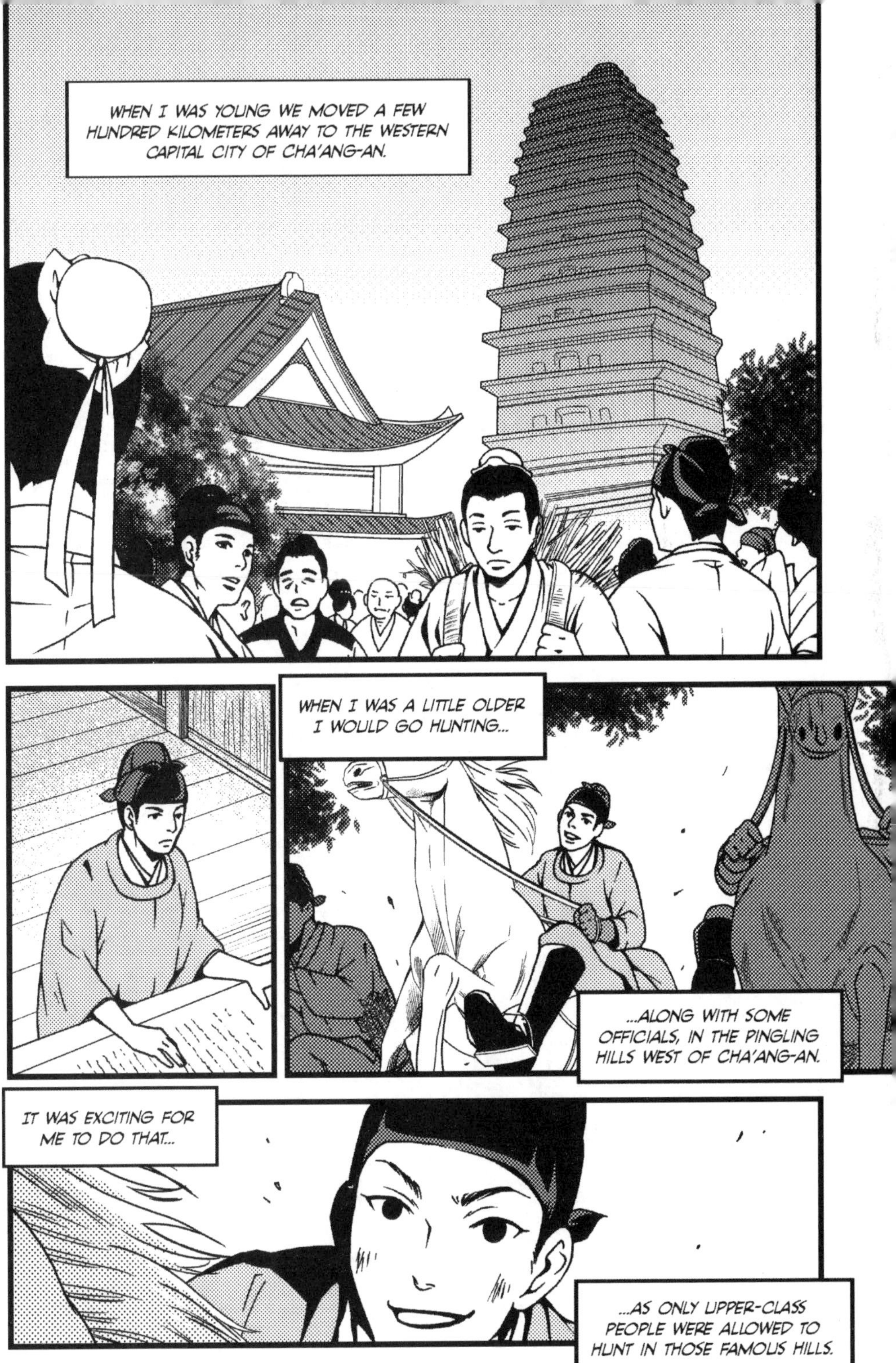
WHEN I WAS YOUNG WE MOVED A FEW HUNDRED KILOMETERS AWAY TO THE WESTERN CAPITAL CITY OF CHA'ANG-AN.
WHEN I WAS A LITTLE OLDER I WOULD GO HUNTING...
...ALONG WITH SOME OFFICIALS, IN THE PINGLING HILLS WEST OF CHA'ANG-AN.
IT WAS EXCITING FOR ME TO DO THAT...
...AS ONLY UPPER-CLASS PEOPLE WERE ALLOWED TO HUNT IN THOSE FAMOUS HILLS.

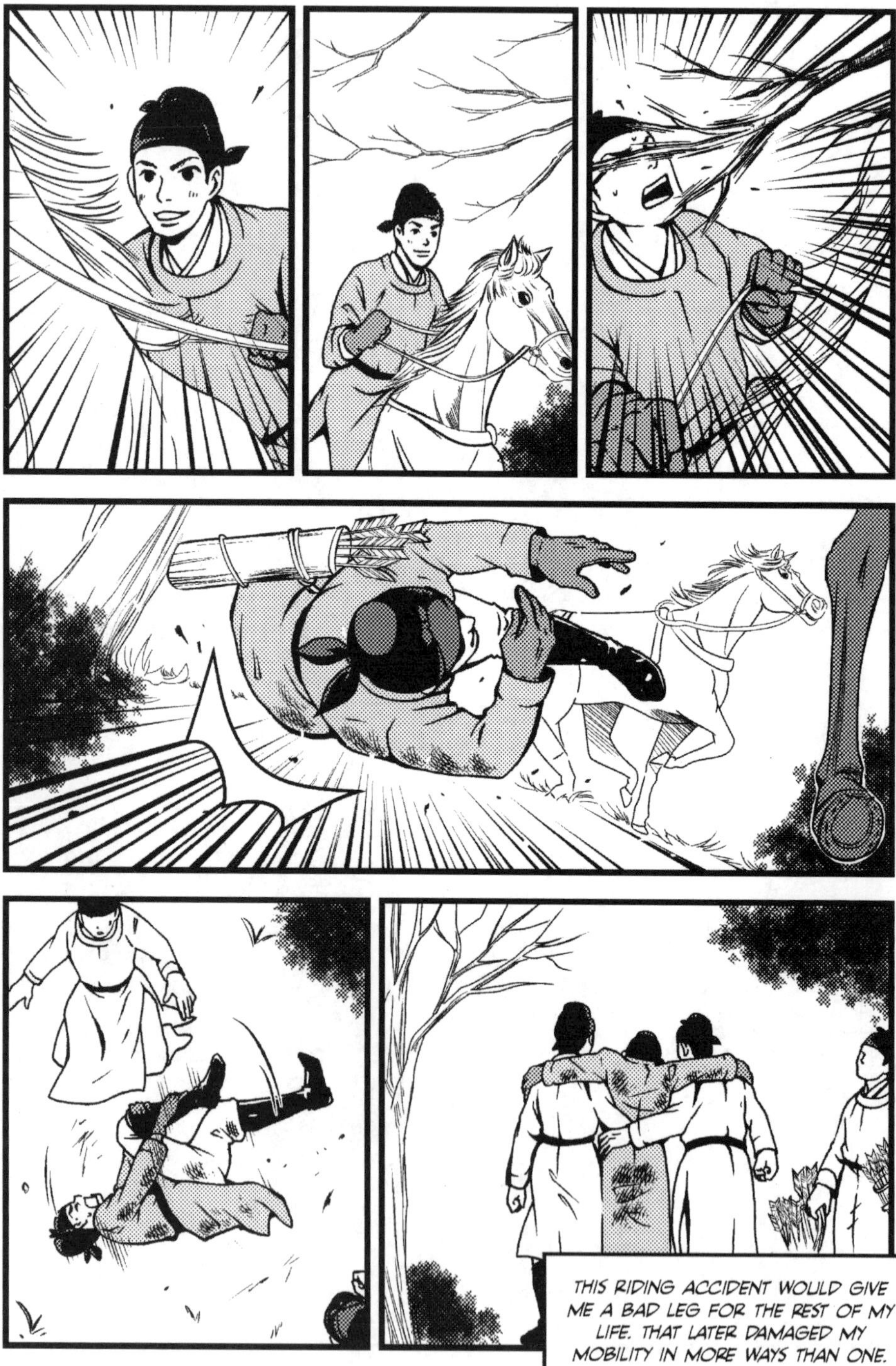
THIS RIDING ACCIDENT WOULD GIVE ME A BAD LEG FOR THE REST OF MY LIFE. THAT LATER DAMAGED MY MOBILITY IN MORE WAYS THAN ONE.

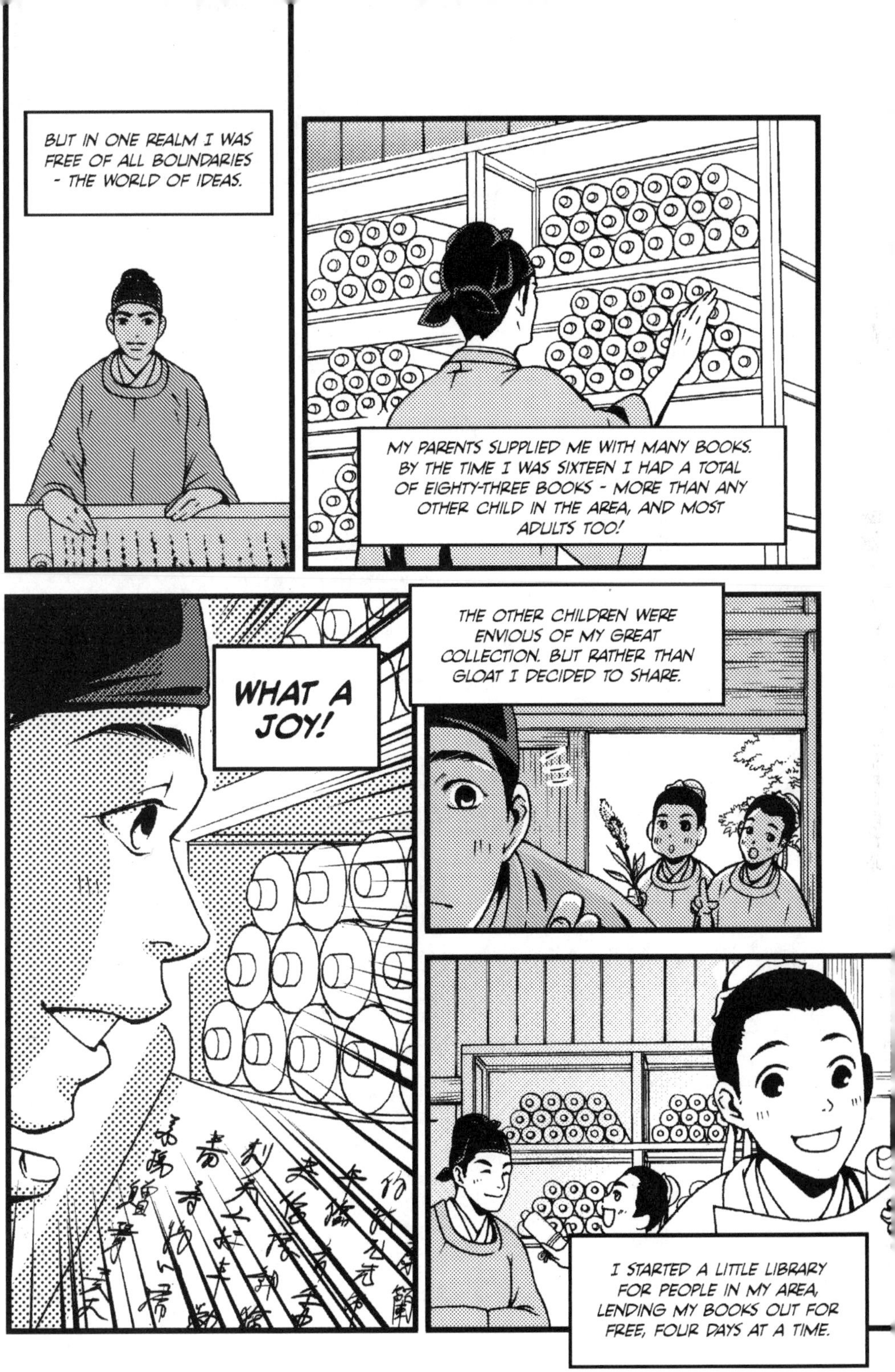
BUT IN ONE REALM I WAS FREE OF ALL BOUNDARIES - THE WORLD OF IDEAS.
MY PARENTS SUPPLIED ME WITH MANY BOOKS. BY THE TIME I WAS SIXTEEN I HAD A TOTAL OF EIGHTY-THREE BOOKS - MORE THAN ANY OTHER CHILD IN THE AREA, AND MOST ADULTS TOO!
WHAT A JOY!
THE OTHER CHILDREN WERE ENVIOUS OF MY GREAT COLLECTION. BUT RATHER THAN GLOAT I DECIDED TO SHARE.
I STARTED A LITTLE LIBRARY FOR PEOPLE IN MY AREA, LENDING MY BOOKS OUT FOR FREE, FOUR DAYS AT A TIME.

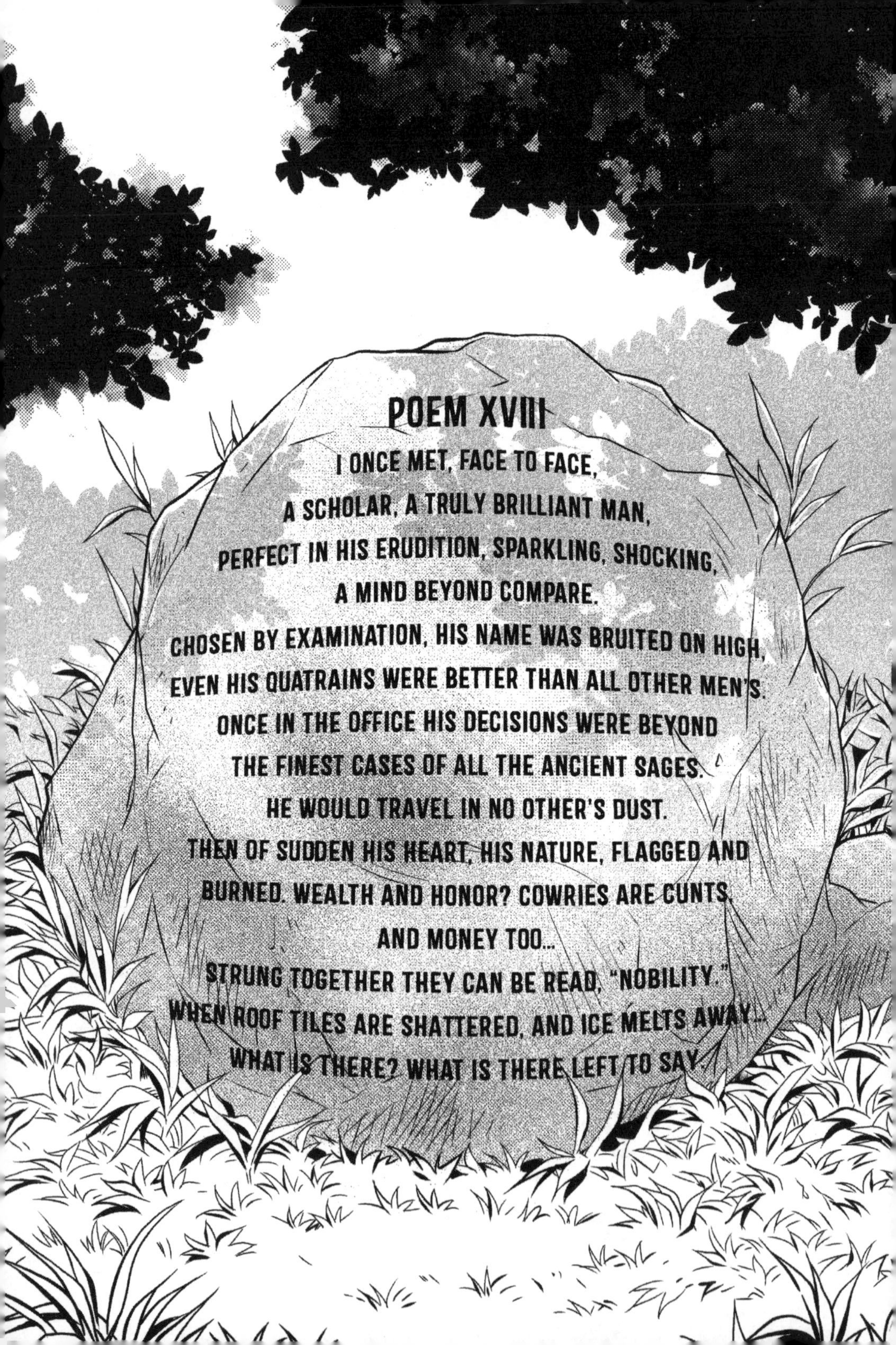
POEM XVIII
I ONCE MET, FACE TO FACE,
A SCHOLAR, A TRULY BRILLIANT MAN,
PERFECT IN HIS ERUDITION, SPARKLING, SHOCKING,
A MIND BEYOND COMPARE.
CHOSEN BY EXAMINATION, HIS NAME WAS BRUITED ON HIGH,
EVEN HIS QUATRAINS WERE BETTER THAN ALL OTHER MEN'S.
ONCE IN THE OFFICE HIS DECISIONS WERE BEYOND
THE FINEST CASES OF ALL THE ANCIENT SAGES.
HE WOULD TRAVEL IN NO OTHER'S DUST.
THEN OF SUDDEN HIS HEART, HIS NATURE, FLAGGED AND
BURNED. WEALTH AND HONOR? COWRIES ARE CUNTS
AND MONEY TOO...
STRUNG TOGETHER THEY CAN BE READ, "NOBILITY."
WHEN ROOF TILES ARE SHATTERED, AND ICE MELTS AWAY...
WHAT IS THERE? WHAT IS THERE LEFT TO SAY.

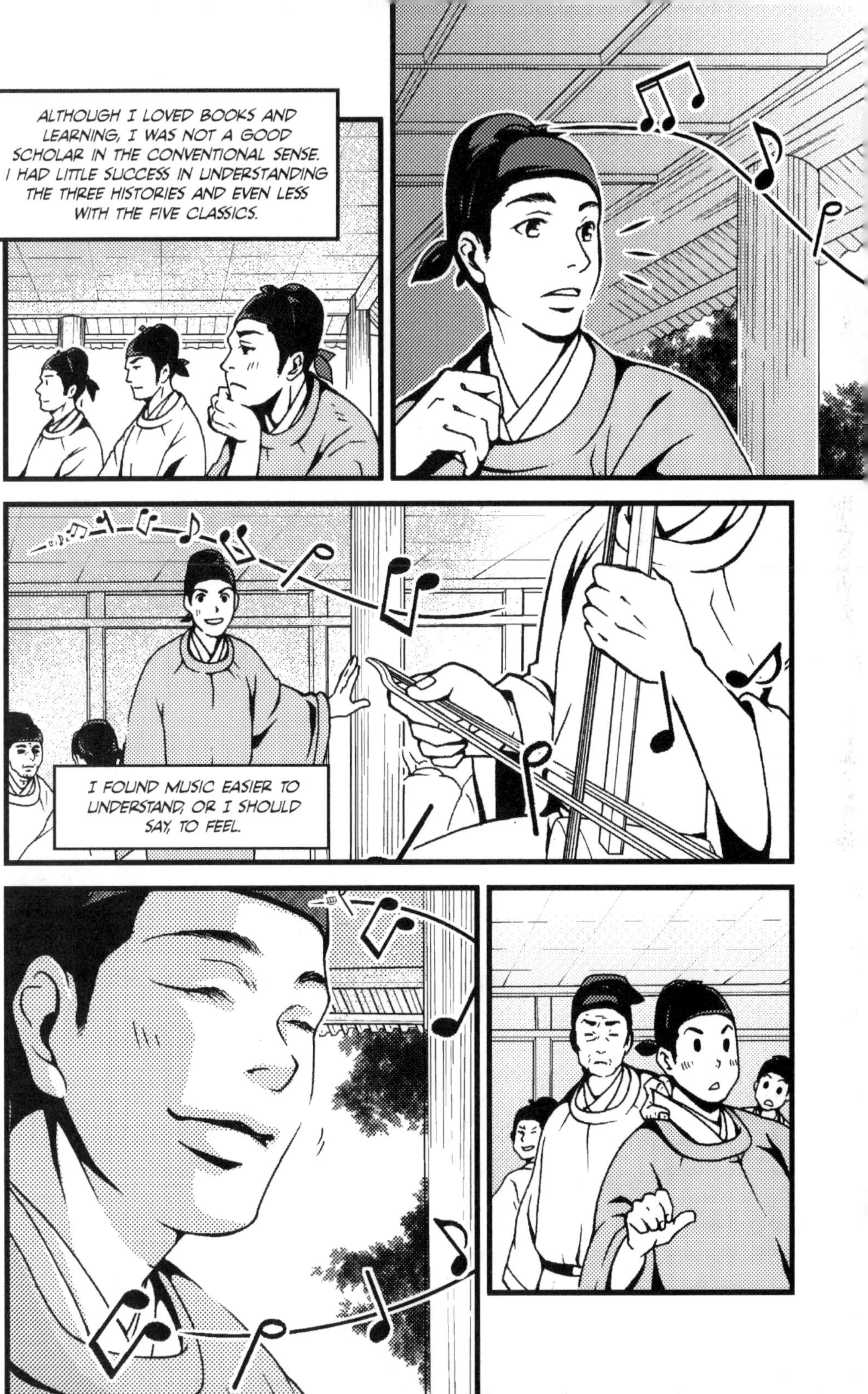
ALTHOUGH I LOVED BOOKS AND LEARNING, I WAS NOT A GOOD SCHOLAR IN THE CONVENTIONAL SENSE. I HAD LITTLE SUCCESS IN UNDERSTANDING THE THREE HISTORIES AND EVEN LESS WITH THE FIVE CLASSICS.
I FOUND MUSIC EASIER TO UNDERSTAND, OR I SHOULD SAY, TO FEEL.

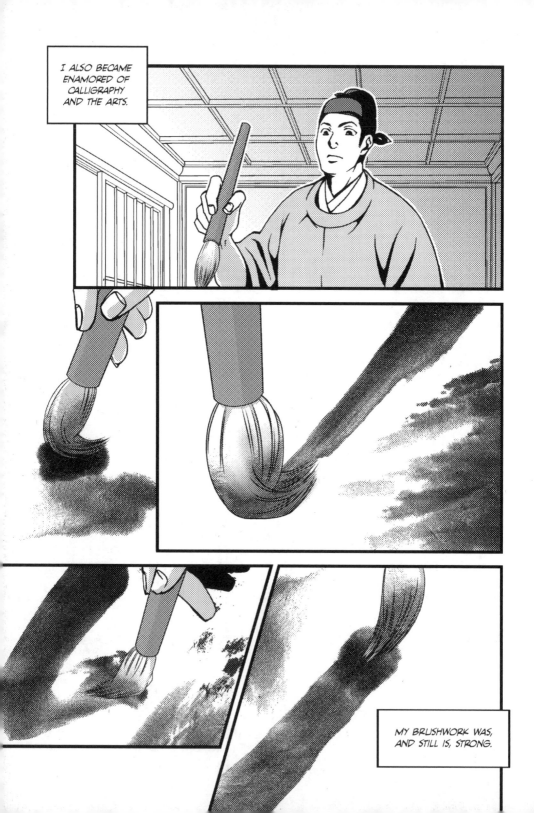

I ALSO BECAME ENAMORED OF CALLIGRAPHY AND THE ARTS.

MY BRUSHWORK WAS, AND STILL IS, STRONG.

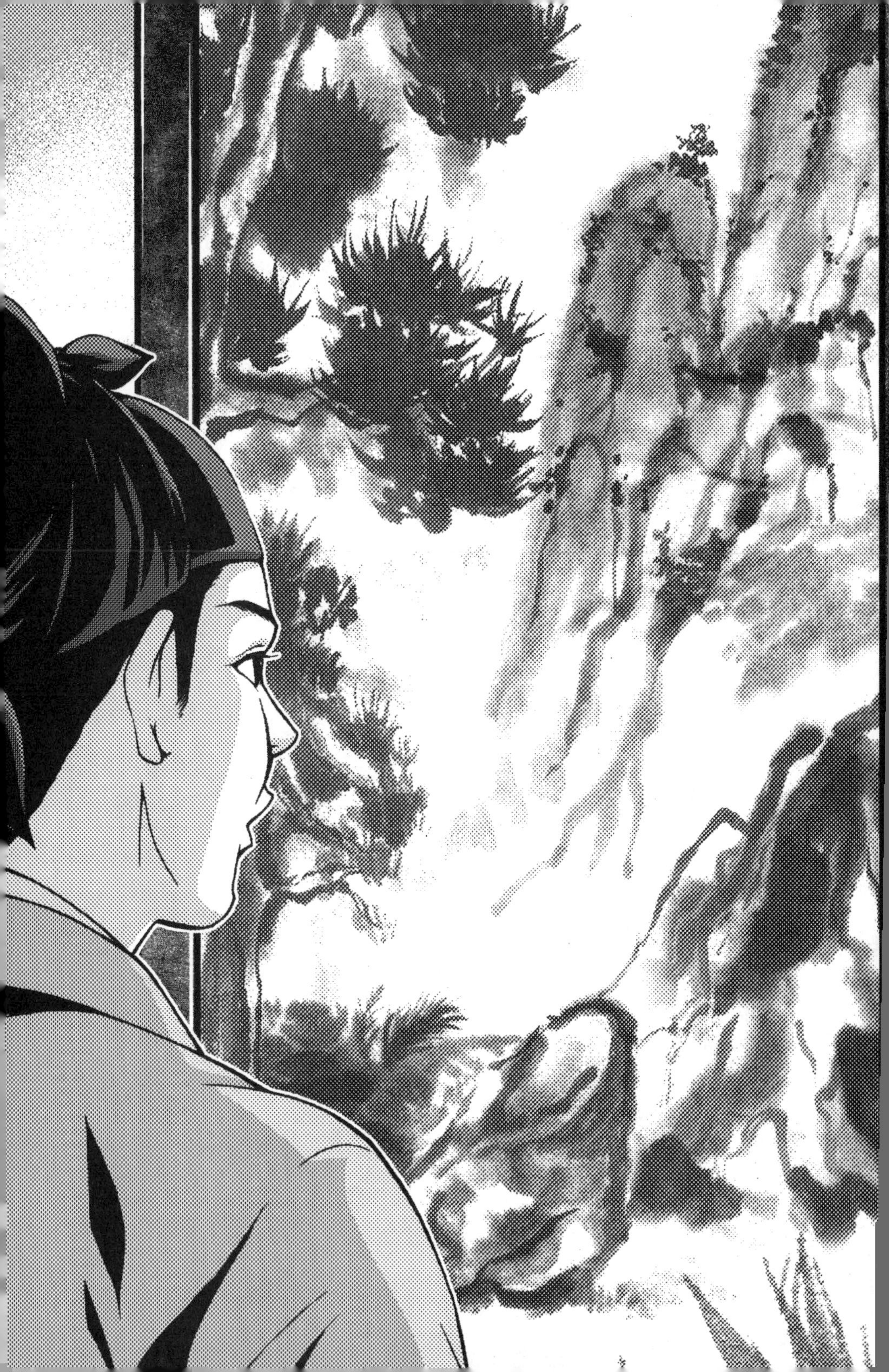

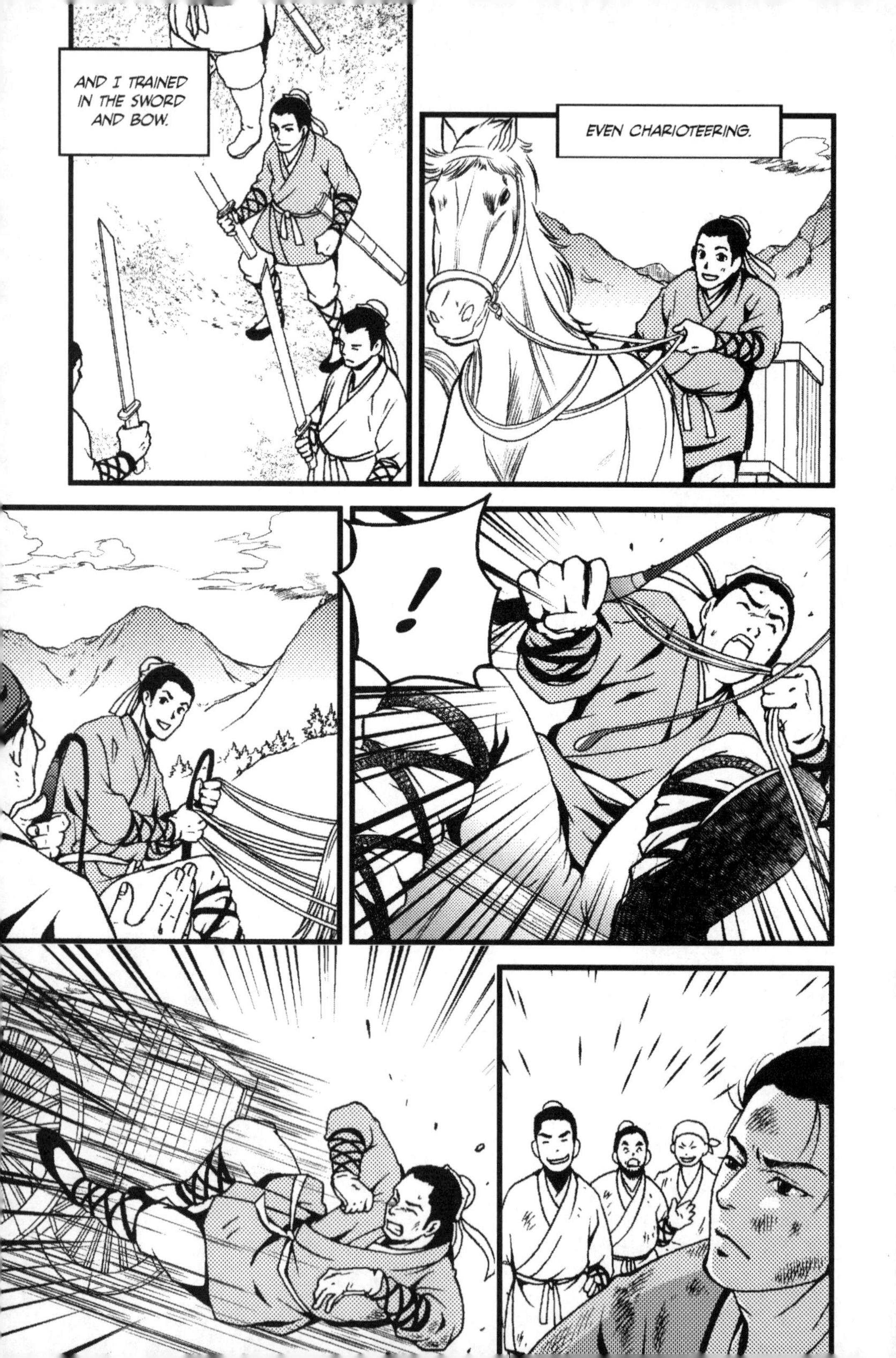
AND I TRAINED IN THE SWORD AND BOW.
EVEN CHARIOTEERING.
!

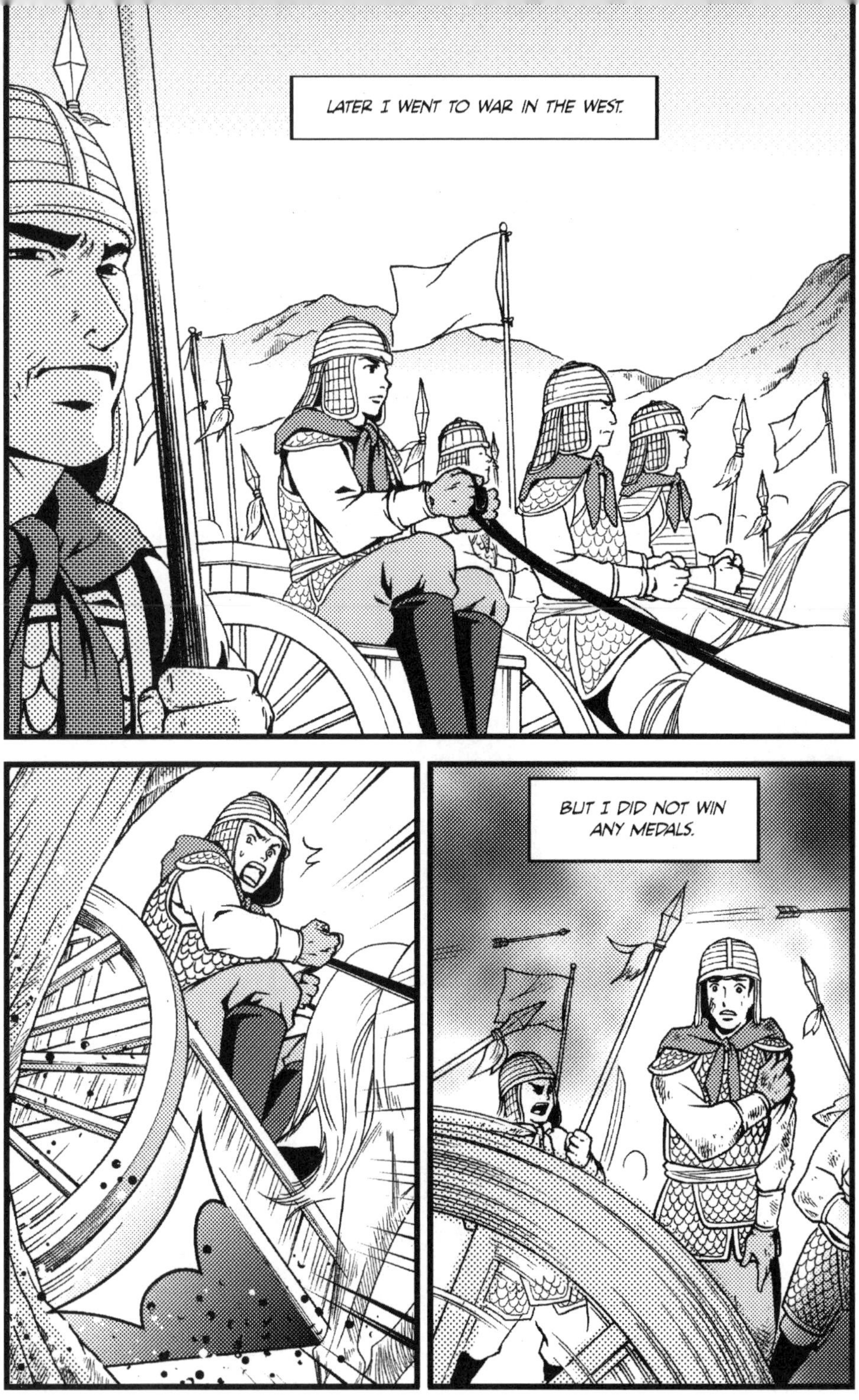
LATER I WENT TO WAR IN THE WEST.
BUT I DID NOT WIN ANY MEDALS.

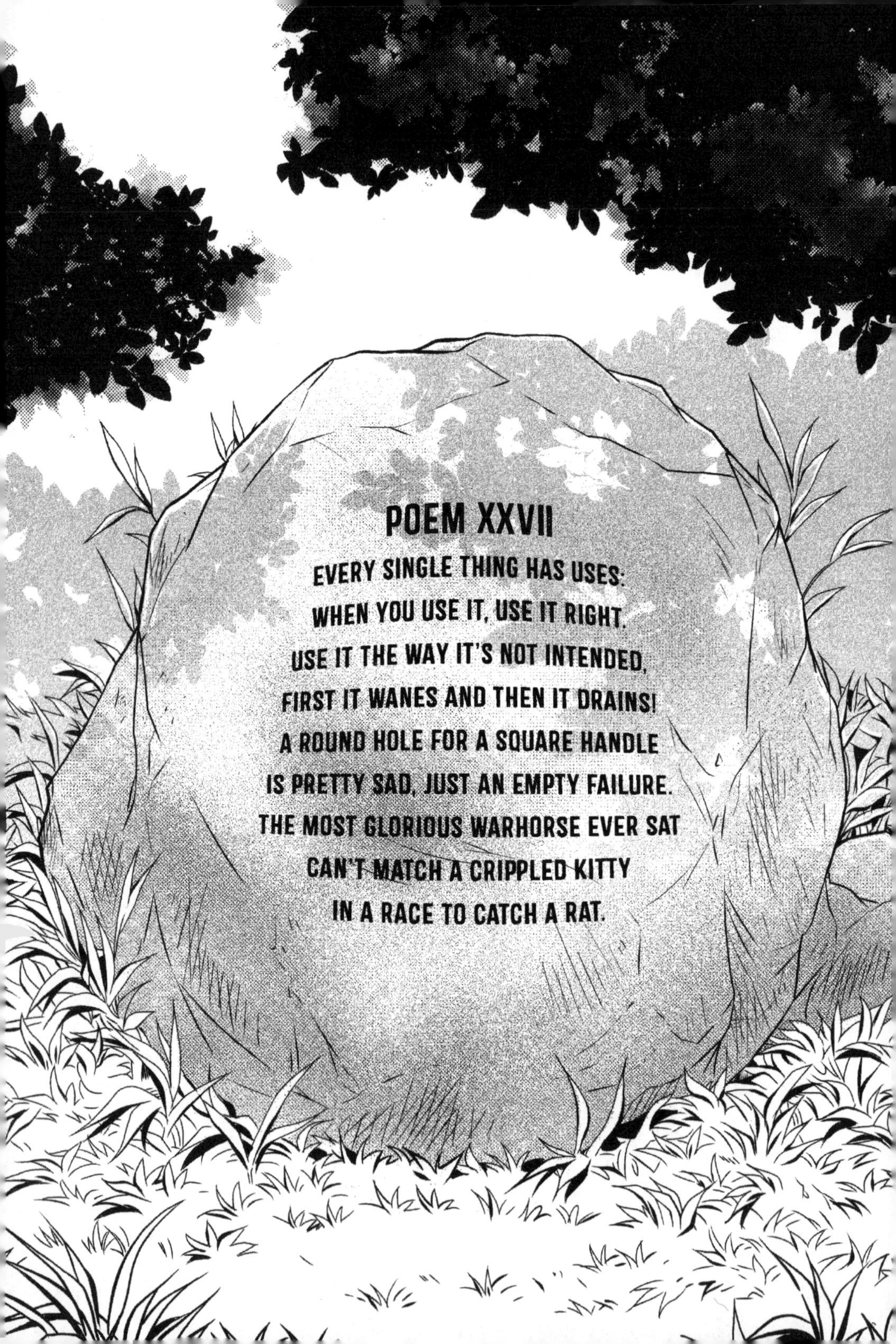
POEM XXVII
EVERY SINGLE THING HAS USES:
WHEN YOU USE IT, USE IT RIGHT.
USE IT THE WAY IT'S NOT INTENDED,
FIRST IT WANES AND THEN IT DRAINS!
A ROUND HOLE FOR A SQUARE HANDLE
IS PRETTY SAD, JUST AN EMPTY FAILURE.
THE MOST GLORIOUS WARHORSE EVER SAT
CAN'T MATCH A CRIPPLED KITTY
IN A RACE TO CATCH A RAT.

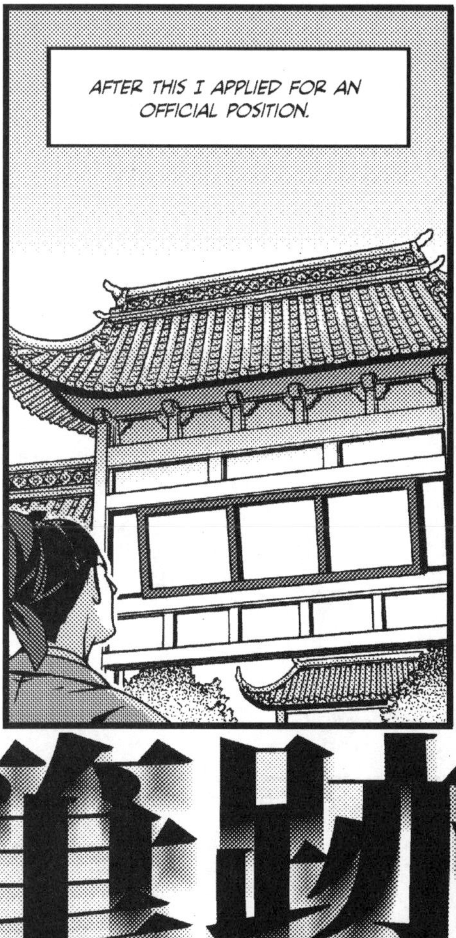
AFTER THIS I APPLIED FOR AN OFFICIAL POSITION.

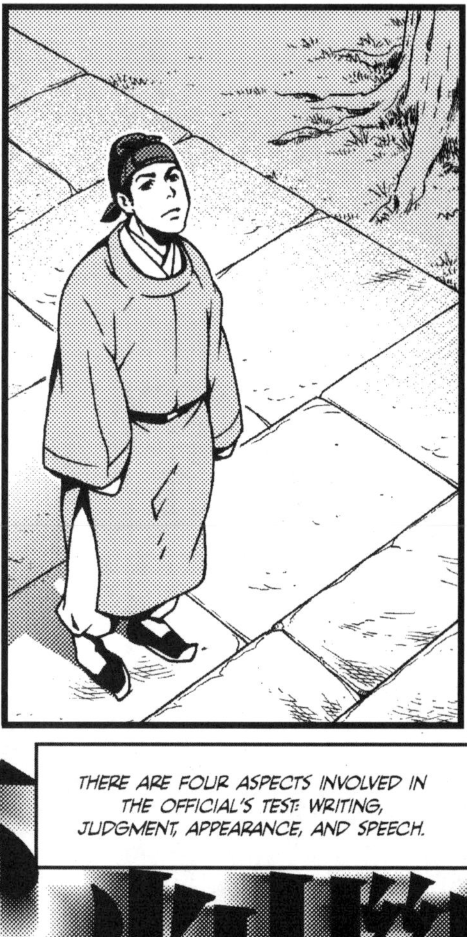

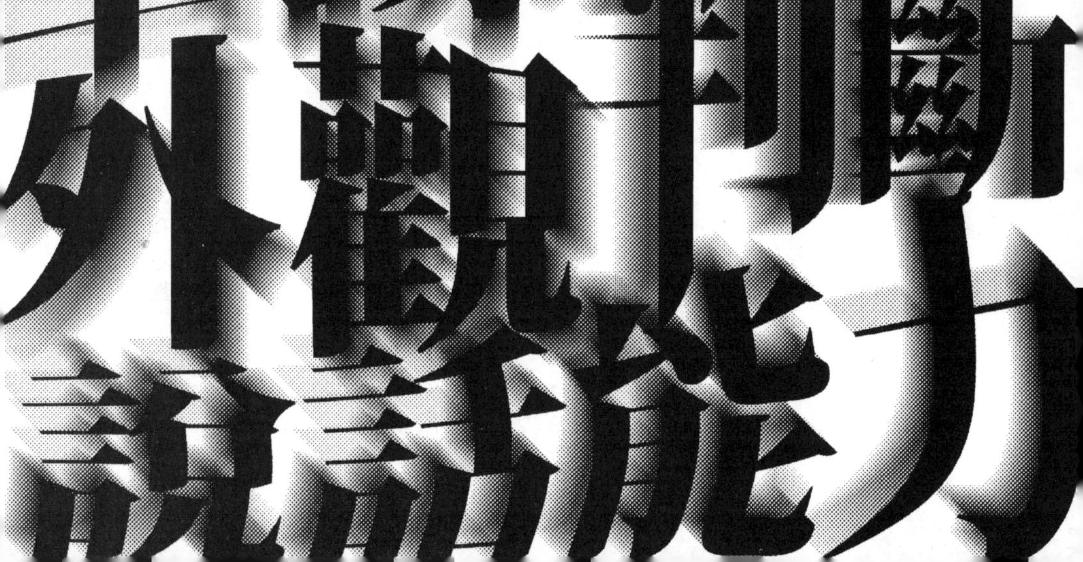
THERE ARE FOUR ASPECTS INVOLVED IN THE OFFICIAL'S TEST: WRITING, JUDGMENT, APPEARANCE, AND SPEECH.
筆跡
判斷
外觀
說話能力

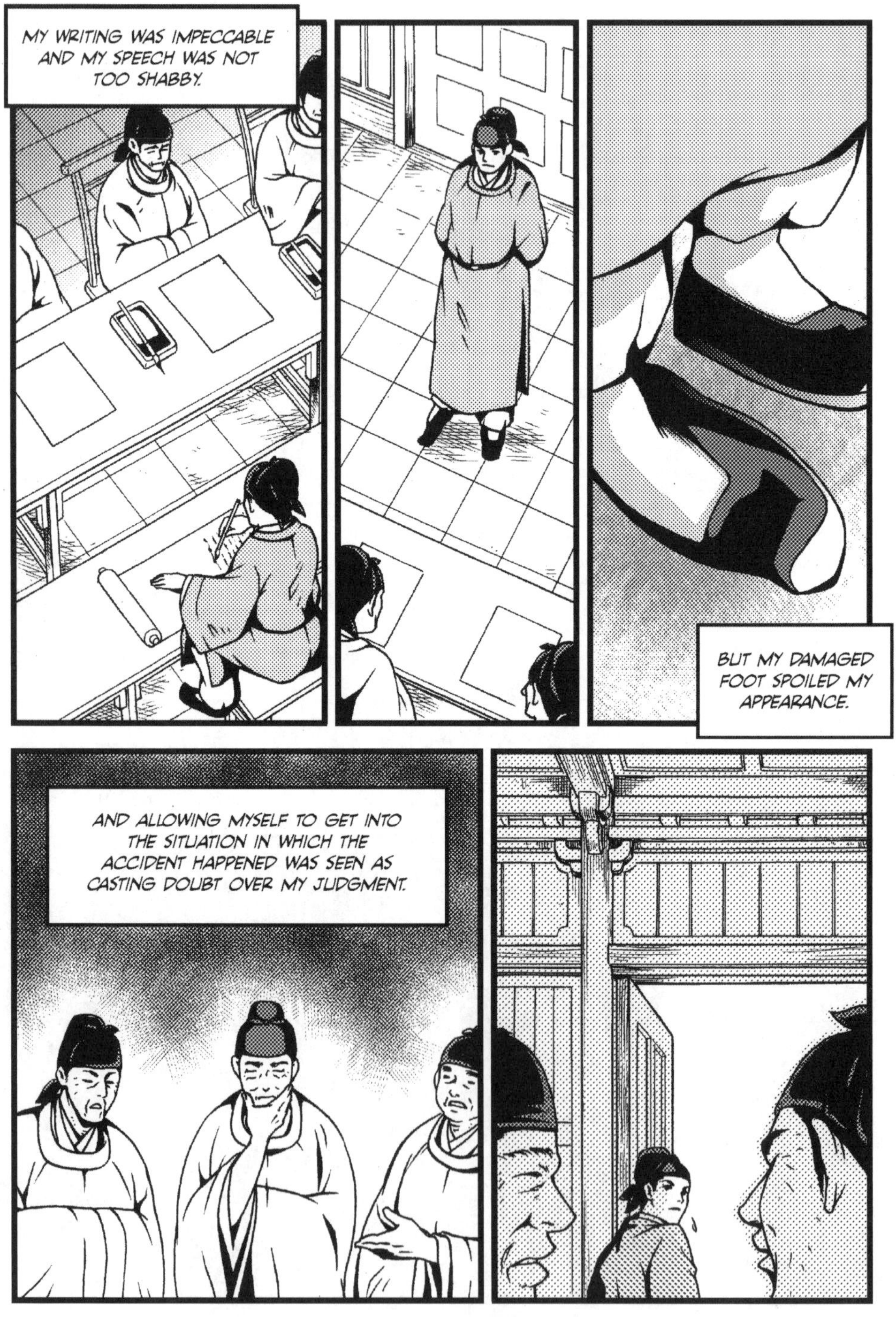
MY WRITING WAS IMPECCABLE AND MY SPEECH WAS NOT TOO SHABBY.
BUT MY DAMAGED FOOT SPOILED MY APPEARANCE.
AND ALLOWING MYSELF TO GET INTO THE SITUATION IN WHICH THE ACCIDENT HAPPENED WAS SEEN AS CASTING DOUBT OVER MY JUDGMENT.

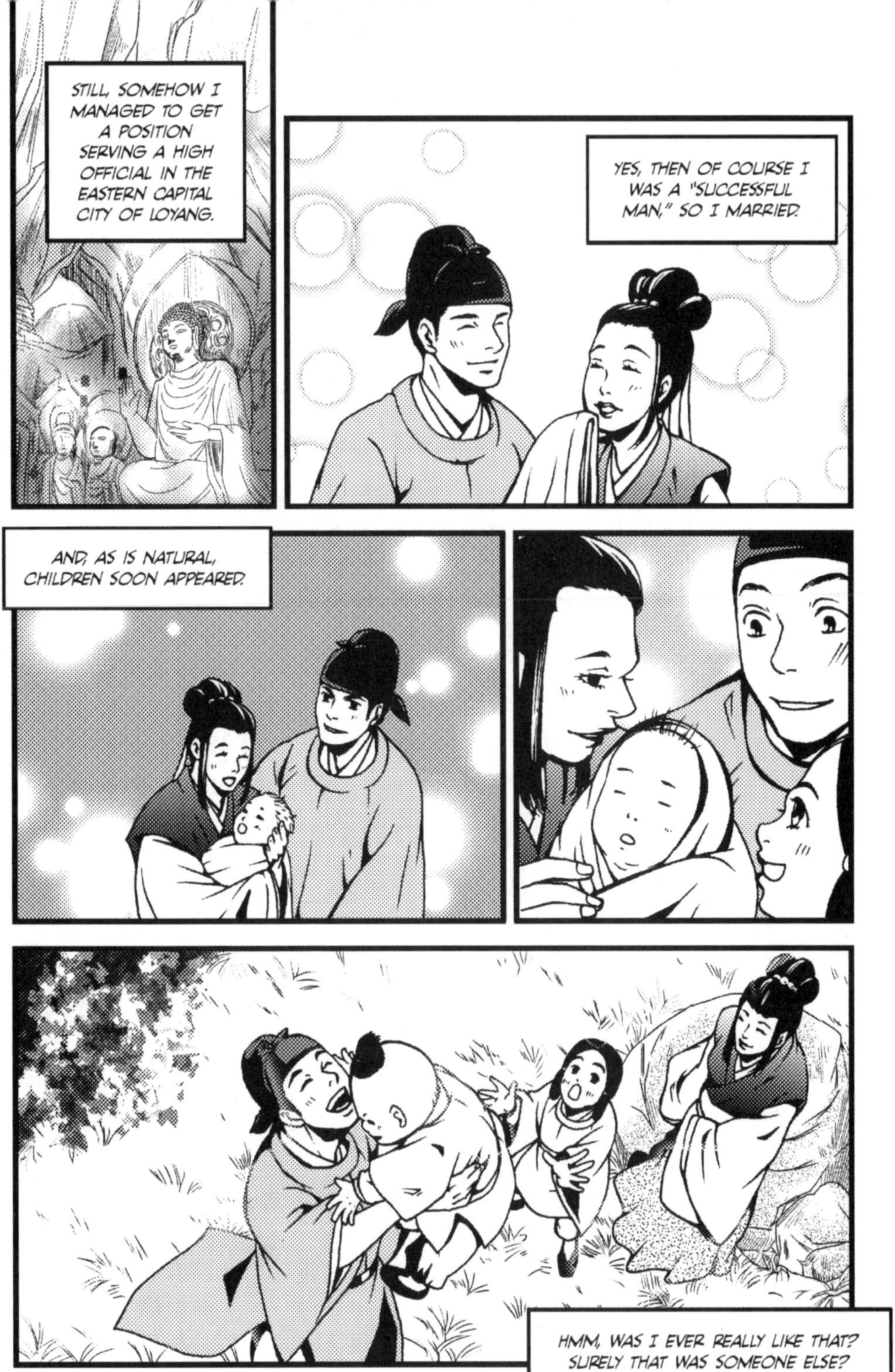
STILL, SOMEHOW I MANAGED TO GET A POSITION SERVING A HIGH OFFICIAL IN THE EASTERN CAPITAL CITY OF LOYANG.
YES, THEN OF COURSE I WAS A "SUCCESSFUL MAN," SO I MARRIED.
AND, AS IS NATURAL, CHILDREN SOON APPEARED.
HMM, WAS I EVER REALLY LIKE THAT? SURELY THAT WAS SOMEONE ELSE?

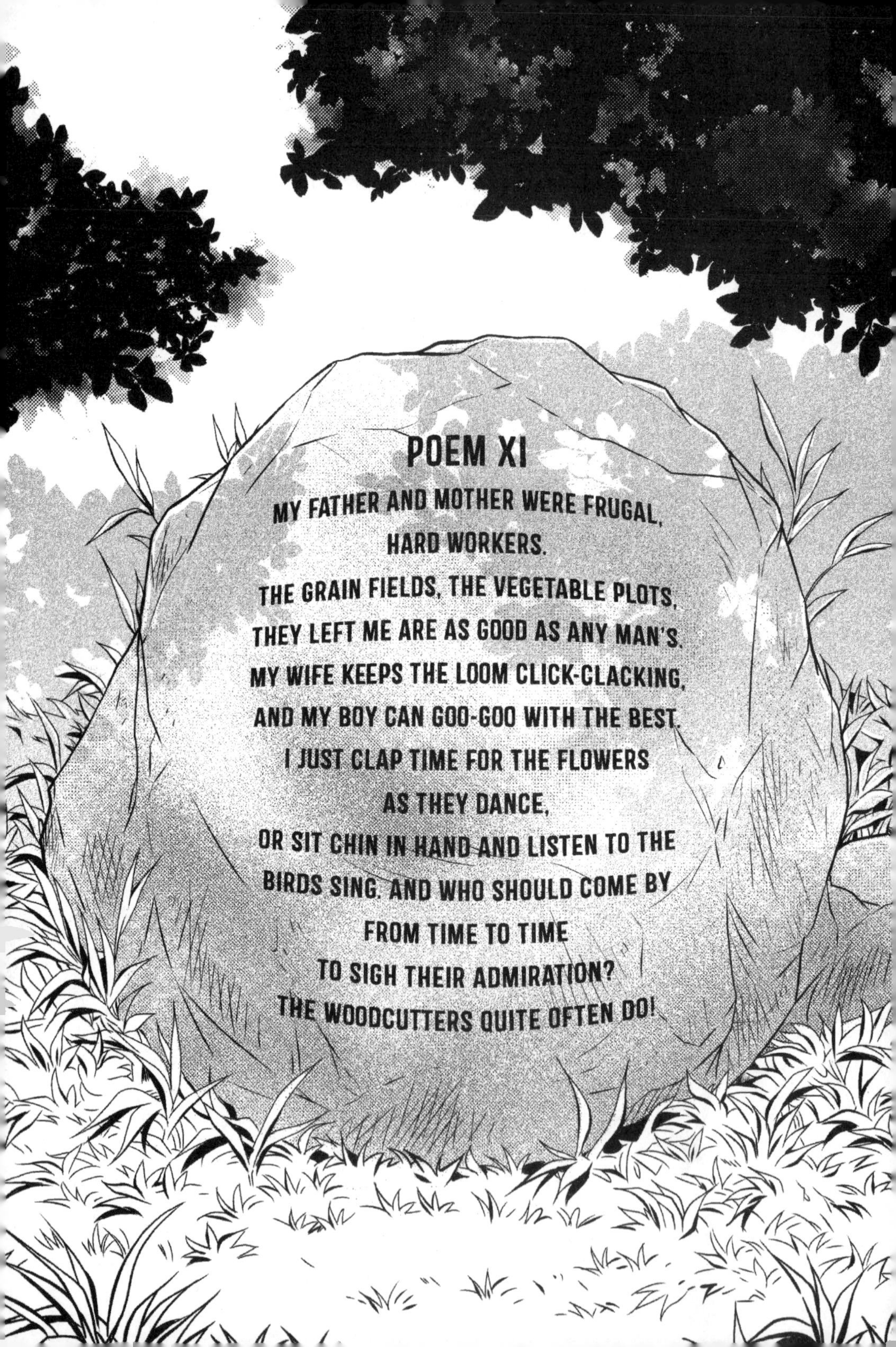
POEM XI
MY FATHER AND MOTHER WERE FRUGAL,
HARD WORKERS.
THE GRAIN FIELDS, THE VEGETABLE PLOTS,
THEY LEFT ME ARE AS GOOD AS ANY MAN'S.
MY WIFE KEEPS THE LOOM CLICK-CLACKING,
AND MY BOY CAN GOO-GOO WITH THE BEST.
I JUST CLAP TIME FOR THE FLOWERS
AS THEY DANCE,
OR SIT CHIN IN HAND AND LISTEN TO THE
BIRDS SING. AND WHO SHOULD COME BY
FROM TIME TO TIME
TO SIGH THEIR ADMIRATION?
THE WOODCUTTERS QUITE OFTEN DO!

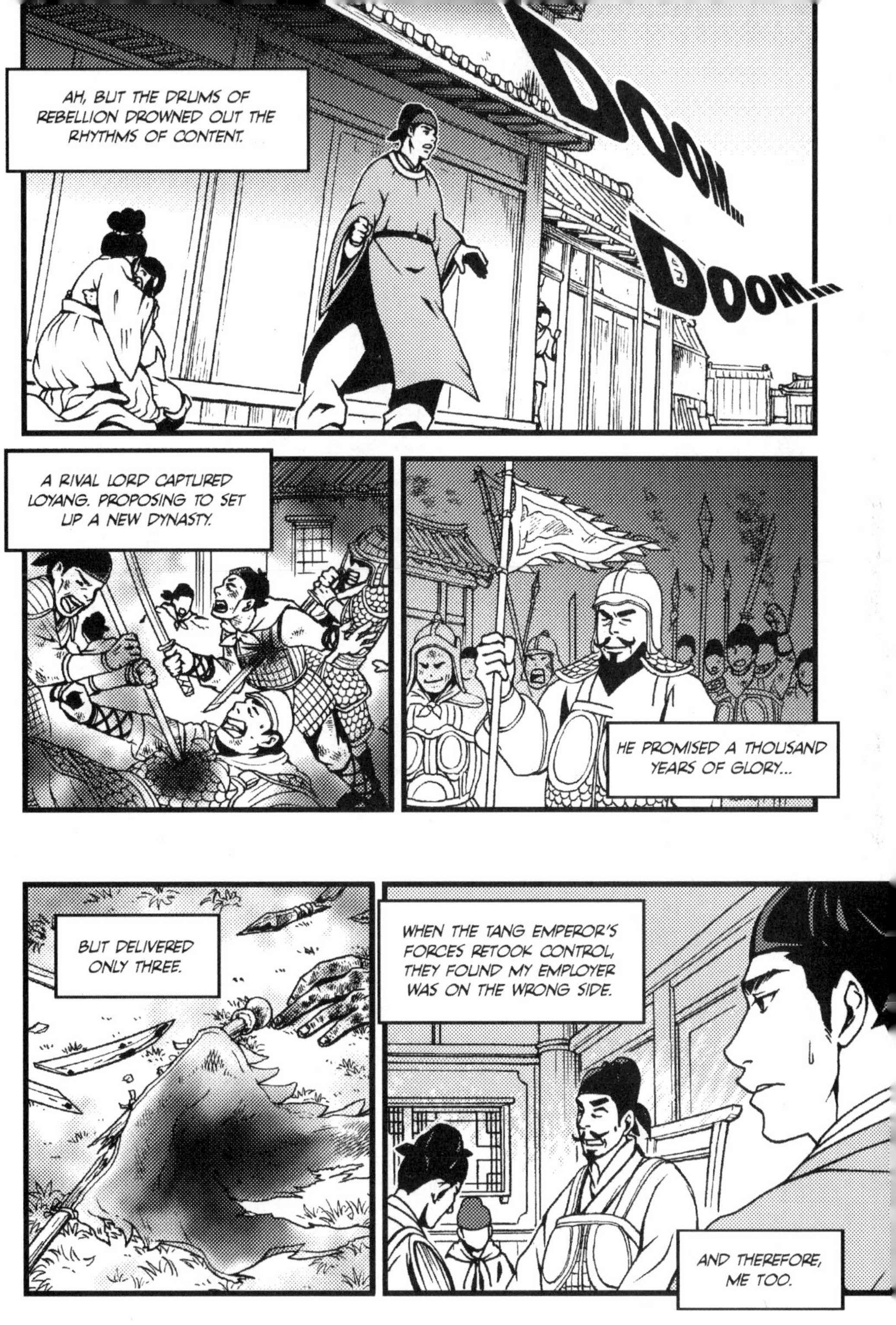
AH, BUT THE DRUMS OF REBELLION DROWNED OUT THE RHYTHMS OF CONTENT.
DOOM...
DOOM...
A RIVAL LORD CAPTURED LOYANG. PROPOSING TO SET UP A NEW DYNASTY.
HE PROMISED A THOUSAND YEARS OF GLORY...
BUT DELIVERED ONLY THREE.
WHEN THE TANG EMPEROR'S FORCES RETOOK CONTROL, THEY FOUND MY EMPLOYER WAS ON THE WRONG SIDE.
AND THEREFORE, ME TOO.

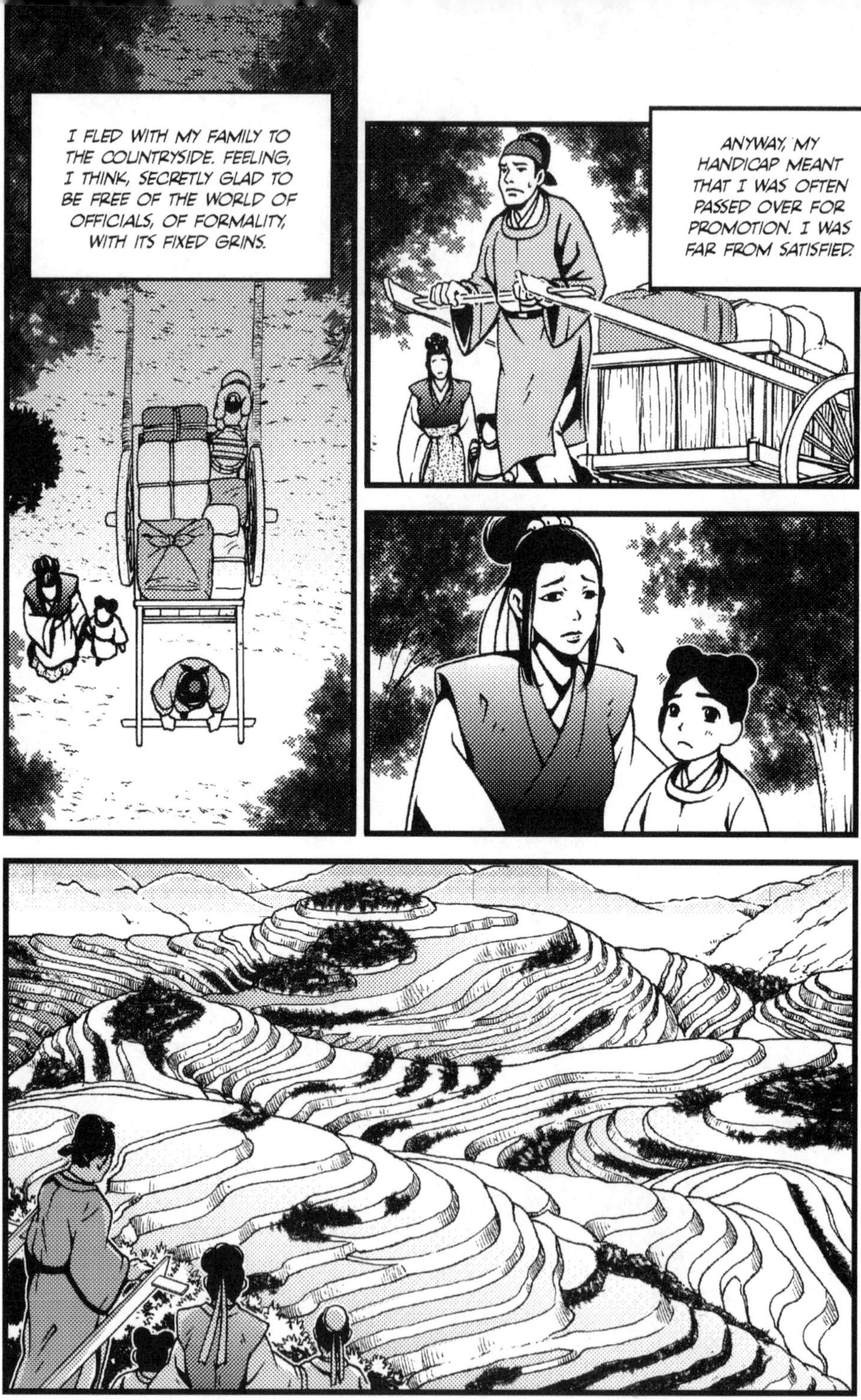
ANYWAY, MY HANDICAP MEANT THAT I WAS OFTEN PASSED OVER FOR PROMOTION. I WAS FAR FROM SATISFIED.
I FLED WITH MY FAMILY TO THE COUNTRYSIDE. FEELING, I THINK, SECRETLY GLAD TO BE FREE OF THE WORLD OF OFFICIALS, OF FORMALITY, WITH ITS FIXED GRINS.

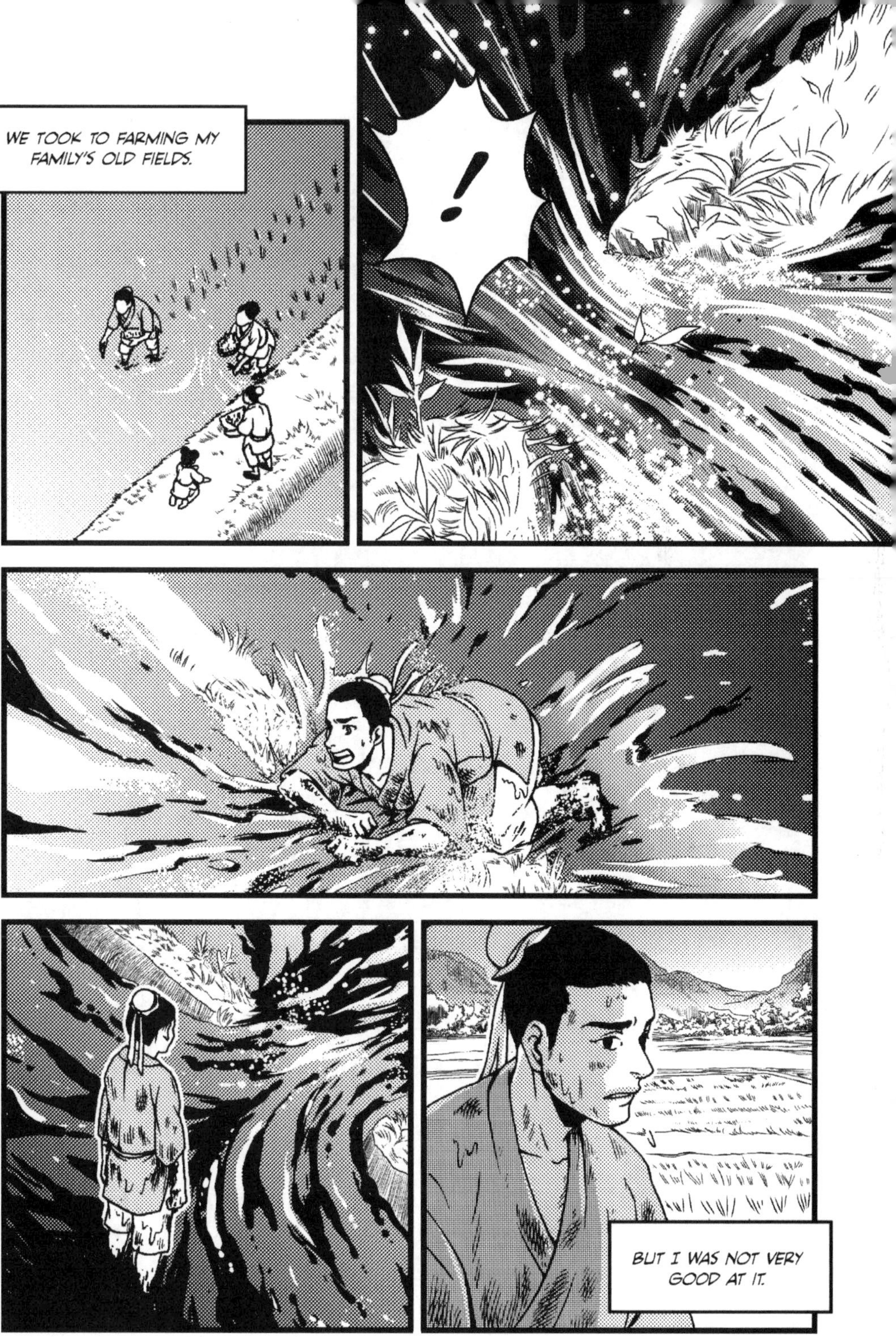
WE TOOK TO FARMING MY FAMILY'S OLD FIELDS.
!
BUT I WAS NOT VERY GOOD AT IT.

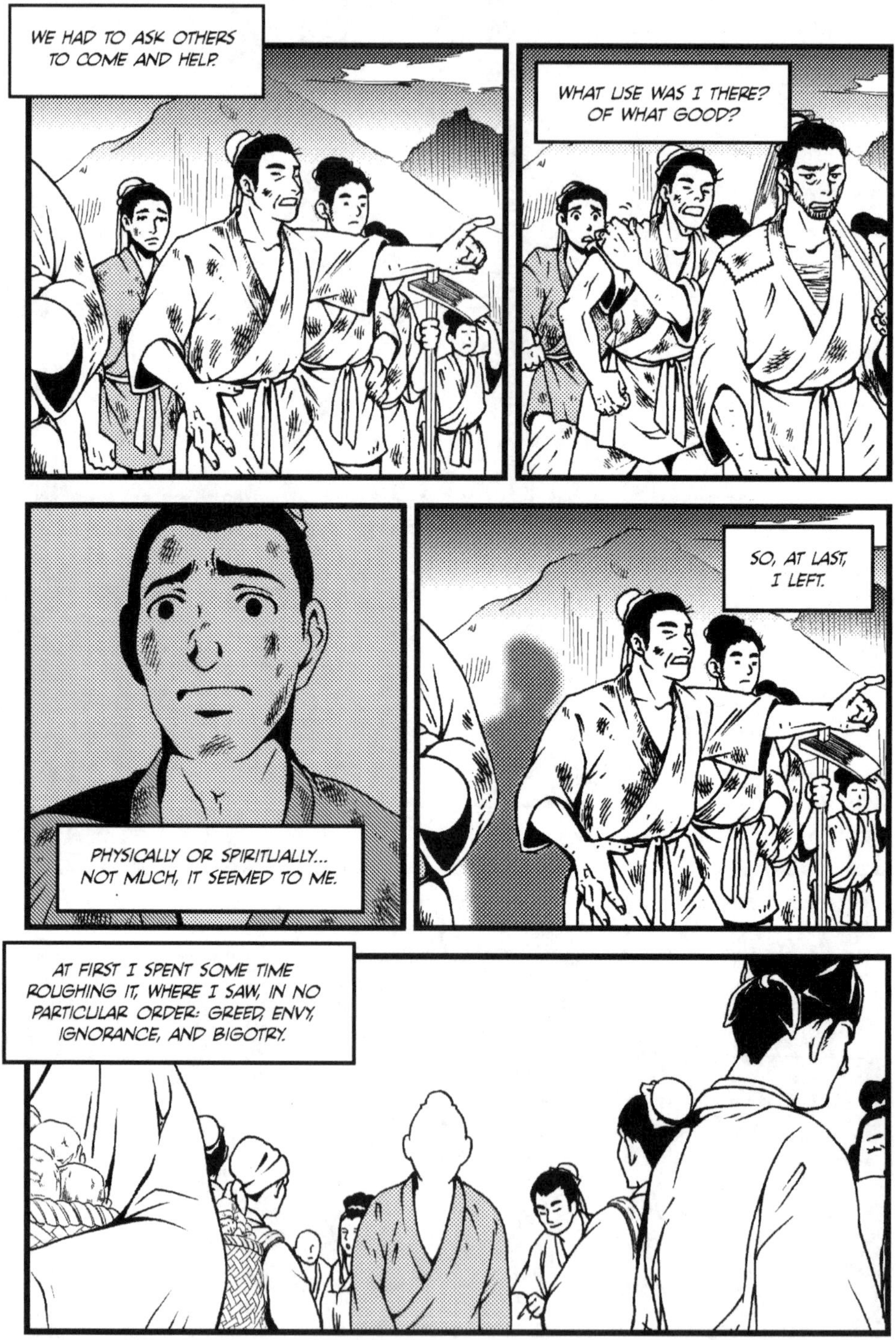
WE HAD TO ASK OTHERS TO COME AND HELP.
WHAT USE WAS I THERE? OF WHAT GOOD?
PHYSICALLY OR SPIRITUALLY... NOT MUCH, IT SEEMED TO ME.
SO, AT LAST, I LEFT.
AT FIRST I SPENT SOME TIME ROUGHING IT, WHERE I SAW, IN NO PARTICULAR ORDER: GREED, ENVY, IGNORANCE, AND BIGOTRY.

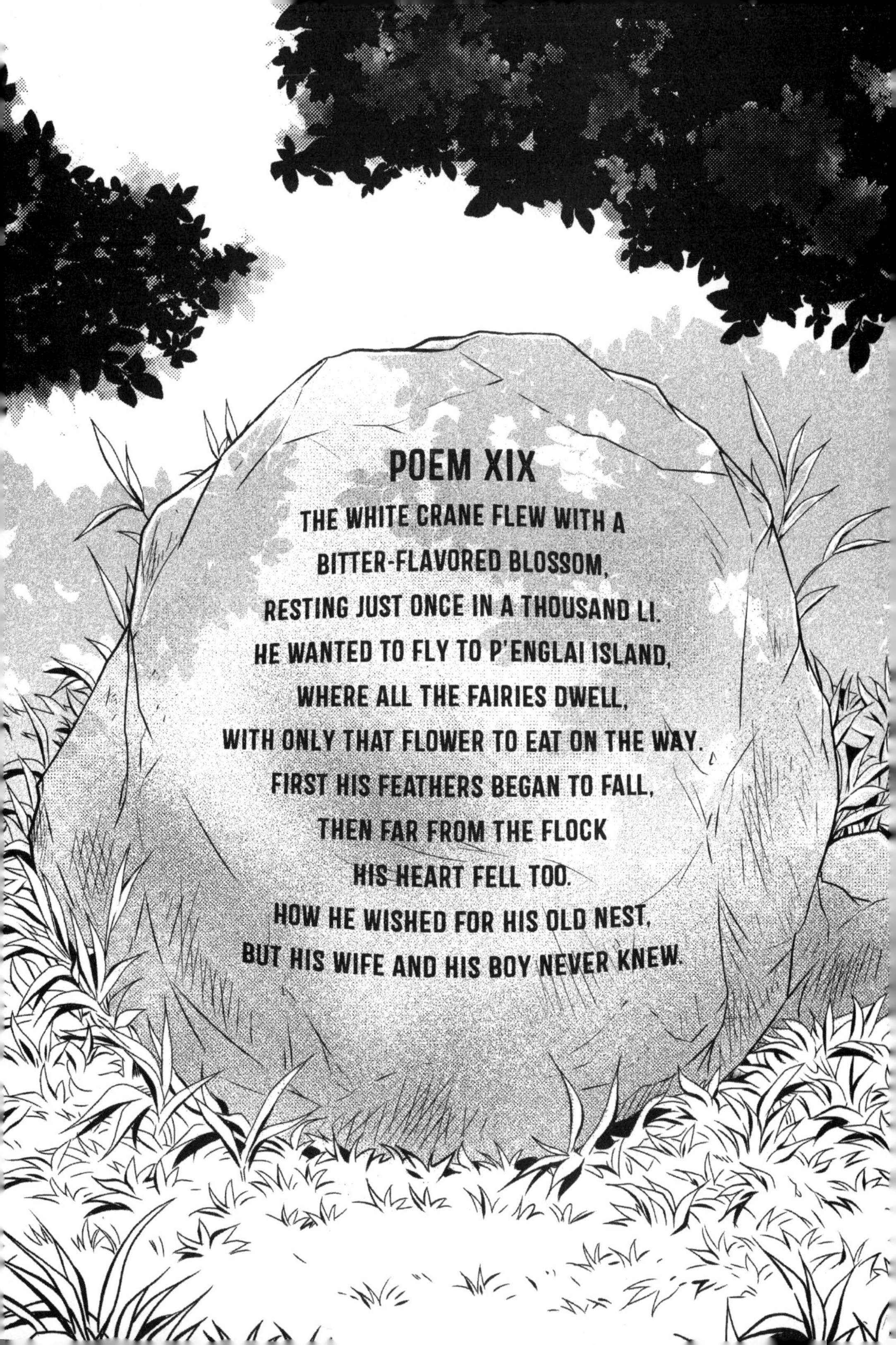
POEM XIX
THE WHITE CRANE FLEW WITH A
BITTER-FLAVORED BLOSSOM,
RESTING JUST ONCE IN A THOUSAND LI.
HE WANTED TO FLY TO P'ENGLAI ISLAND,
WHERE ALL THE FAIRIES DWELL,
WITH ONLY THAT FLOWER TO EAT ON THE WAY.
FIRST HIS FEATHERS BEGAN TO FALL,
THEN FAR FROM THE FLOCK
HIS HEART FELL TOO.
HOW HE WISHED FOR HIS OLD NEST,
BUT HIS WIFE AND HIS BOY NEVER KNEW.

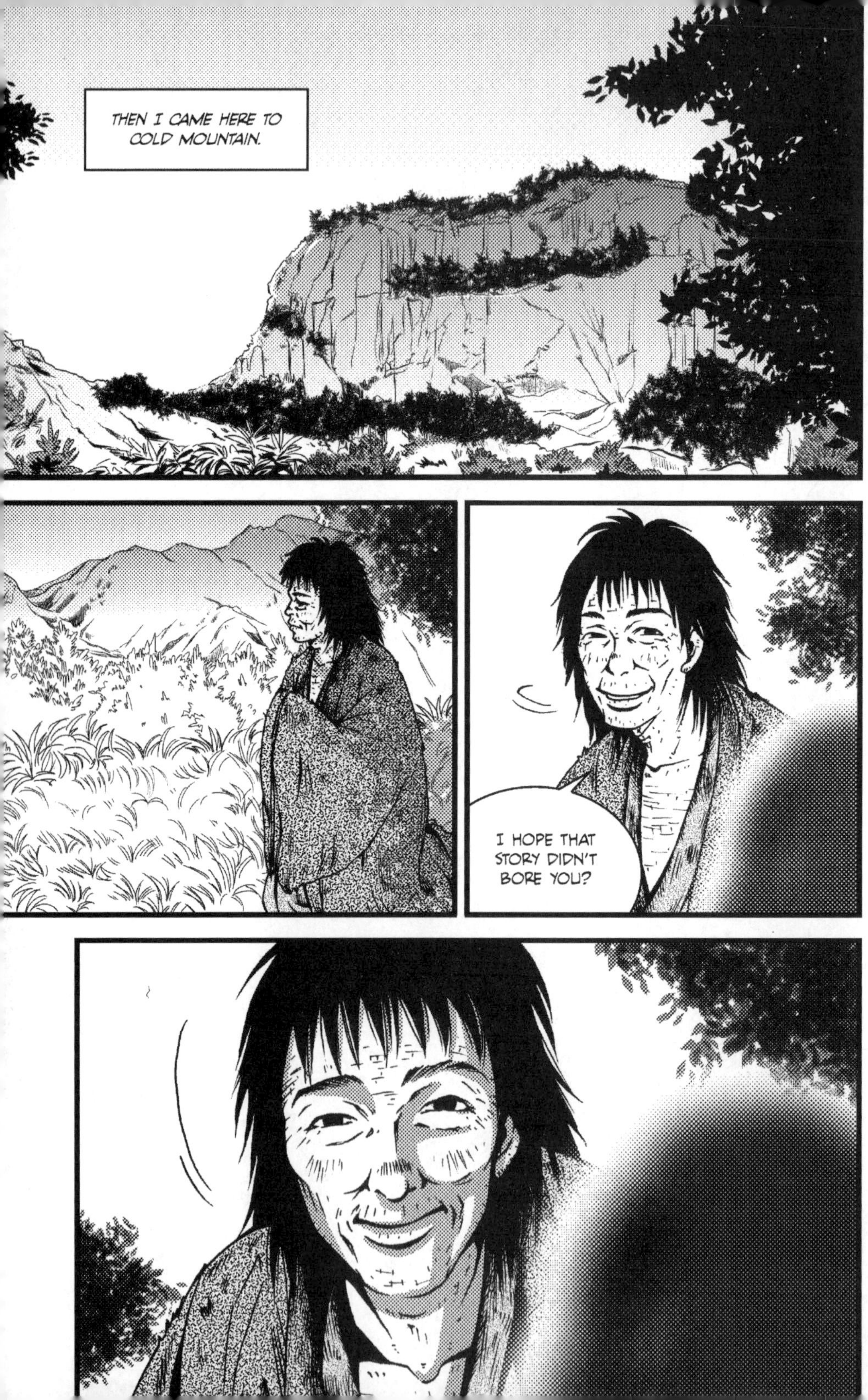
THEN I CAME HERE TO COLD MOUNTAIN.
I HOPE THAT STORY DIDN'T BORE YOU?

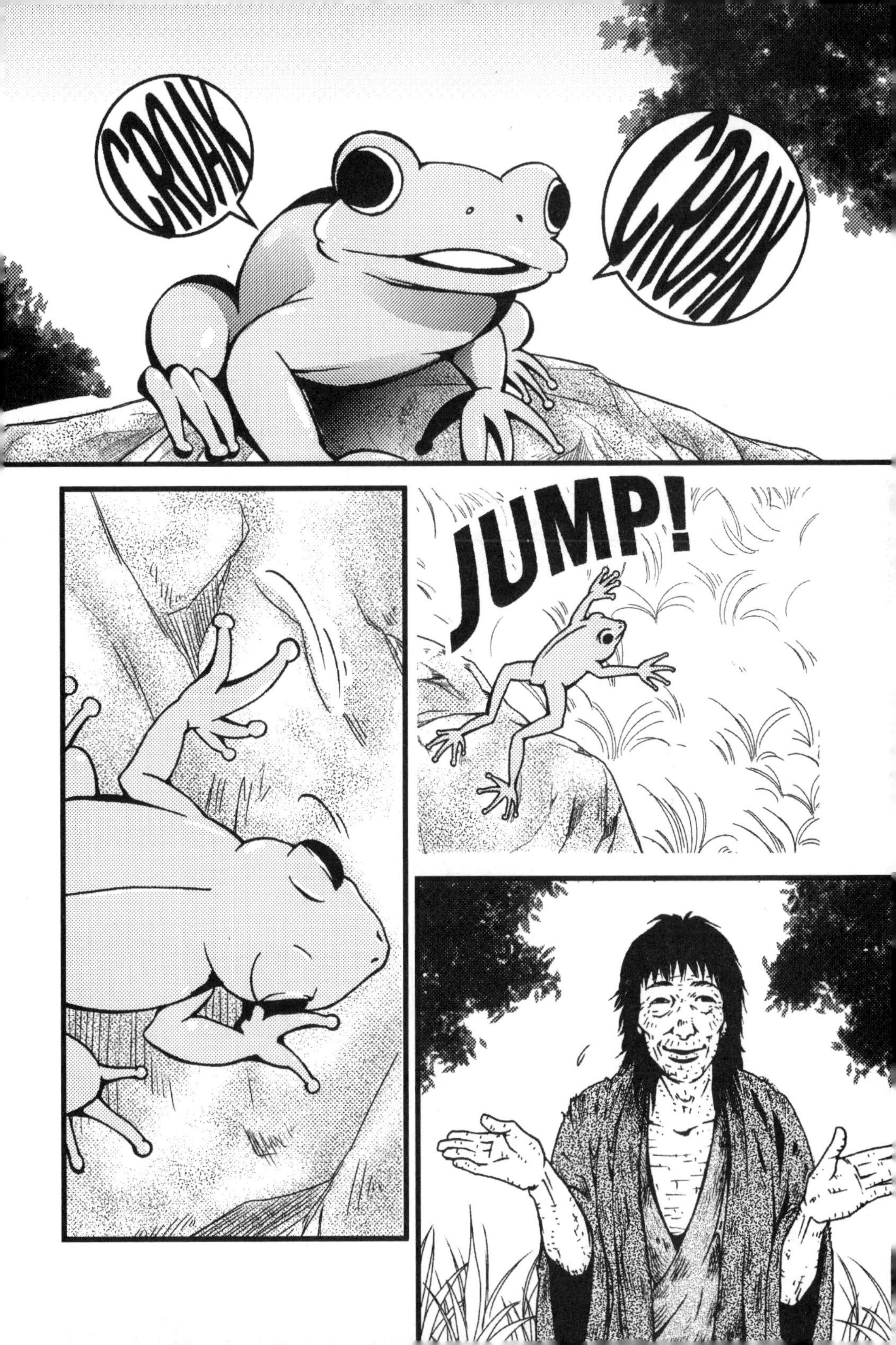
CROAK
CROAK
JUMP!

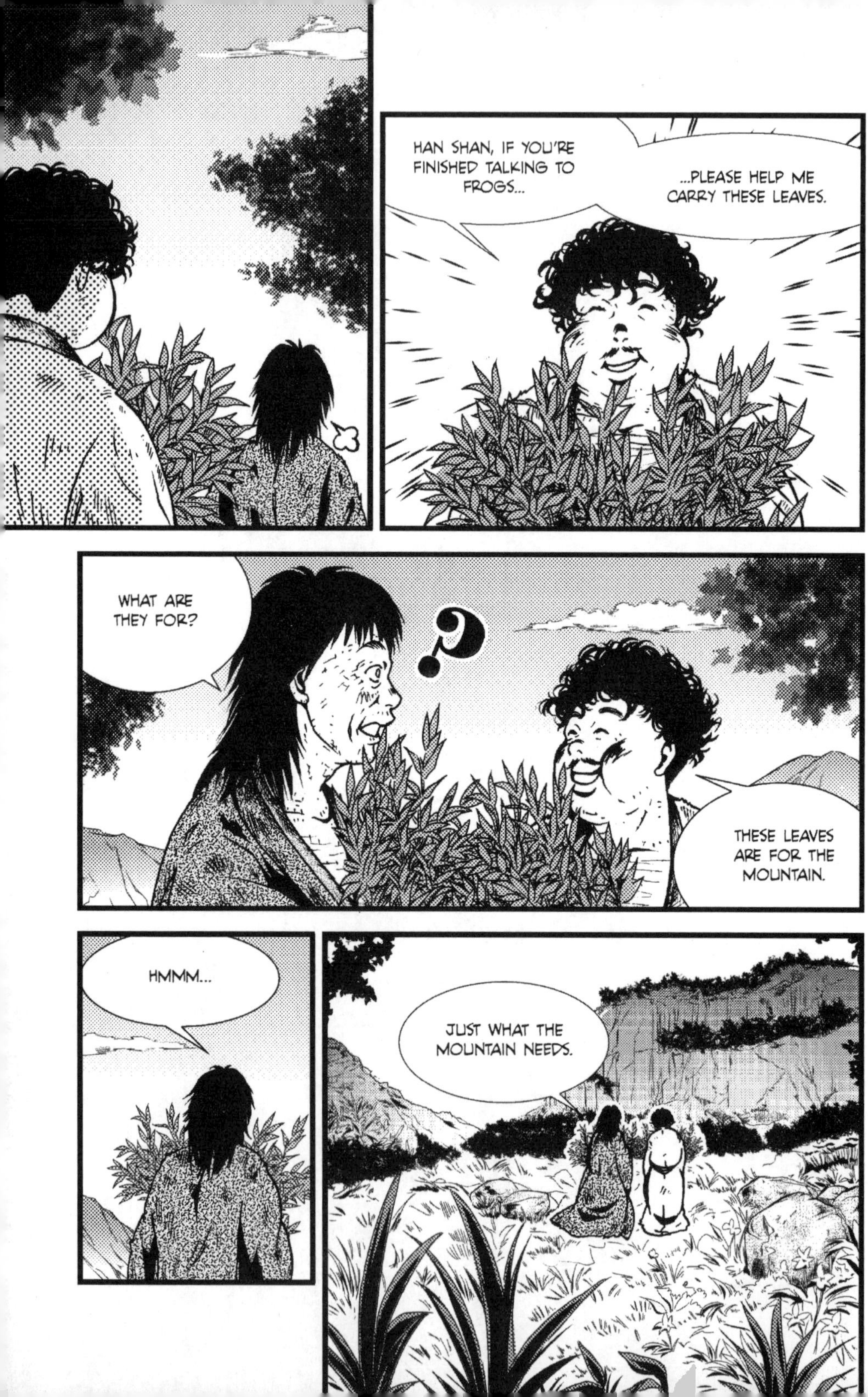
HAN SHAN, IF YOU'RE FINISHED TALKING TO FROGS...
...PLEASE HELP ME CARRY THESE LEAVES.
WHAT ARE THEY FOR?
?
THESE LEAVES ARE FOR THE MOUNTAIN.
HMMM...
JUST WHAT THE MOUNTAIN NEEDS.

PART 2

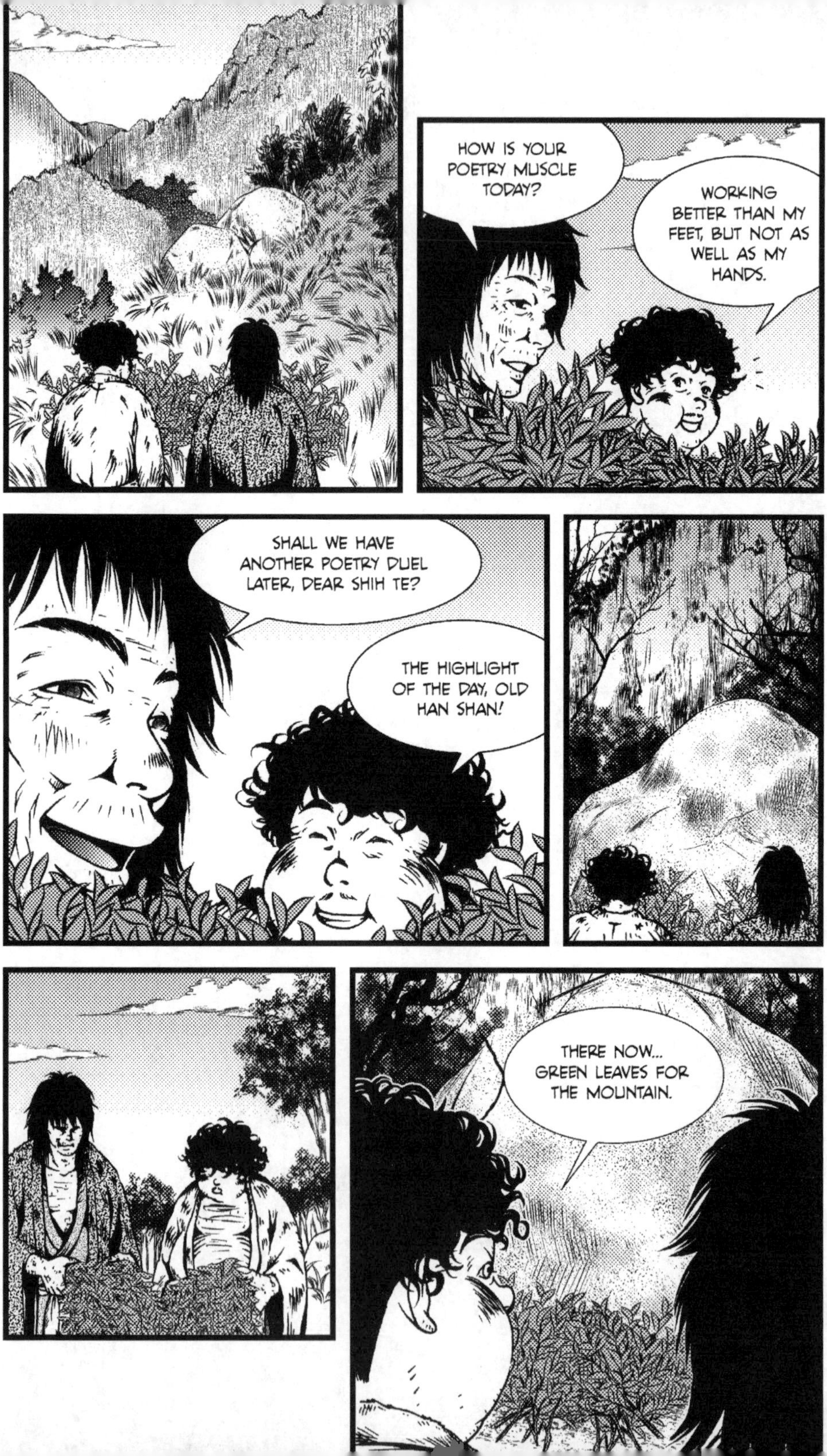
HOW IS YOUR POETRY MUSCLE TODAY?
WORKING BETTER THAN MY FEET, BUT NOT AS WELL AS MY HANDS.
SHALL WE HAVE ANOTHER POETRY DUEL LATER, DEAR SHIH TE?
THE HIGHLIGHT OF THE DAY, OLD HAN SHAN!
THERE NOW... GREEN LEAVES FOR THE MOUNTAIN.

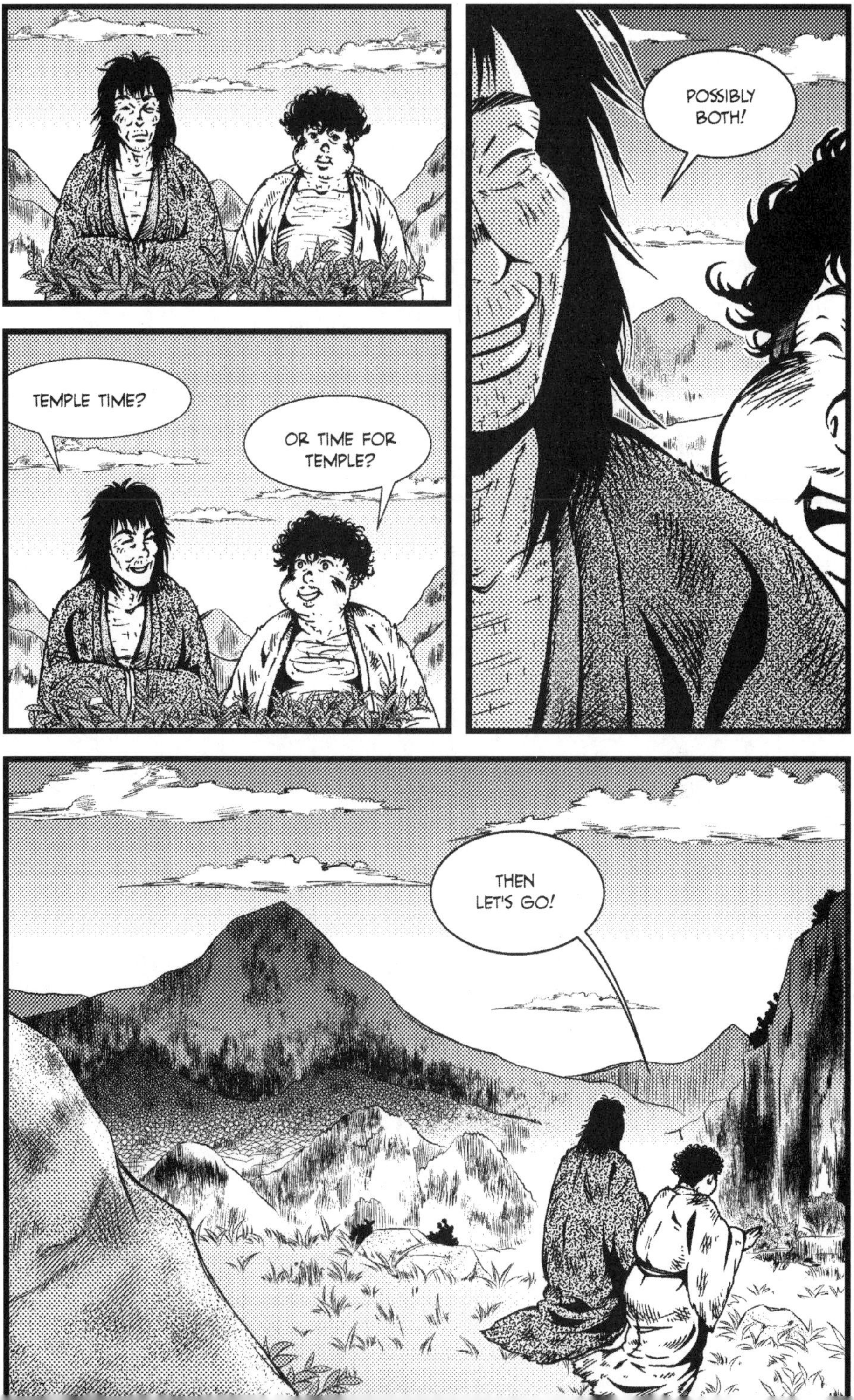
TEMPLE TIME?
OR TIME FOR TEMPLE?
POSSIBLY BOTH!
THEN LET'S GO!

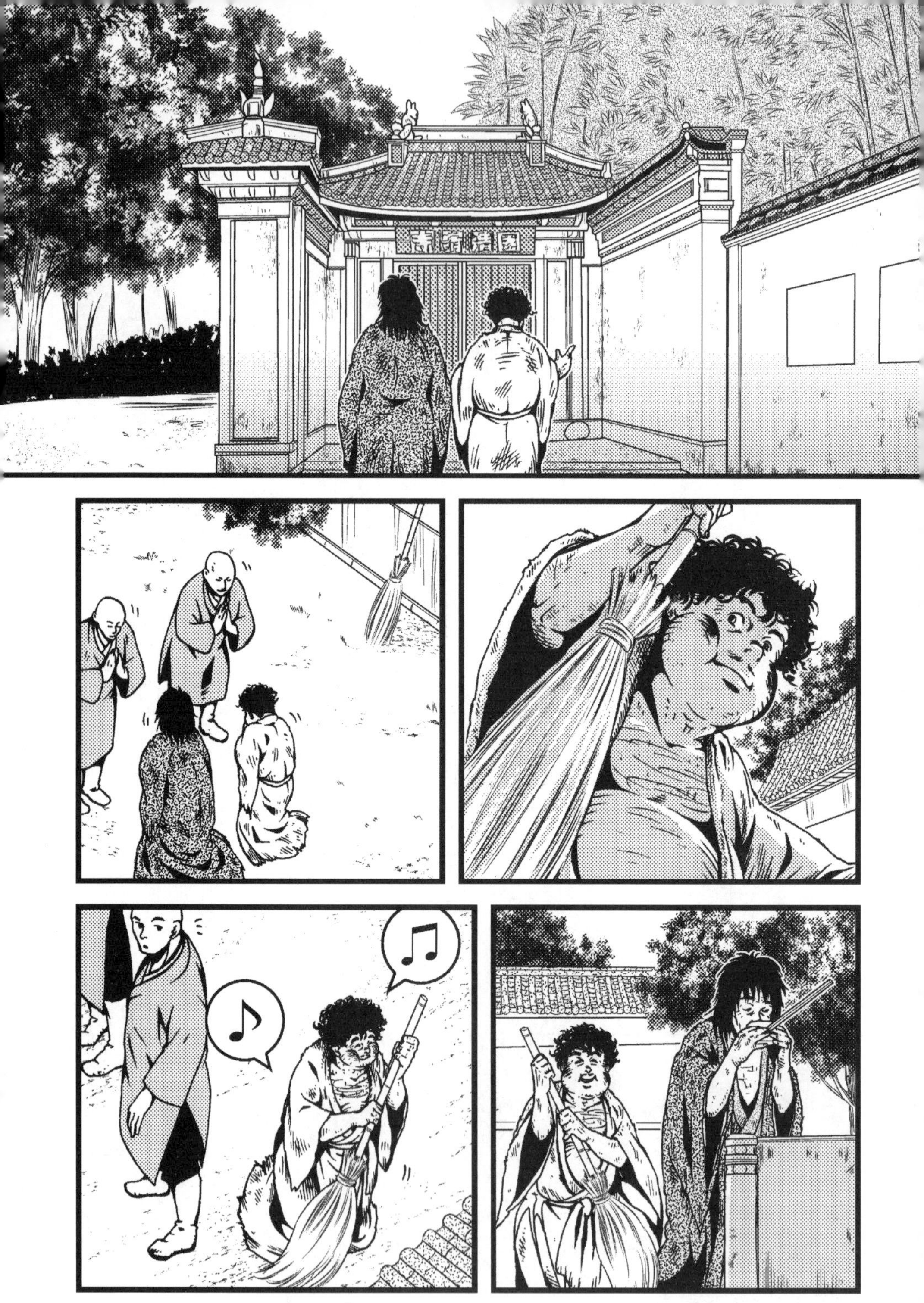

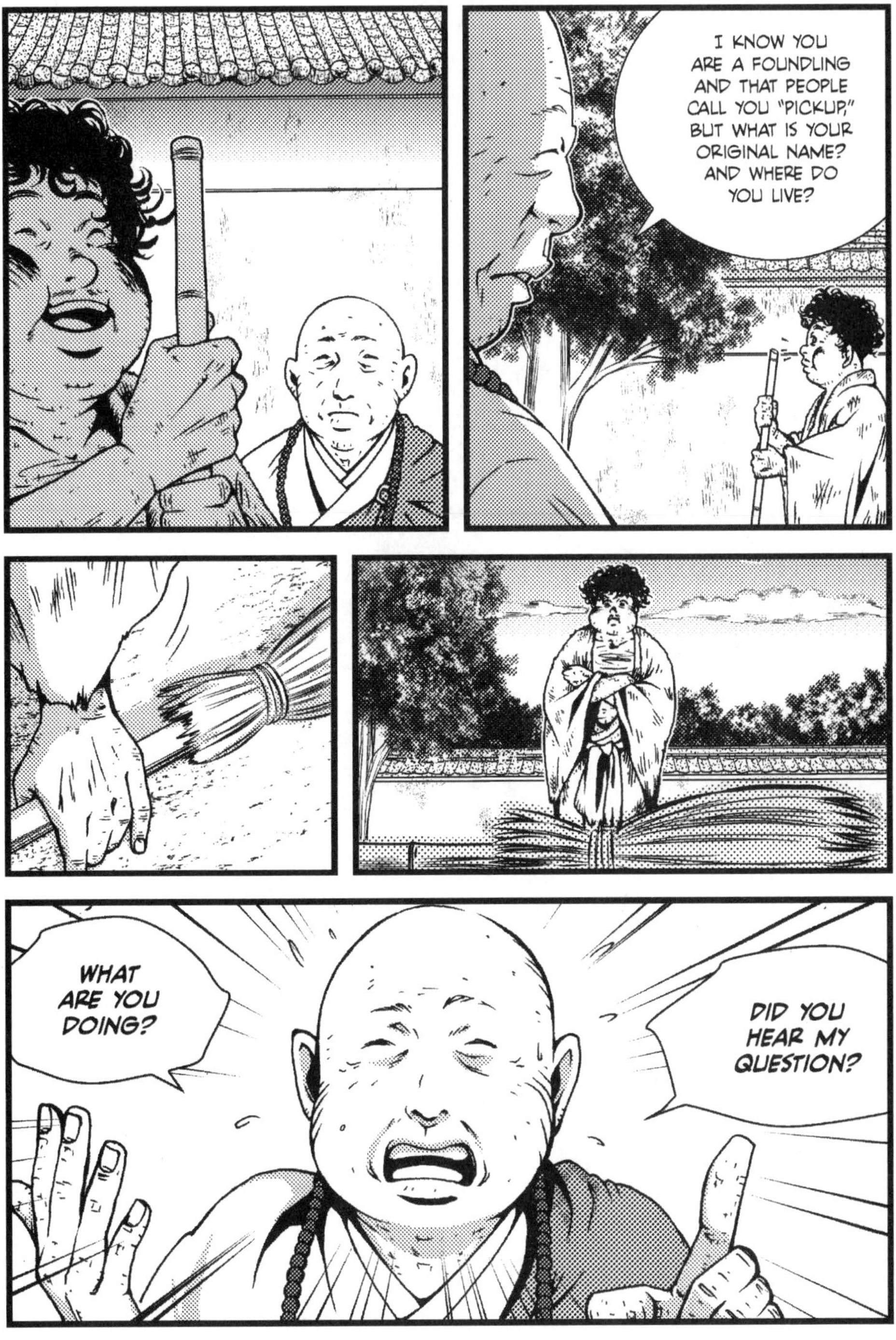
I KNOW YOU ARE A FOUNDLING AND THAT PEOPLE CALL YOU "PICKUP," BUT WHAT IS YOUR ORIGINAL NAME? AND WHERE DO YOU LIVE?
DID YOU HEAR MY QUESTION?
WHAT ARE YOU DOING?

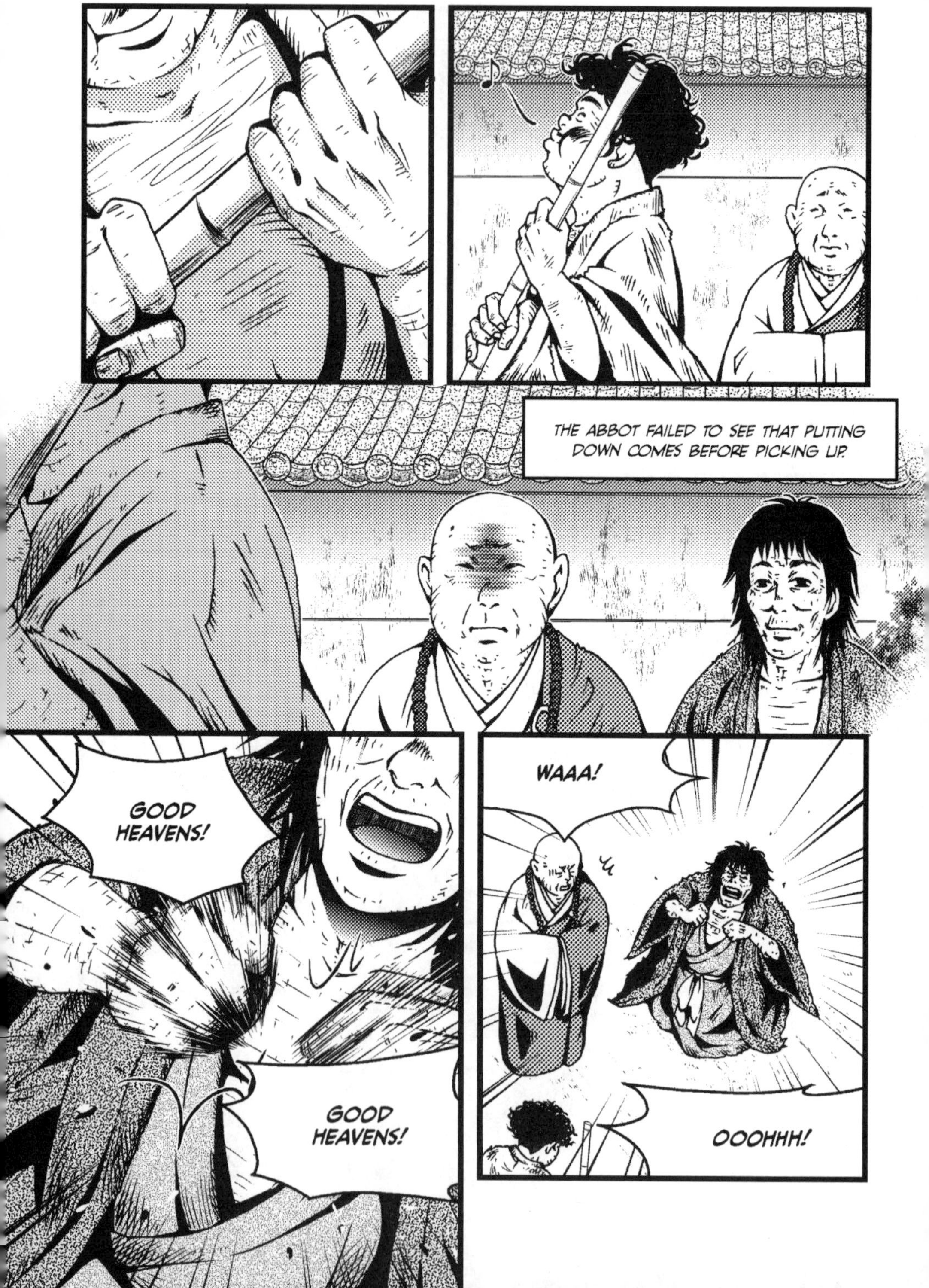
THE ABBOT FAILED TO SEE THAT PUTTING DOWN COMES BEFORE PICKING UP.
WAAA!
OOOHHH!
GOOD HEAVENS!
GOOD HEAVENS!

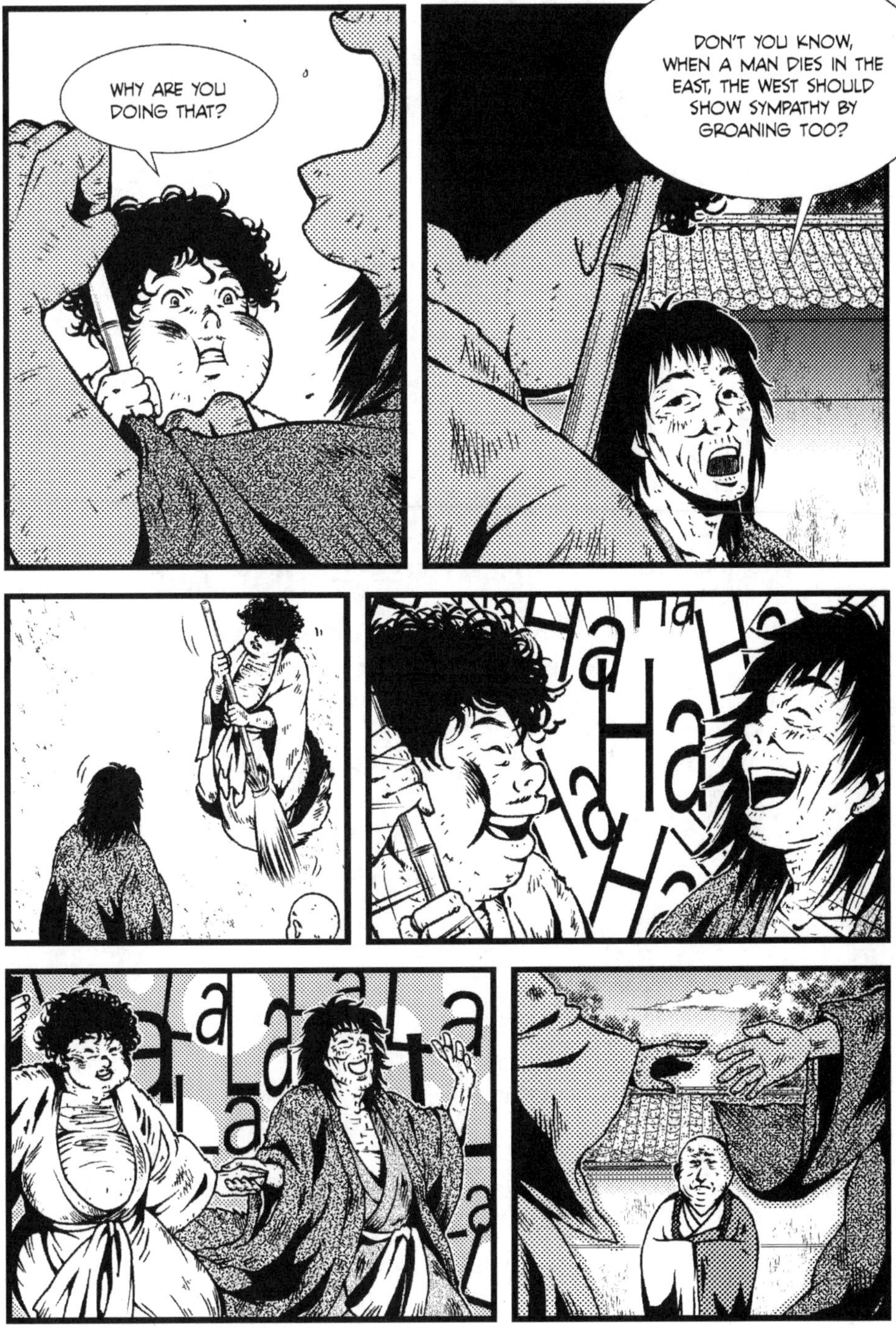
WHY ARE YOU DOING THAT?
DON'T YOU KNOW, WHEN A MAN DIES IN THE EAST, THE WEST SHOULD SHOW SYMPATHY BY GROANING TOO?

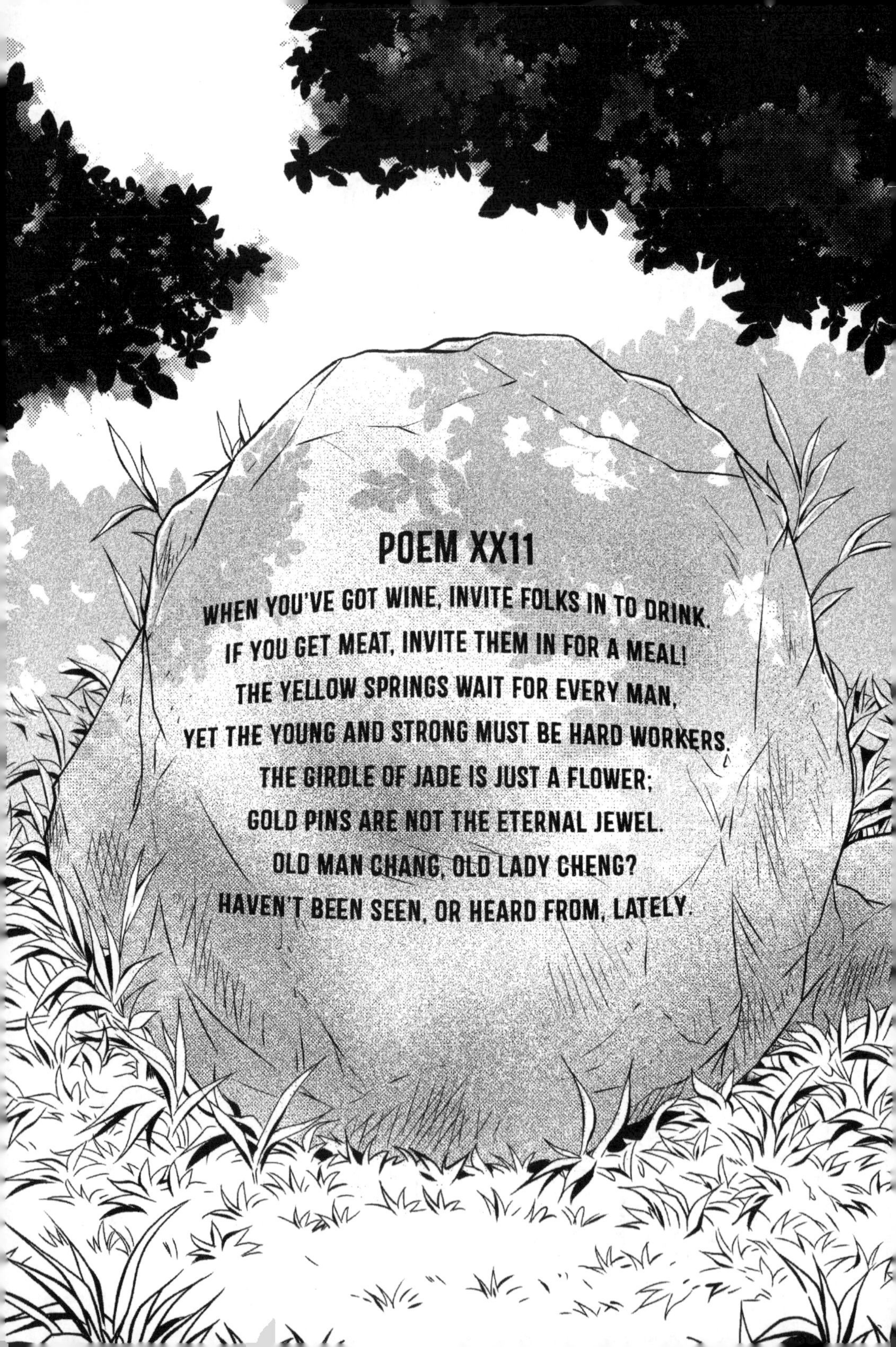
POEM XX11
WHEN YOU'VE GOT WINE, INVITE FOLKS IN TO DRINK.
IF YOU GET MEAT, INVITE THEM IN FOR A MEAL!
THE YELLOW SPRINGS WAIT FOR EVERY MAN,
YET THE YOUNG AND STRONG MUST BE HARD WORKERS.
THE GIRDLE OF JADE IS JUST A FLOWER;
GOLD PINS ARE NOT THE ETERNAL JEWEL.
OLD MAN CHANG, OLD LADY CHENG?
HAVEN'T BEEN SEEN, OR HEARD FROM, LATELY.

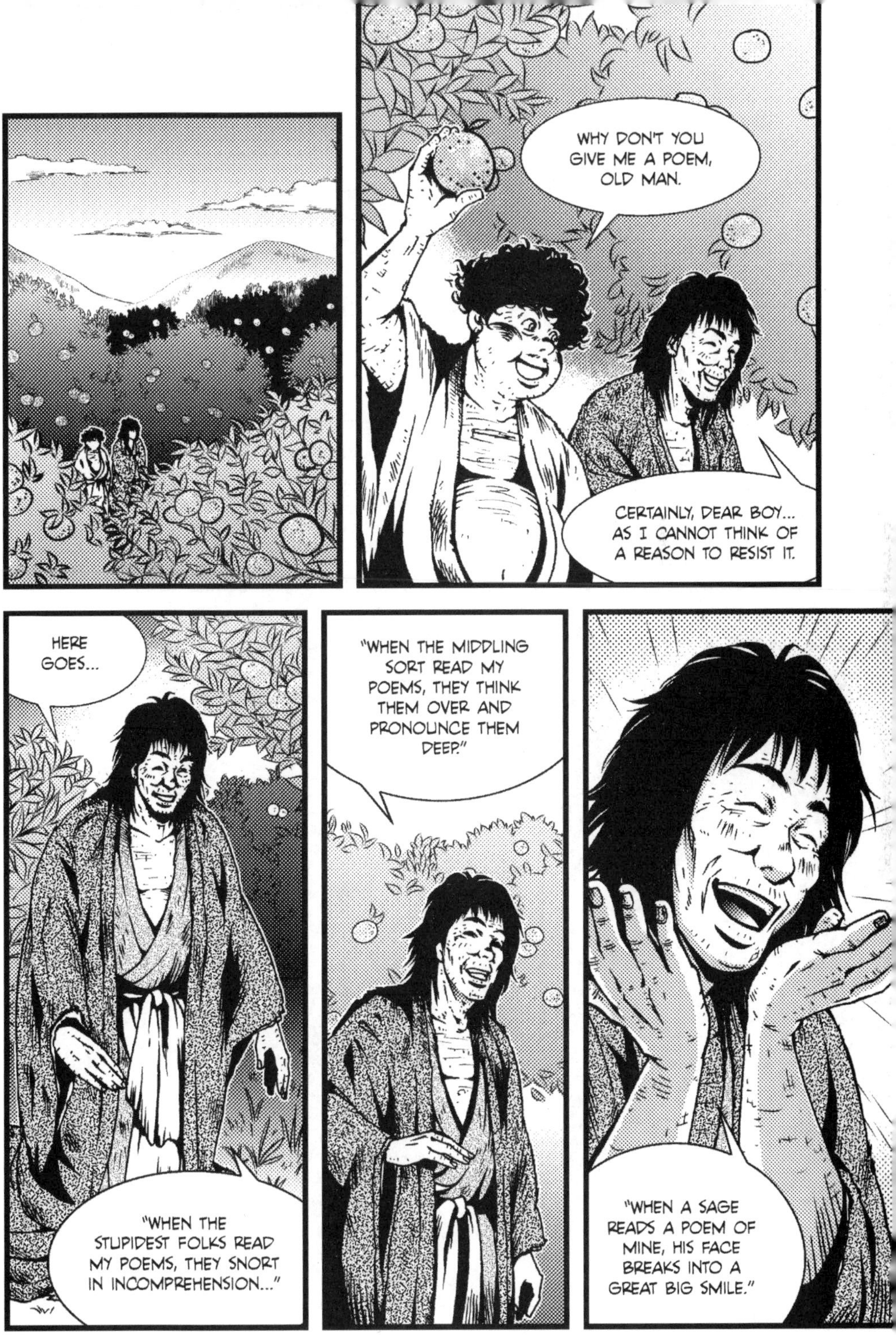
WHY DON'T YOU GIVE ME A POEM, OLD MAN.
CERTAINLY, DEAR BOY... AS I CANNOT THINK OF A REASON TO RESIST IT.
HERE GOES...
"WHEN THE STUPIDEST FOLKS READ MY POEMS, THEY SNORT IN INCOMPREHENSION..."
"WHEN THE MIDDLING SORT READ MY POEMS, THEY THINK THEM OVER AND PRONOUNCE THEM DEEP."
"WHEN A SAGE READS A POEM OF MINE, HIS FACE BREAKS INTO A GREAT BIG SMILE."

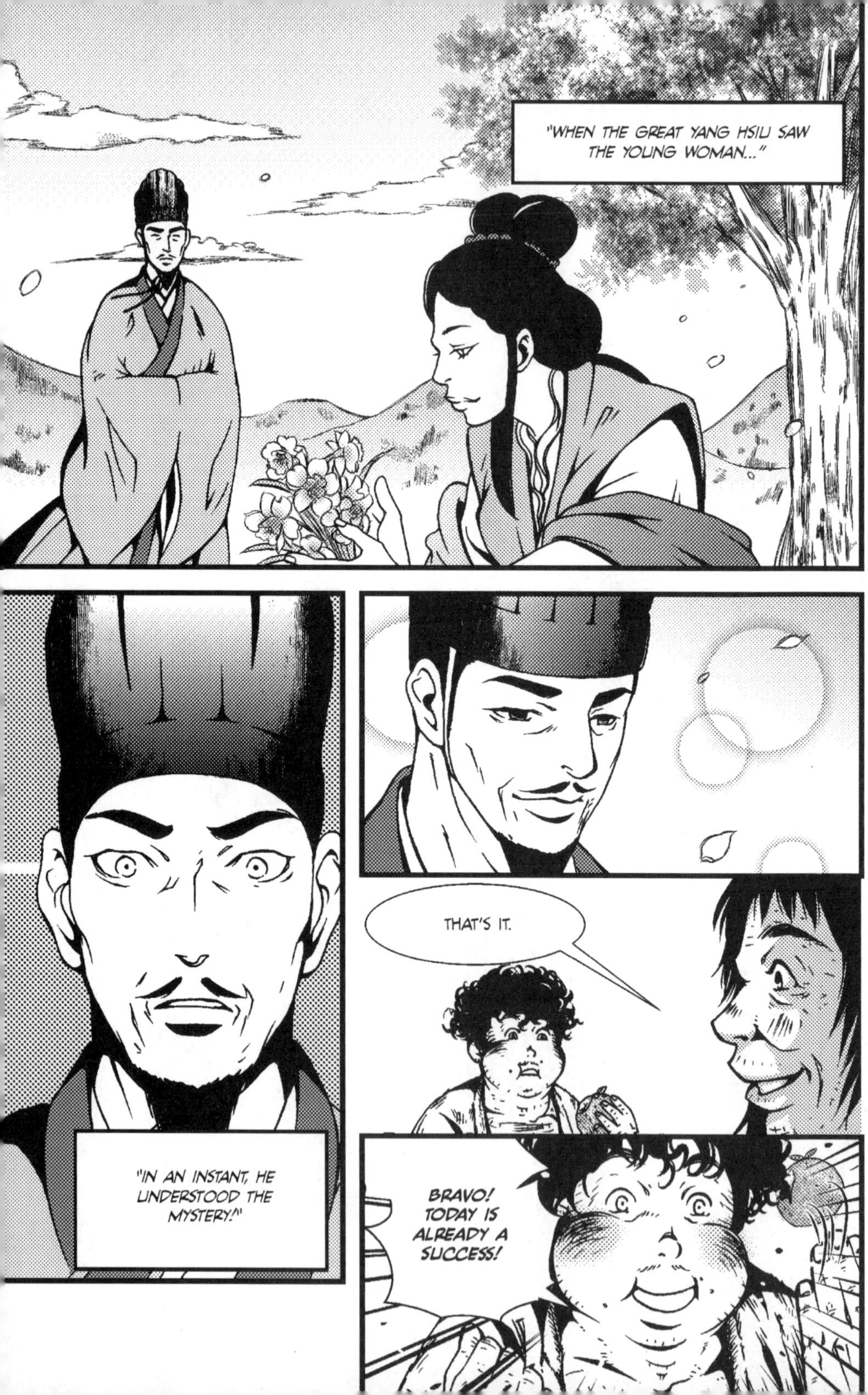
"WHEN THE GREAT YANG HSIU SAW THE YOUNG WOMAN..."
"IN AN INSTANT, HE UNDERSTOOD THE MYSTERY!"
THAT'S IT.
BRAVO! TODAY IS ALREADY A SUCCESS!

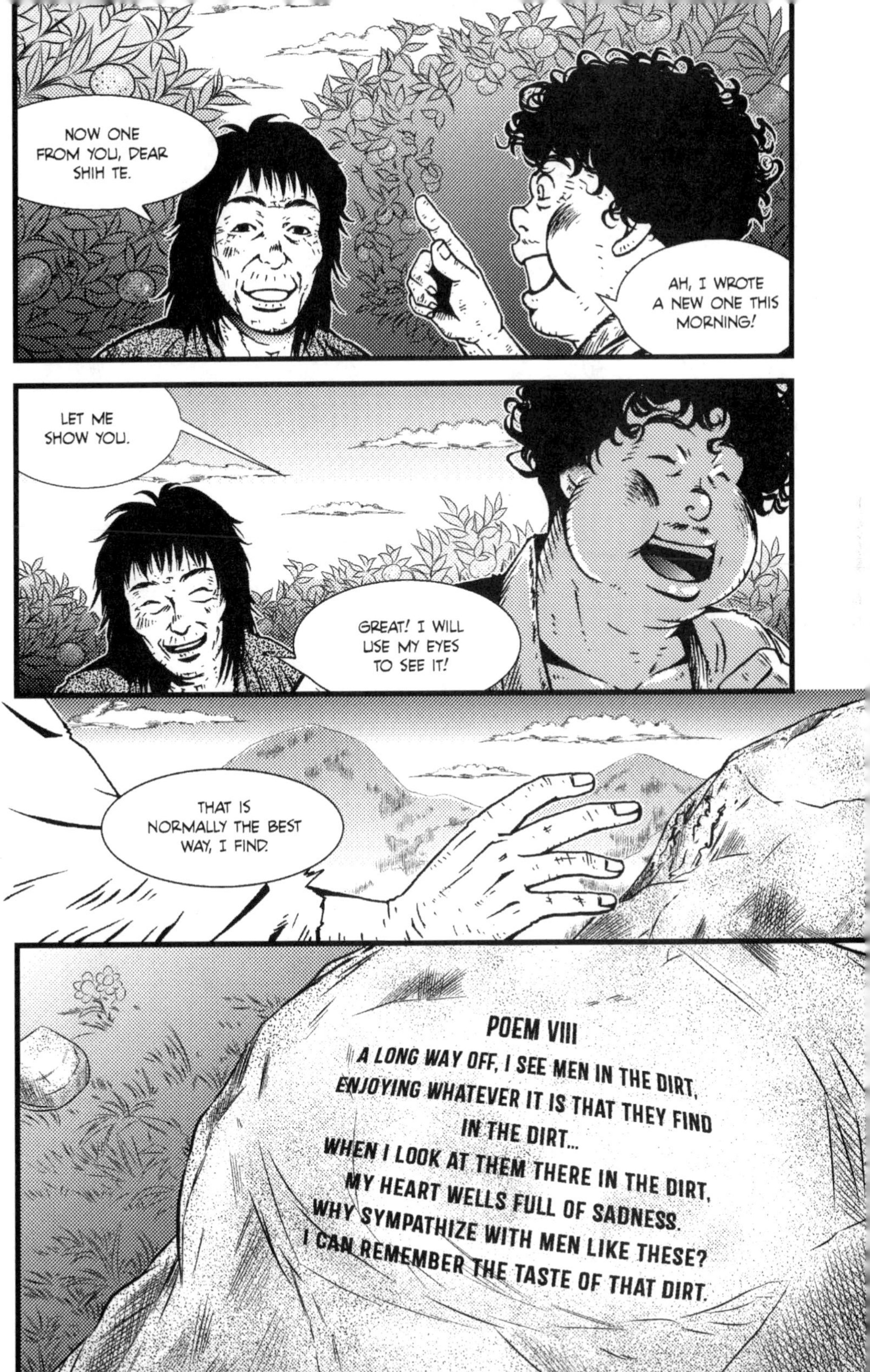
NOW ONE FROM YOU, DEAR SHIH TE.
AH, I WROTE A NEW ONE THIS MORNING!
LET ME SHOW YOU.
GREAT! I WILL USE MY EYES TO SEE IT!
THAT IS NORMALLY THE BEST WAY, I FIND.
POEM VIII
A LONG WAY OFF, I SEE MEN IN THE DIRT,
ENJOYING WHATEVER IT IS THAT THEY FIND
IN THE DIRT...
WHEN I LOOK AT THEM THERE IN THE DIRT,
MY HEART WELLS FULL OF SADNESS.
WHY SYMPATHIZE WITH MEN LIKE THESE?
I CAN REMEMBER THE TASTE OF THAT DIRT.

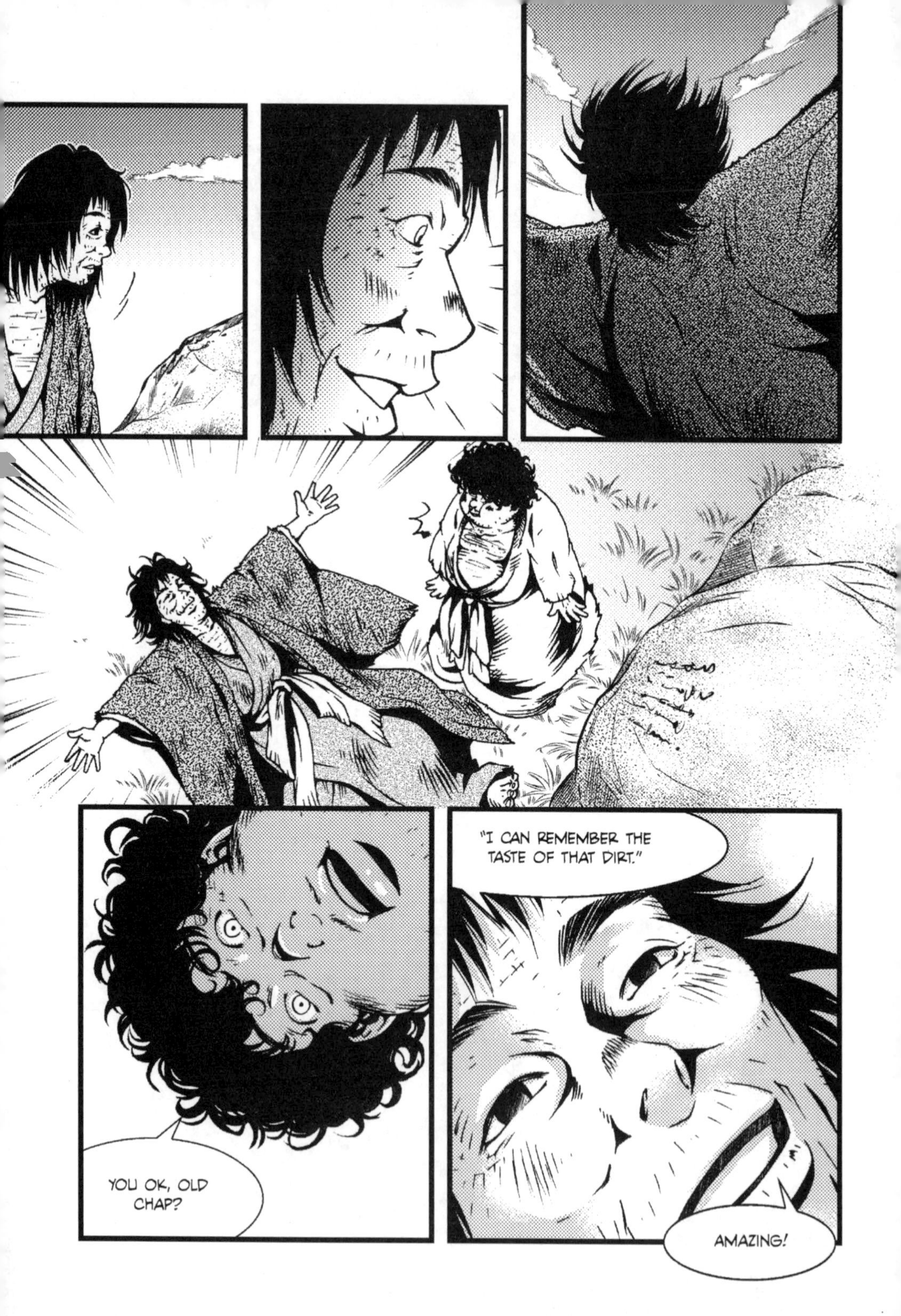
"I CAN REMEMBER THE TASTE OF THAT DIRT."
AMAZING!
YOU OK, OLD CHAP?

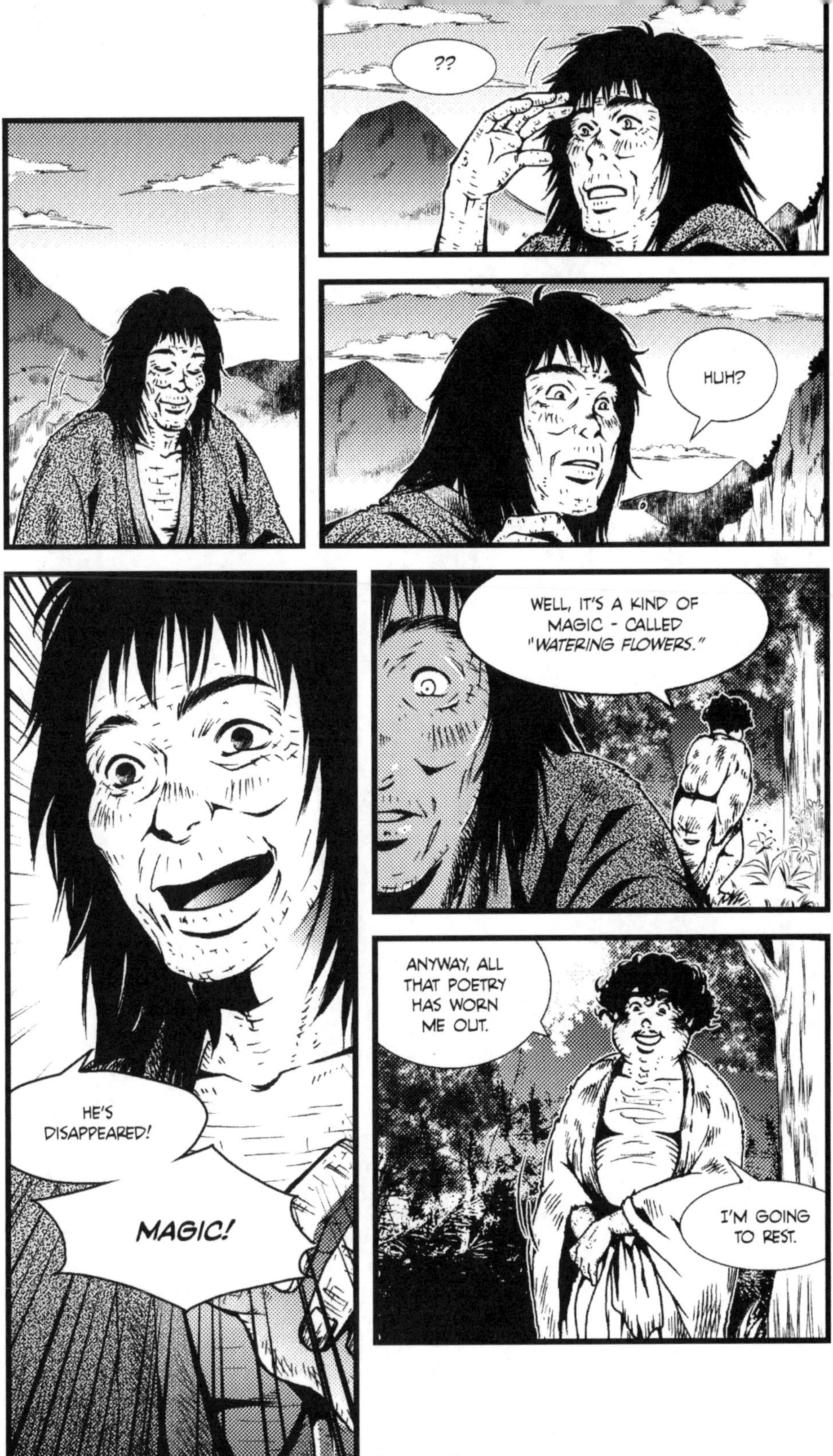
??
HUH?
HE'S DISAPPEARED!
MAGIC!
WELL, IT'S A KIND OF MAGIC - CALLED "WATERING FLOWERS."
ANYWAY, ALL THAT POETRY HAS WORN ME OUT.
I'M GOING TO REST.

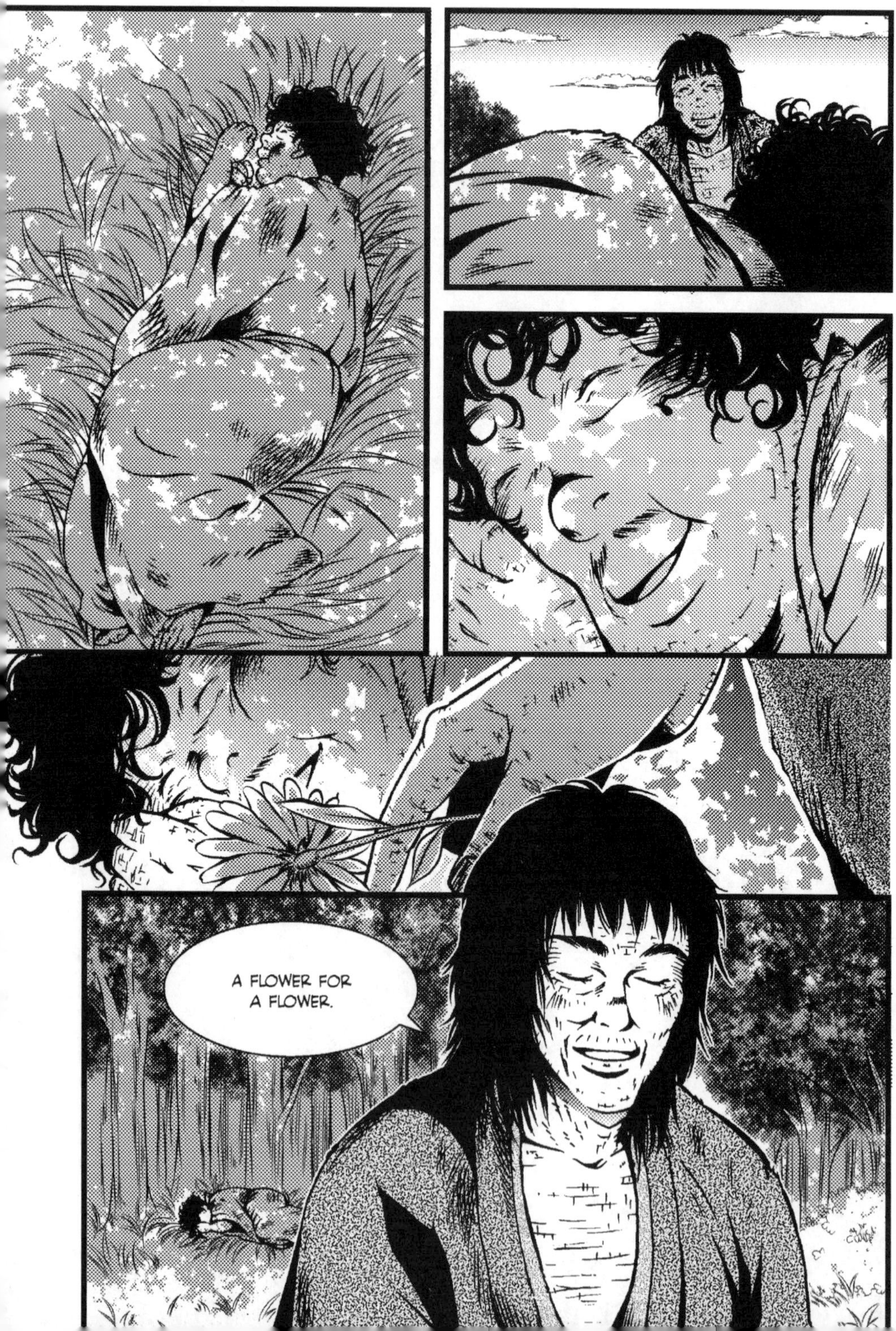
A FLOWER FOR
A FLOWER.

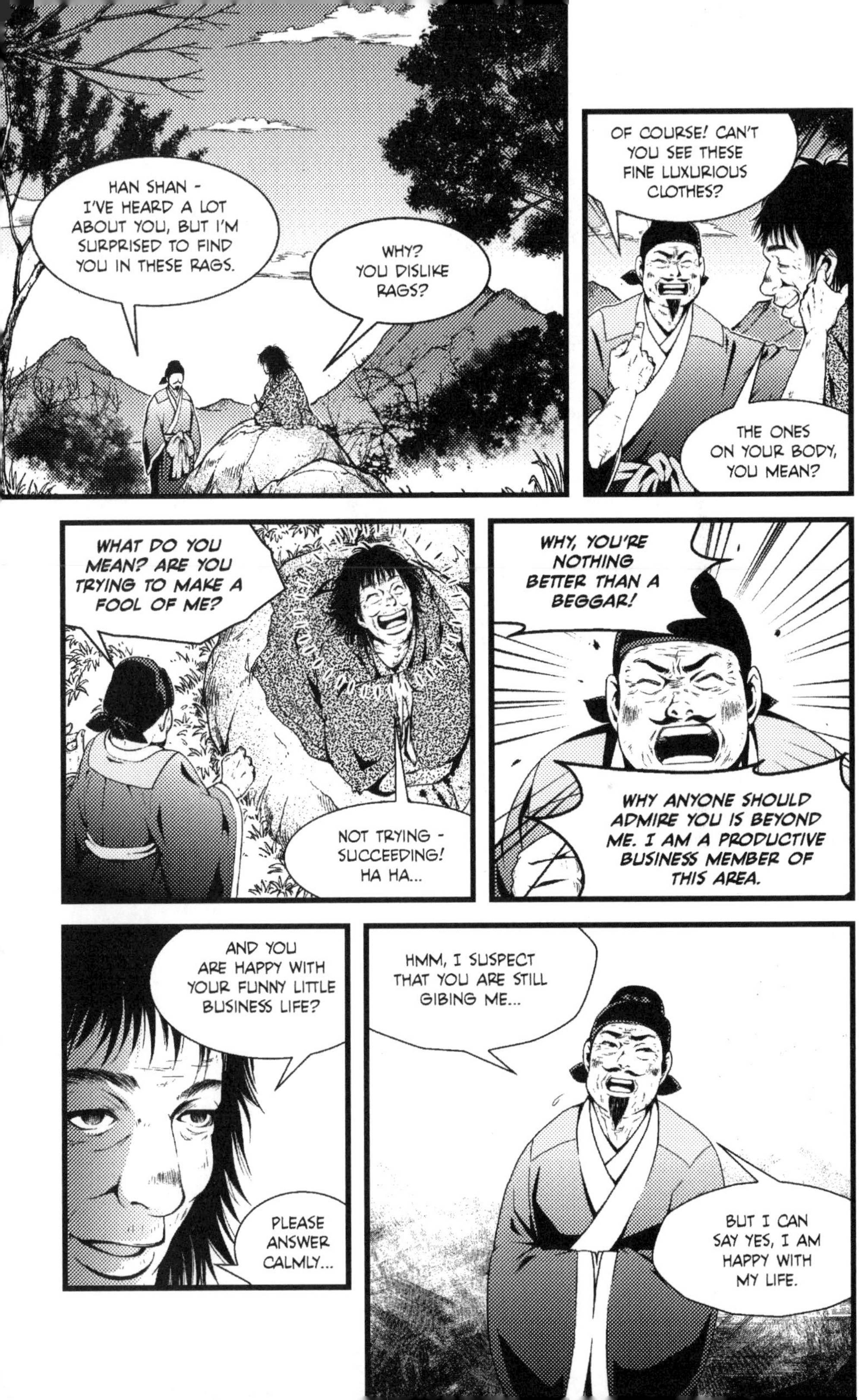
HAN SHAN - I'VE HEARD A LOT ABOUT YOU, BUT I'M SURPRISED TO FIND YOU IN THESE RAGS.
WHY? YOU DISLIKE RAGS?
OF COURSE! CAN'T YOU SEE THESE FINE LUXURIOUS CLOTHES?
THE ONES ON YOUR BODY, YOU MEAN?
WHAT DO YOU MEAN? ARE YOU TRYING TO MAKE A FOOL OF ME?
NOT TRYING - SUCCEEDING! HA HA...
WHY, YOU'RE NOTHING BETTER THAN A BEGGAR!
WHY ANYONE SHOULD ADMIRE YOU IS BEYOND ME. I AM A PRODUCTIVE BUSINESS MEMBER OF THIS AREA.
AND YOU ARE HAPPY WITH YOUR FUNNY LITTLE BUSINESS LIFE?
PLEASE ANSWER CALMLY...
HMM, I SUSPECT THAT YOU ARE STILL GIBING ME...
BUT I CAN SAY YES, I AM HAPPY WITH MY LIFE.

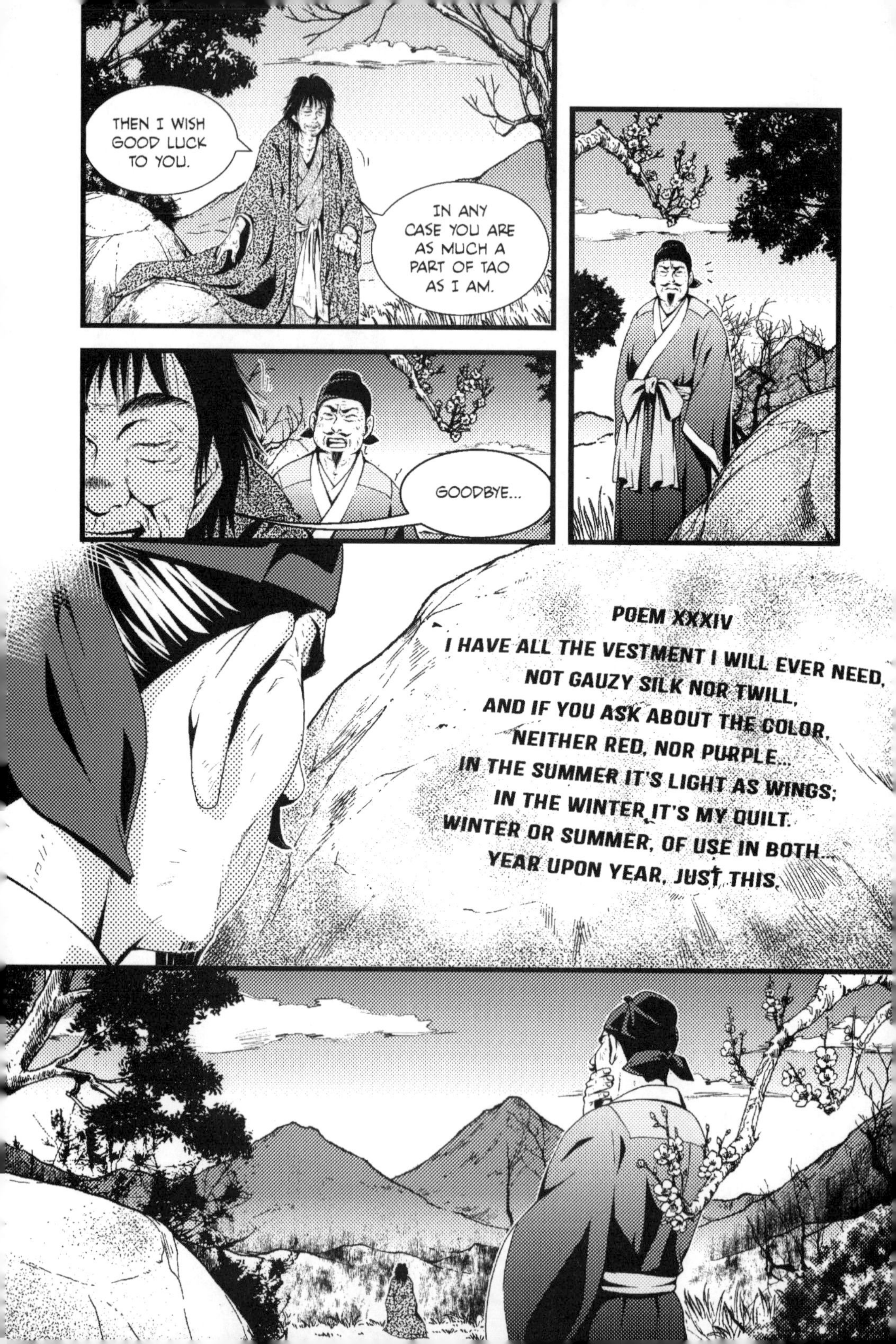
THEN I WISH GOOD LUCK TO YOU.
IN ANY CASE YOU ARE AS MUCH A PART OF TAO AS I AM.
GOODBYE...
POEM XXXIV
I HAVE ALL THE VESTMENT I WILL EVER NEED,
NOT GAUZY SILK NOR TWILL,
AND IF YOU ASK ABOUT THE COLOR,
NEITHER RED, NOR PURPLE...
IN THE SUMMER IT'S LIGHT AS WINGS;
IN THE WINTER IT'S MY QUILT.
WINTER OR SUMMER, OF USE IN BOTH...
YEAR UPON YEAR, JUST THIS.

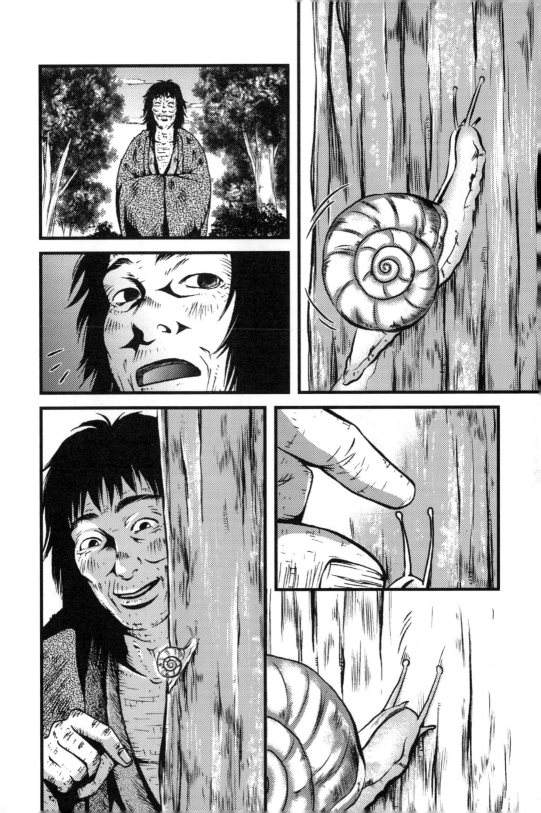

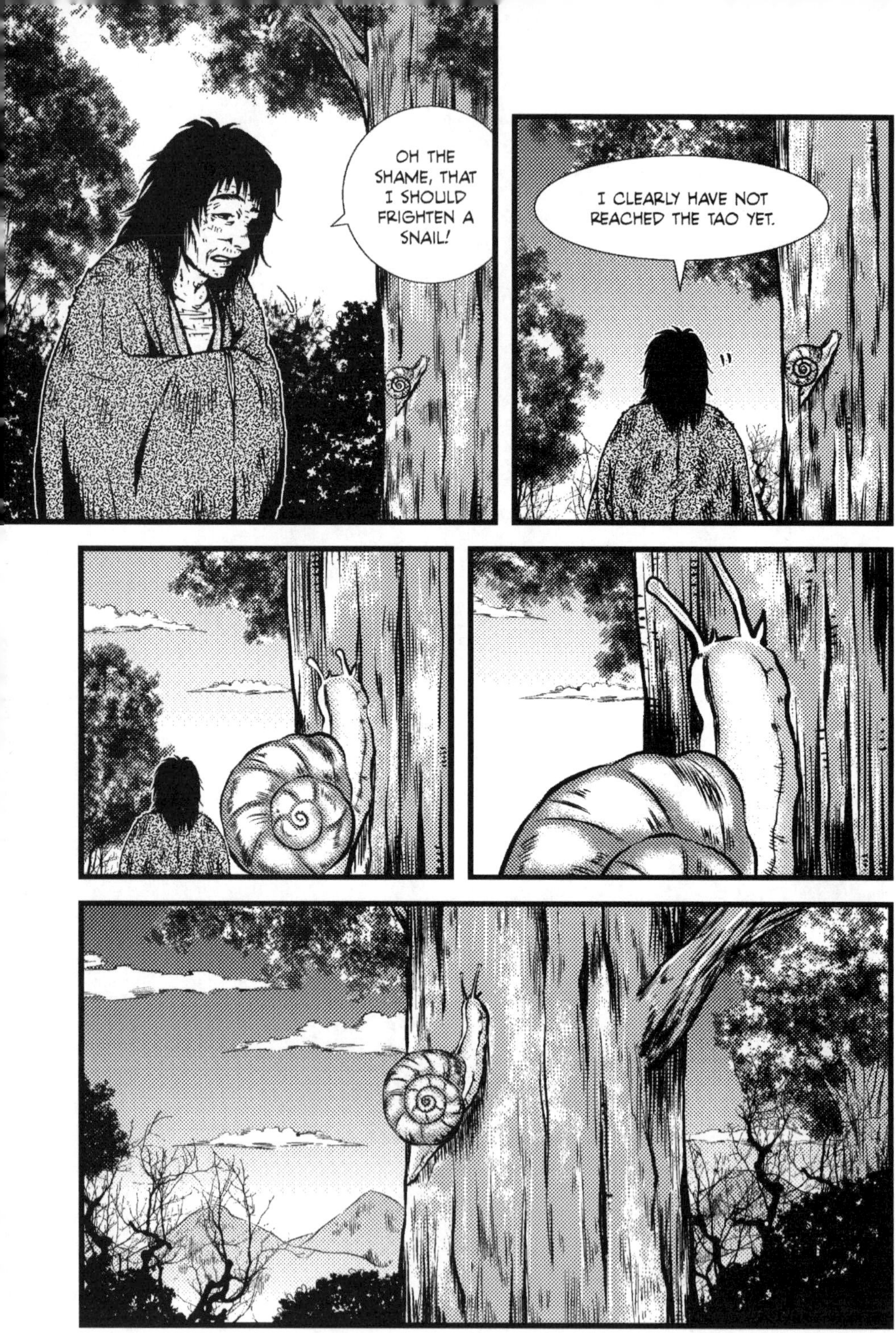
OH THE SHAME, THAT I SHOULD FRIGHTEN A SNAIL!
I CLEARLY HAVE NOT REACHED THE TAO YET.

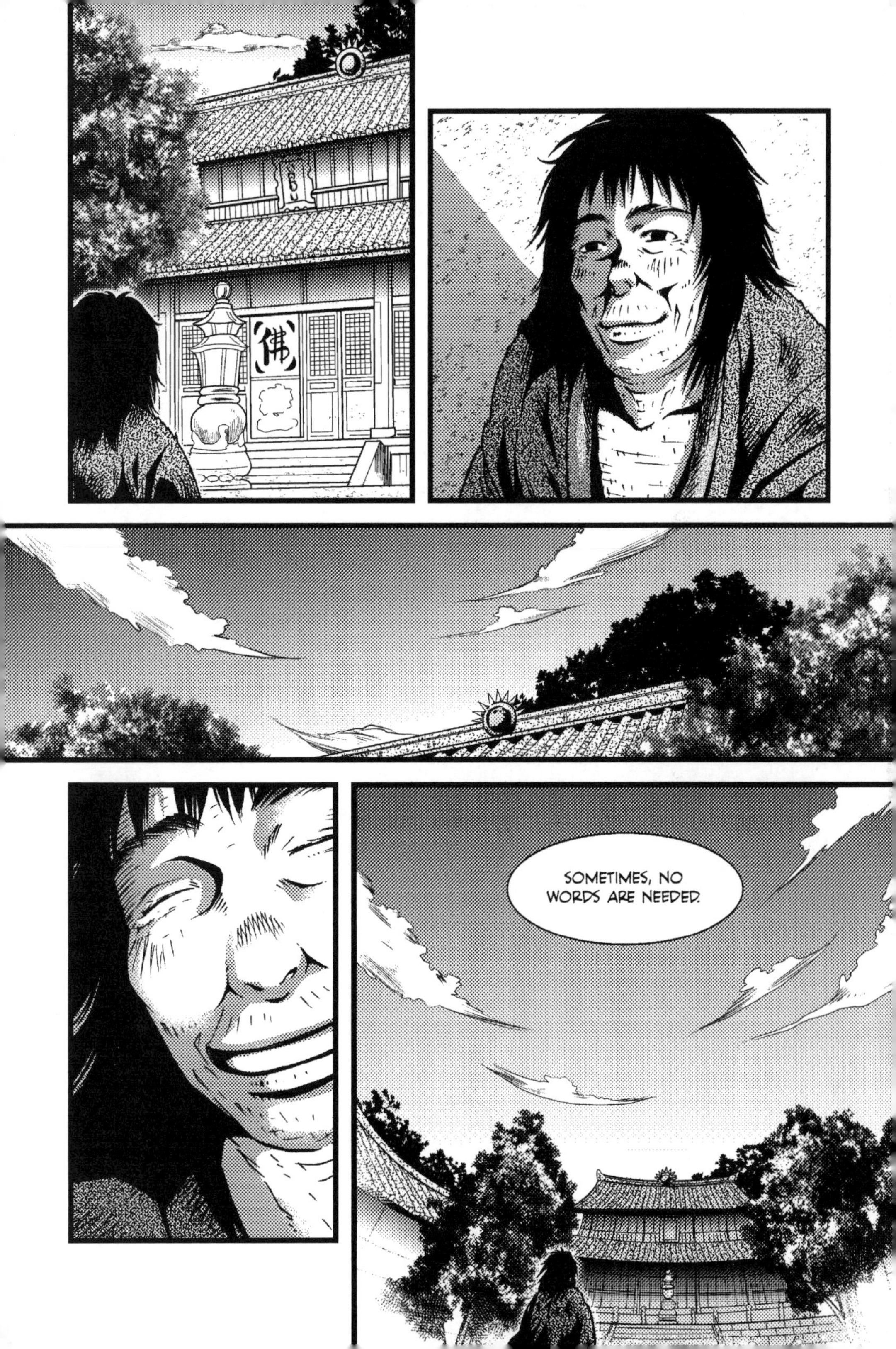
SOMETIMES, NO WORDS ARE NEEDED.

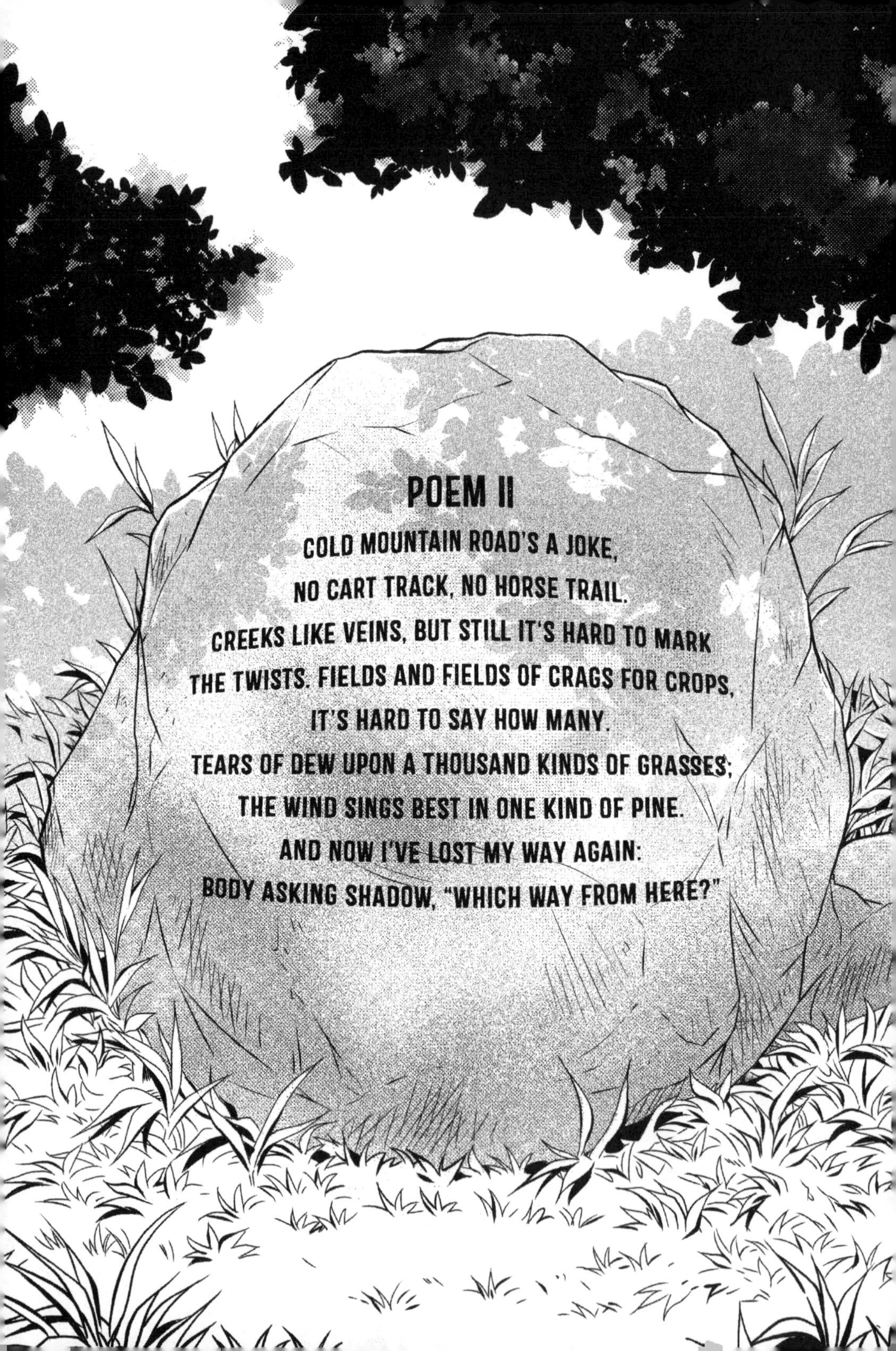
POEM II
COLD MOUNTAIN ROAD'S A JOKE,
NO CART TRACK, NO HORSE TRAIL.
CREEKS LIKE VEINS, BUT STILL IT'S HARD TO MARK
THE TWISTS. FIELDS AND FIELDS OF CRAGS FOR CROPS,
IT'S HARD TO SAY HOW MANY.
TEARS OF DEW UPON A THOUSAND KINDS OF GRASSES;
THE WIND SINGS BEST IN ONE KIND OF PINE.
AND NOW I'VE LOST MY WAY AGAIN:
BODY ASKING SHADOW, "WHICH WAY FROM HERE?"

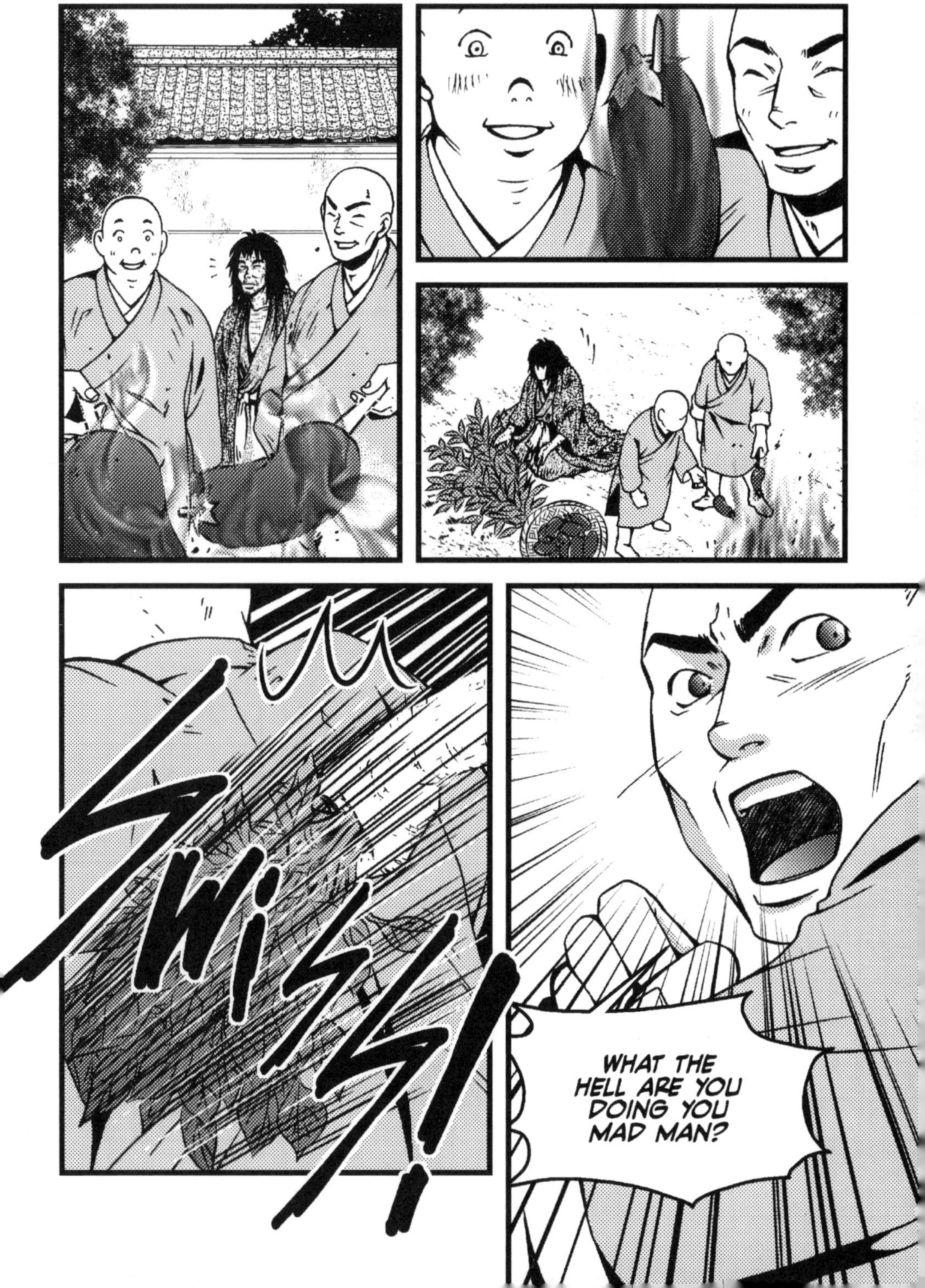
SWISH!
WHAT THE HELL ARE YOU DOING YOU MAD MAN?

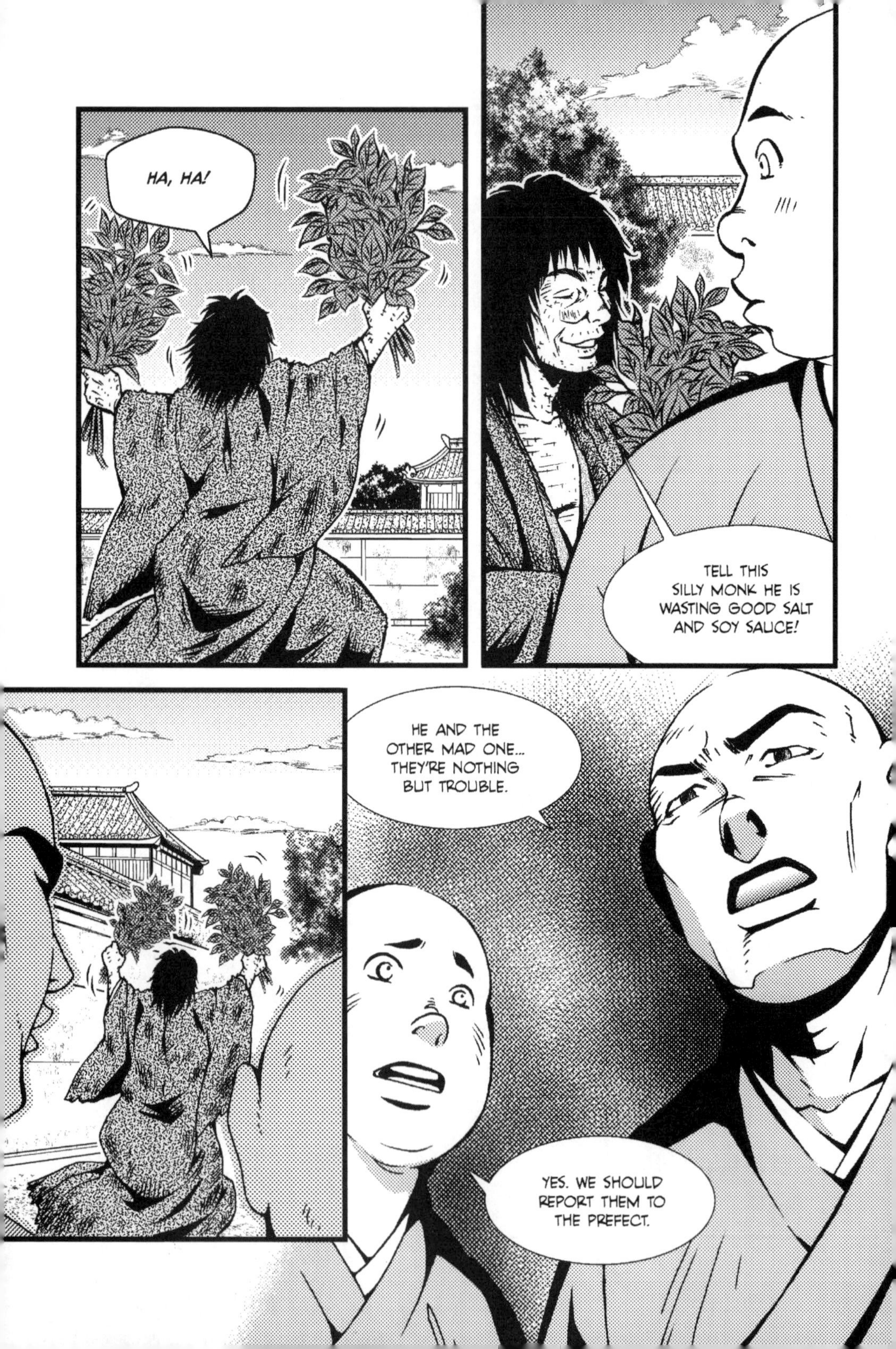
TELL THIS SILLY MONK HE IS WASTING GOOD SALT AND SOY SAUCE!
HA, HA!
HE AND THE OTHER MAD ONE... THEY'RE NOTHING BUT TROUBLE.
YES. WE SHOULD REPORT THEM TO THE PREFECT.

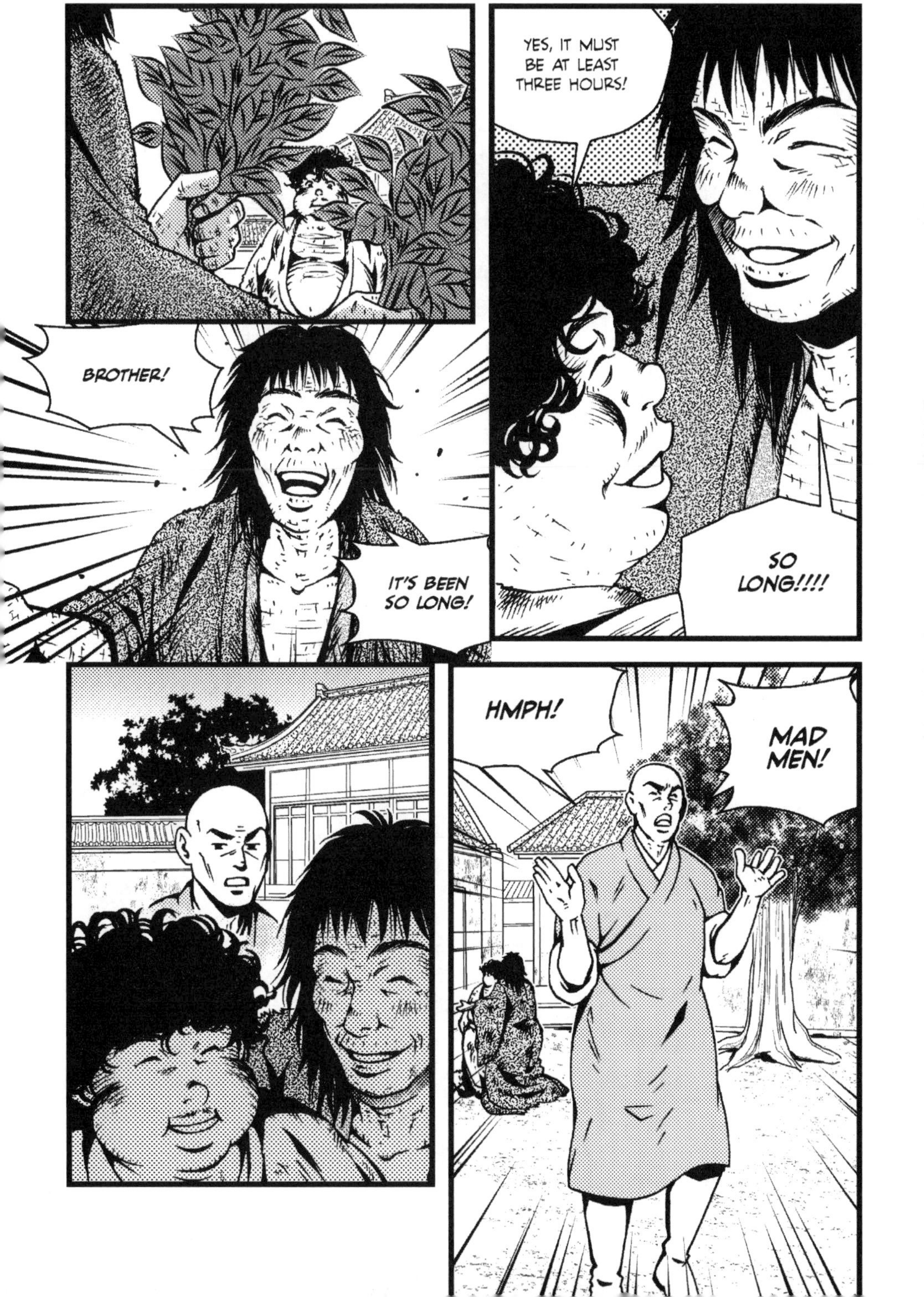
BROTHER!
IT'S BEEN SO LONG!
YES, IT MUST BE AT LEAST THREE HOURS!
SO LONG!!!!
HMPH!
MAD MEN!

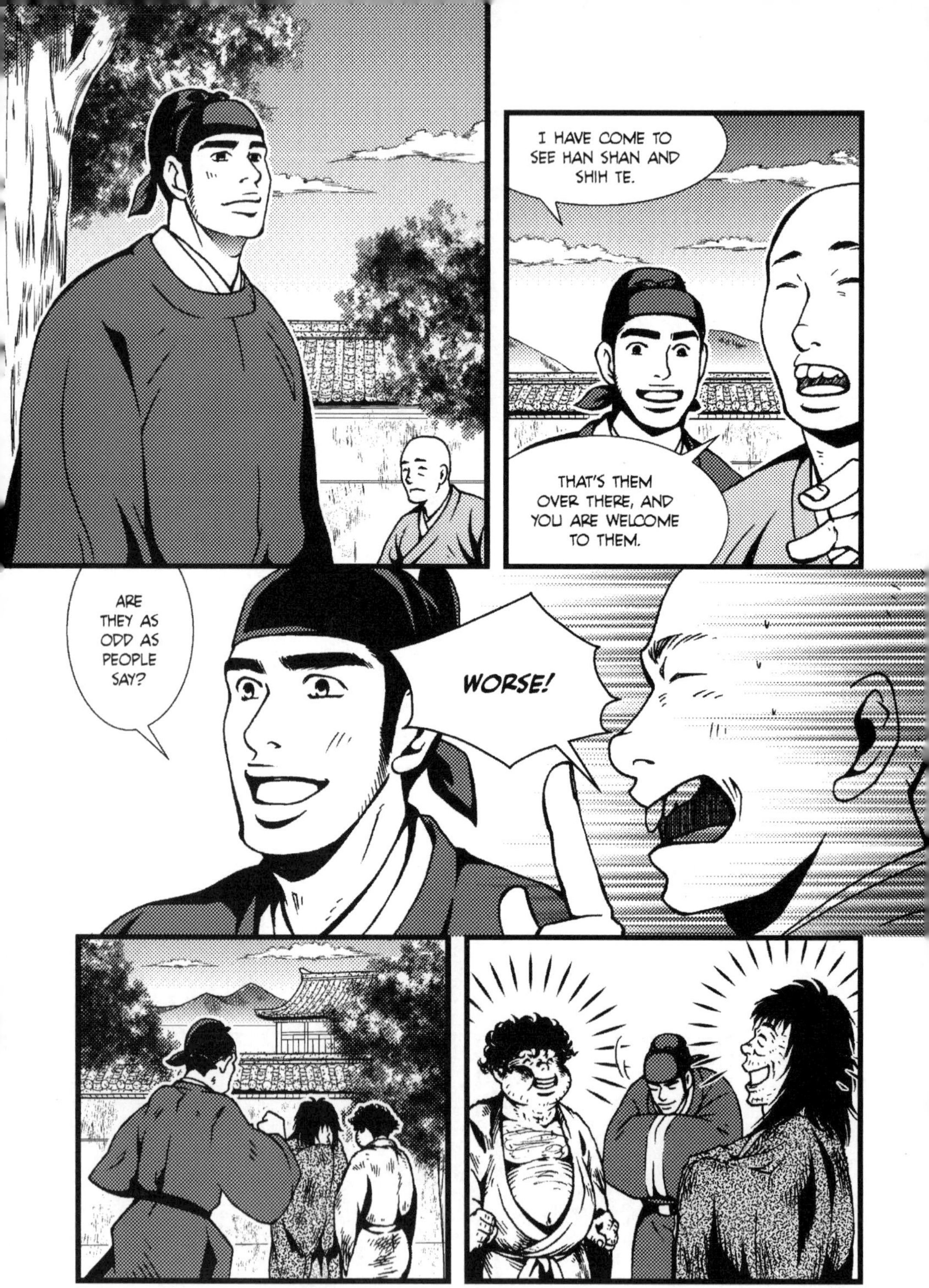
I HAVE COME TO SEE HAN SHAN AND SHIH TE.
THAT'S THEM OVER THERE, AND YOU ARE WELCOME TO THEM.
ARE THEY AS ODD AS PEOPLE SAY?
WORSE!

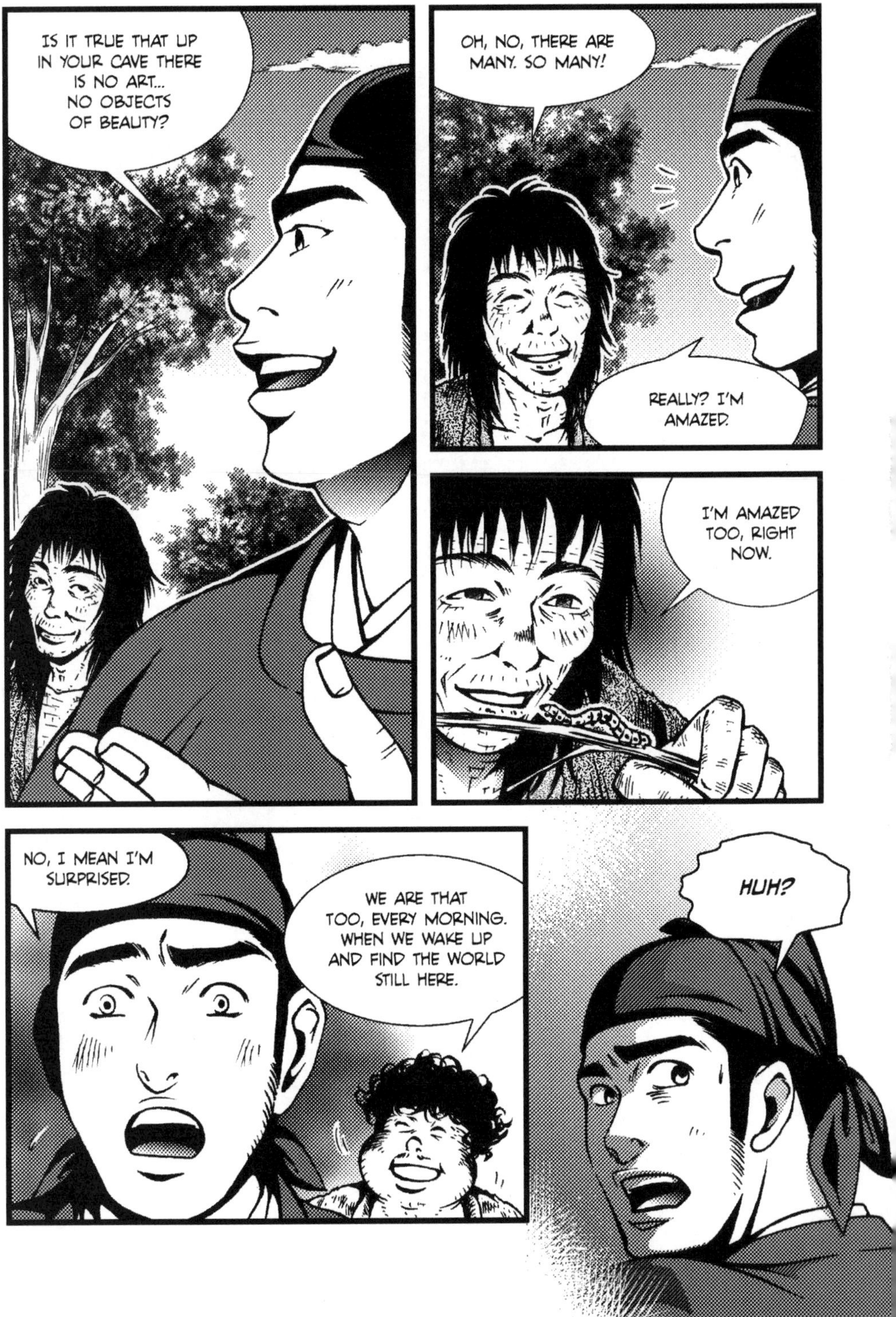
IS IT TRUE THAT UP IN YOUR CAVE THERE IS NO ART... NO OBJECTS OF BEAUTY?
OH, NO, THERE ARE MANY. SO MANY!
REALLY? I'M AMAZED.
I'M AMAZED TOO, RIGHT NOW.
NO, I MEAN I'M SURPRISED.
WE ARE THAT TOO, EVERY MORNING. WHEN WE WAKE UP AND FIND THE WORLD STILL HERE.
HUH?

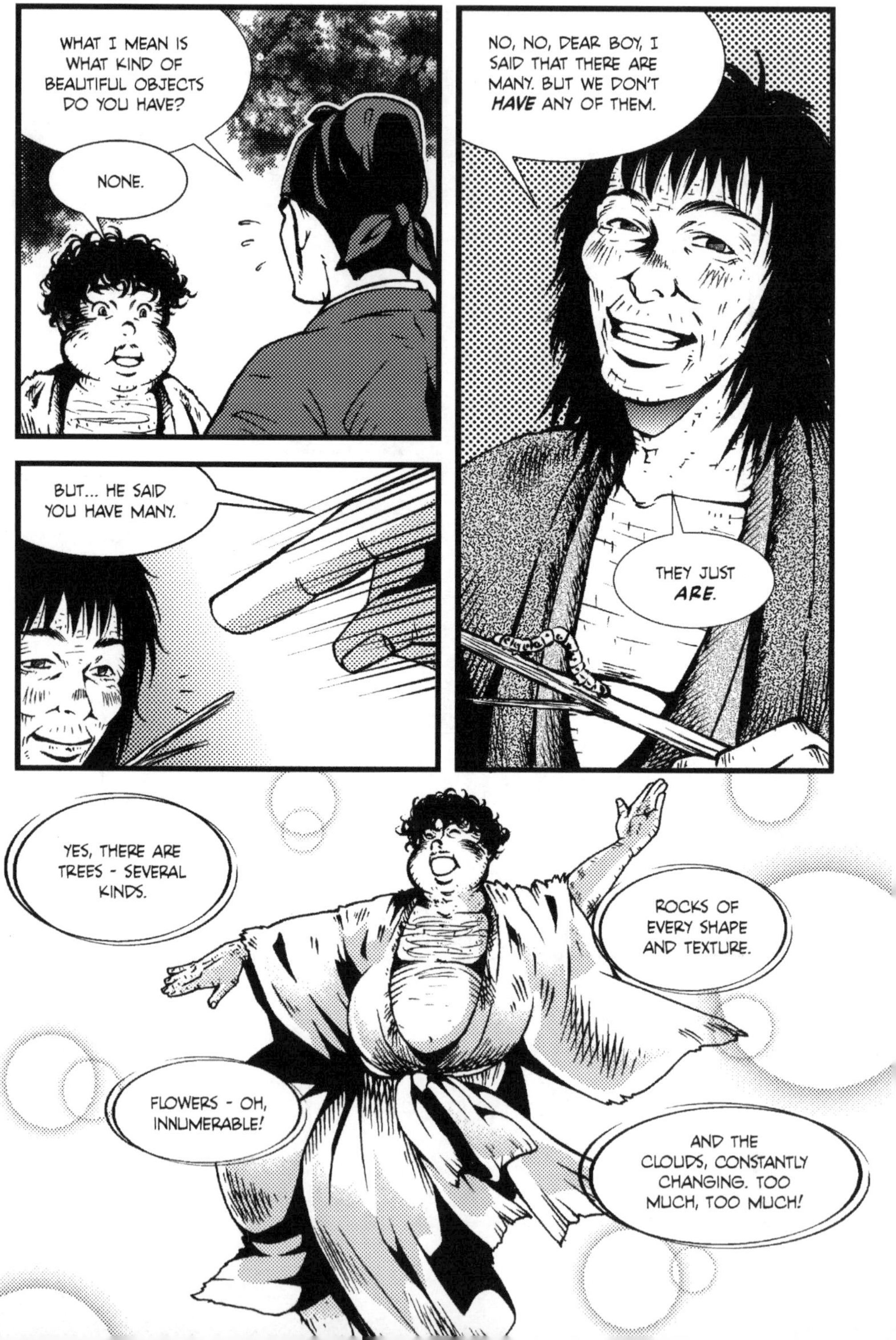
WHAT I MEAN IS WHAT KIND OF BEAUTIFUL OBJECTS DO YOU HAVE?
NONE.
BUT... HE SAID YOU HAVE MANY.
NO, NO, DEAR BOY, I SAID THAT THERE ARE MANY. BUT WE DON'T ***HAVE*** ANY OF THEM.
THEY JUST ***ARE***.
YES, THERE ARE TREES - SEVERAL KINDS.
ROCKS OF EVERY SHAPE AND TEXTURE.
FLOWERS - OH, INNUMERABLE!
AND THE CLOUDS, CONSTANTLY CHANGING. TOO MUCH, TOO MUCH!

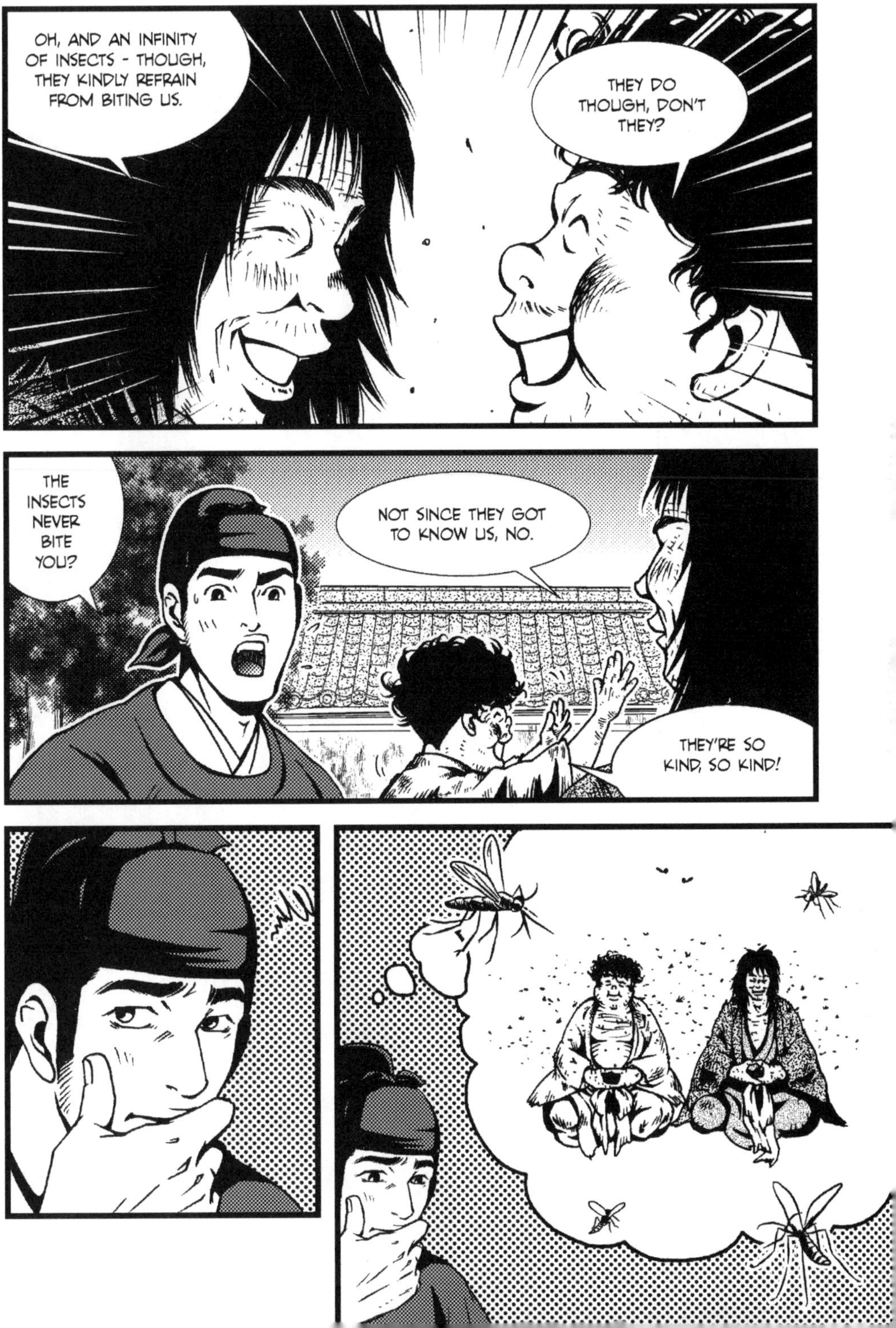

OH, AND AN INFINITY OF INSECTS - THOUGH, THEY KINDLY REFRAIN FROM BITING US.
THEY DO THOUGH, DON'T THEY?
THE INSECTS NEVER BITE YOU?
NOT SINCE THEY GOT TO KNOW US, NO.
THEY'RE SO KIND, SO KIND!

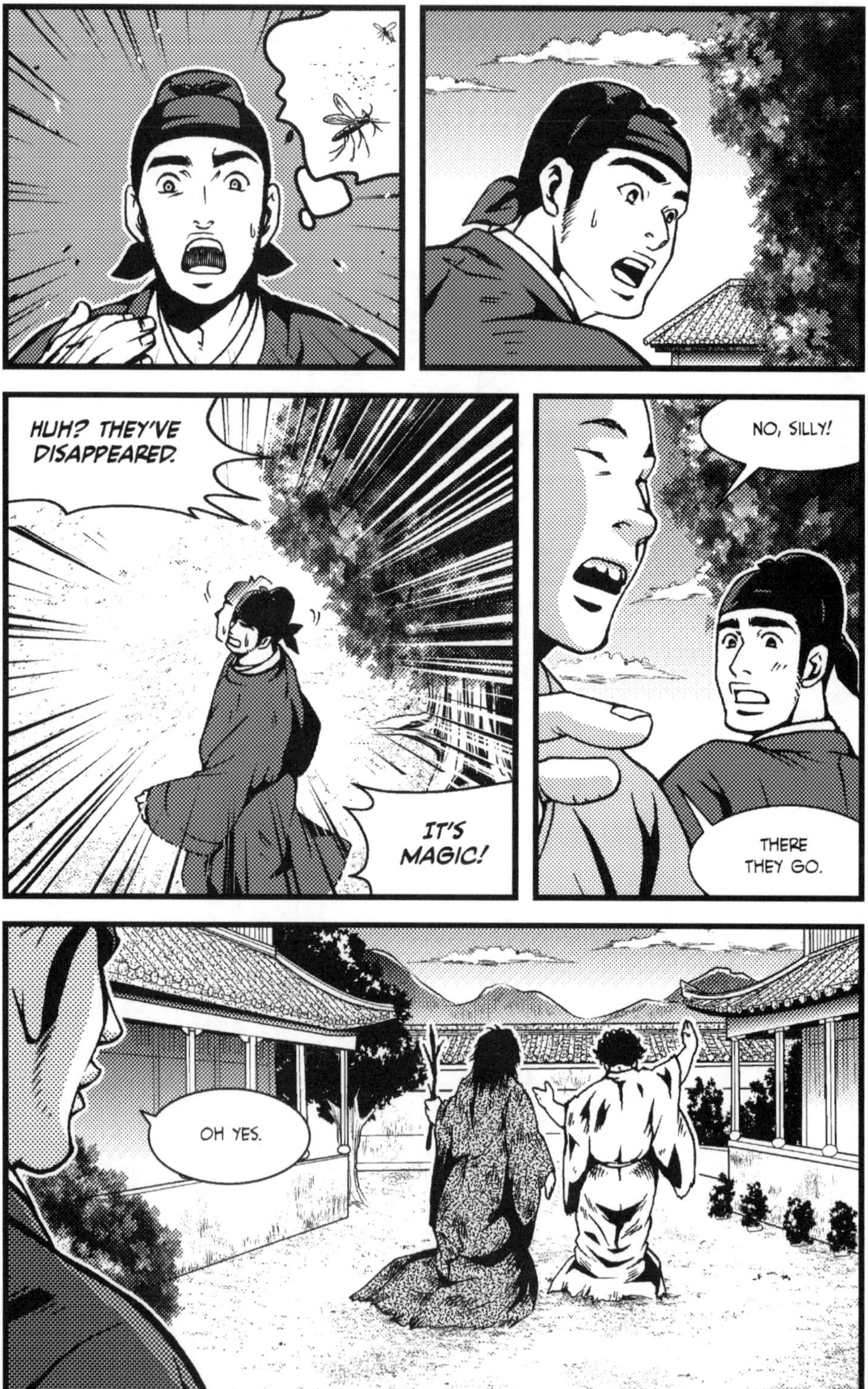
HUH? THEY'VE DISAPPEARED.
IT'S MAGIC!
NO, SILLY!
THERE THEY GO.
OH YES.

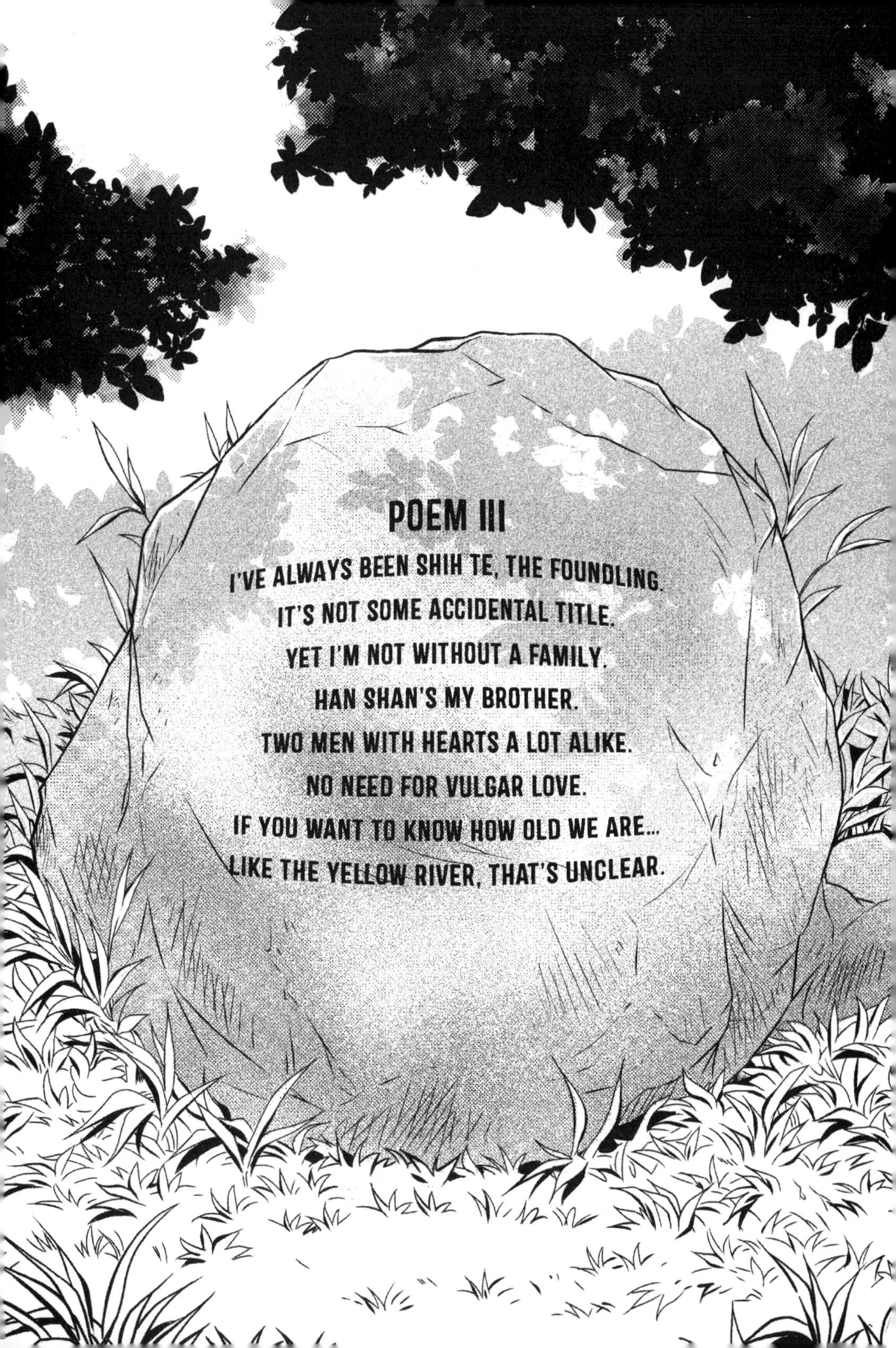
POEM III
I'VE ALWAYS BEEN SHIH TE, THE FOUNDLING.
IT'S NOT SOME ACCIDENTAL TITLE.
YET I'M NOT WITHOUT A FAMILY.
HAN SHAN'S MY BROTHER.
TWO MEN WITH HEARTS A LOT ALIKE.
NO NEED FOR VULGAR LOVE.
IF YOU WANT TO KNOW HOW OLD WE ARE...
LIKE THE YELLOW RIVER, THAT'S UNCLEAR.

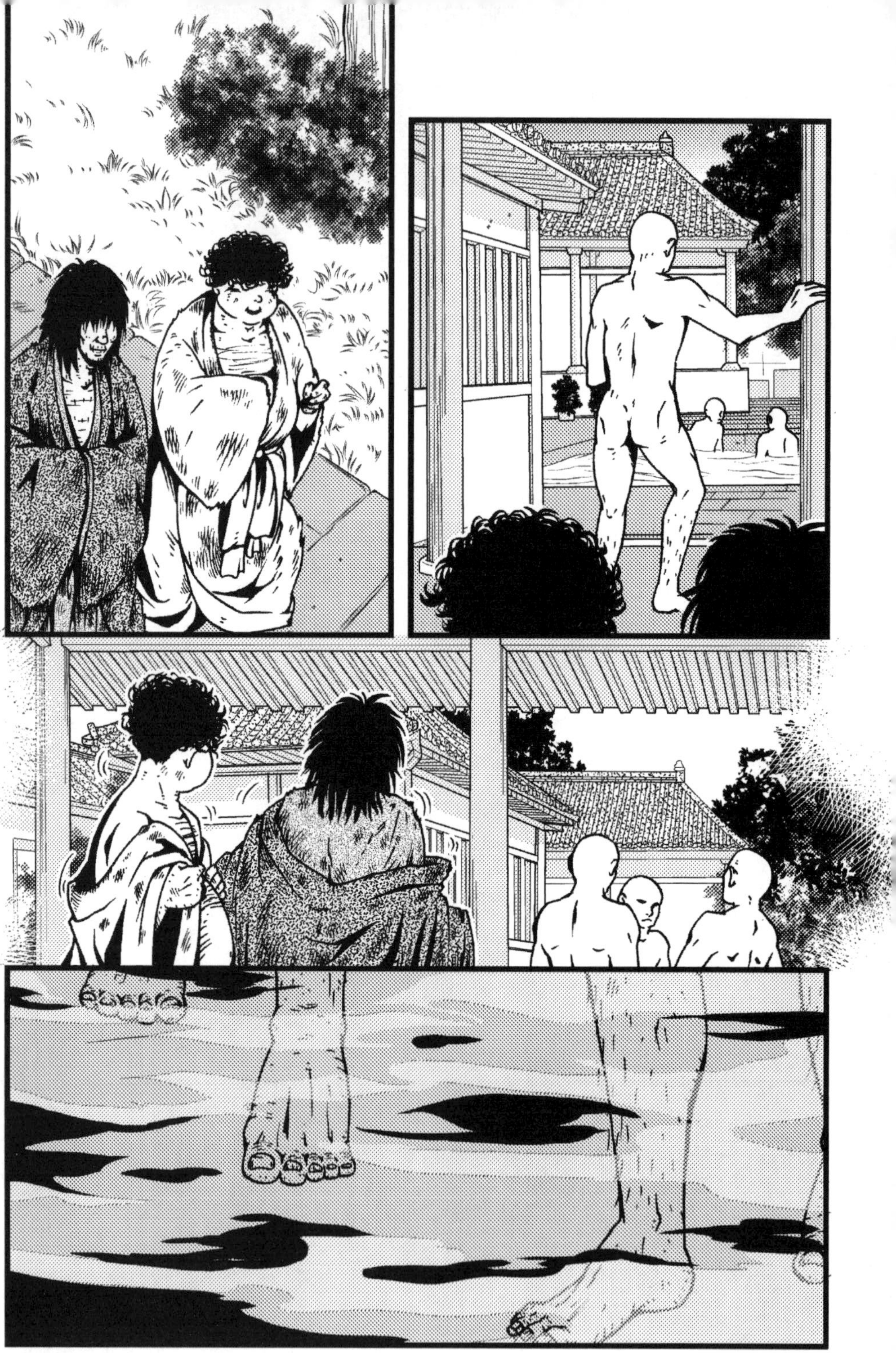

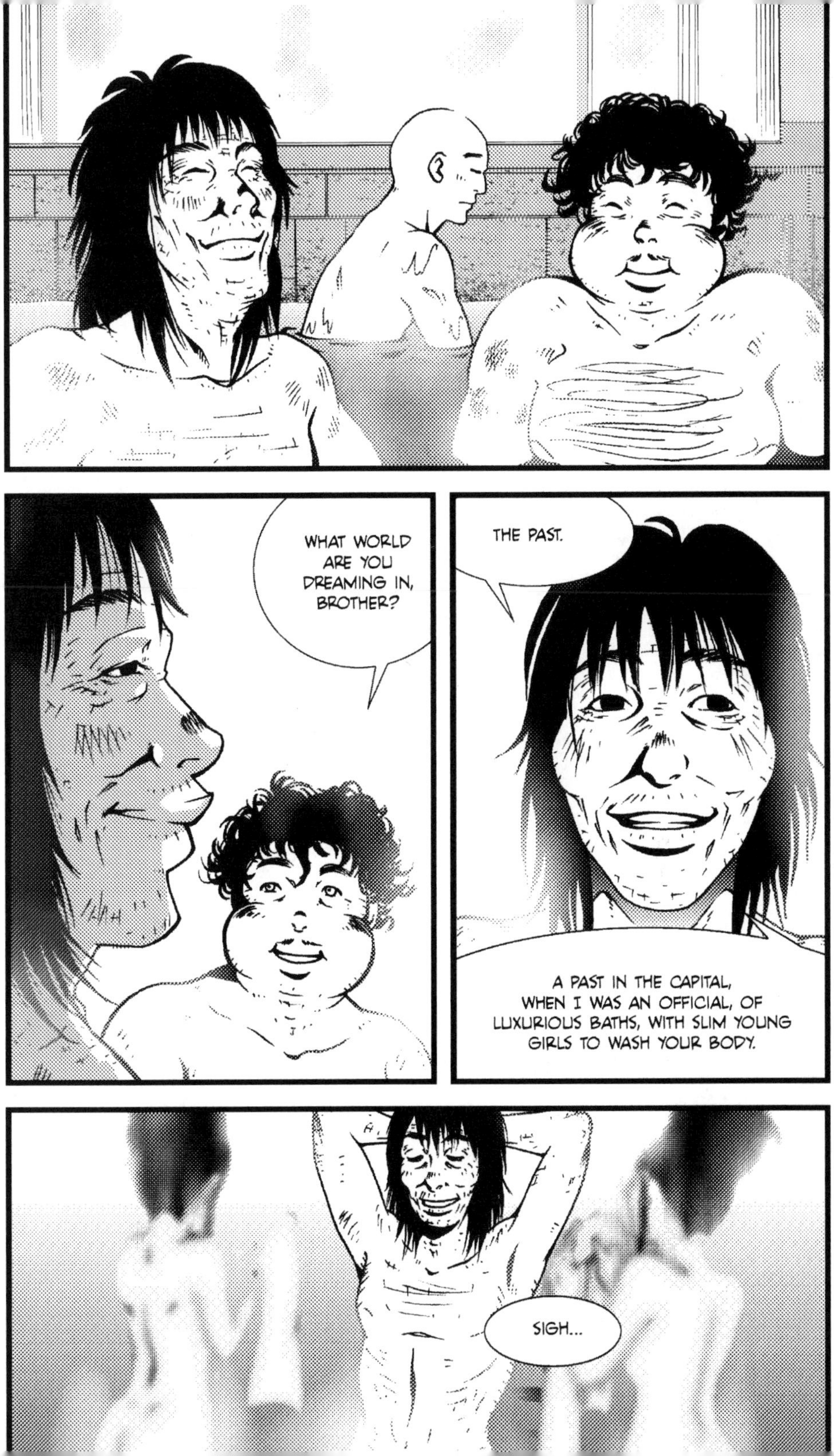
WHAT WORLD ARE YOU DREAMING IN, BROTHER?
THE PAST.
A PAST IN THE CAPITAL, WHEN I WAS AN OFFICIAL, OF LUXURIOUS BATHS, WITH SLIM YOUNG GIRLS TO WASH YOUR BODY.
SIGH...

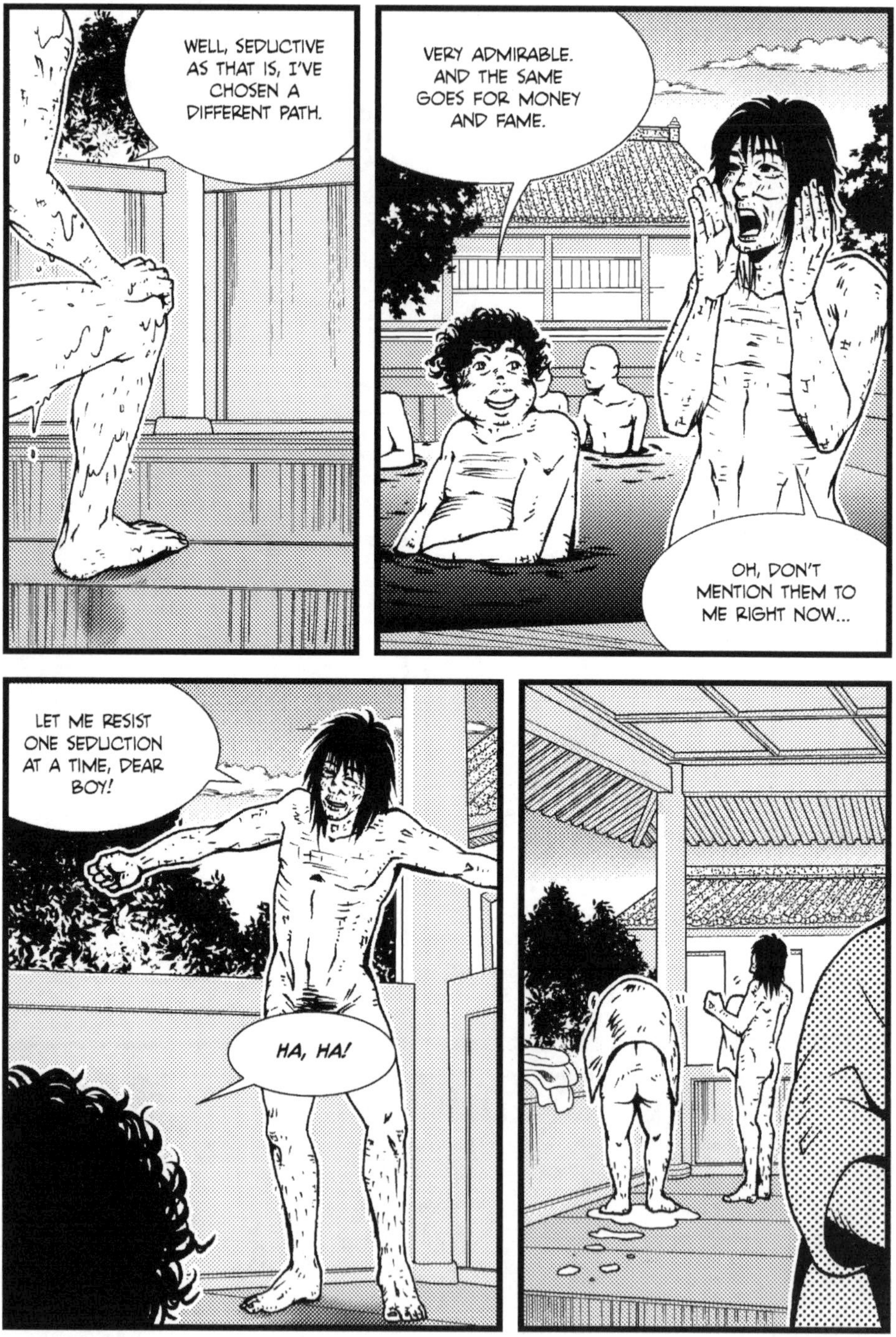
WELL, SEDUCTIVE AS THAT IS, I'VE CHOSEN A DIFFERENT PATH.
VERY ADMIRABLE. AND THE SAME GOES FOR MONEY AND FAME.
OH, DON'T MENTION THEM TO ME RIGHT NOW...
LET ME RESIST ONE SEDUCTION AT A TIME, DEAR BOY!
HA, HA!

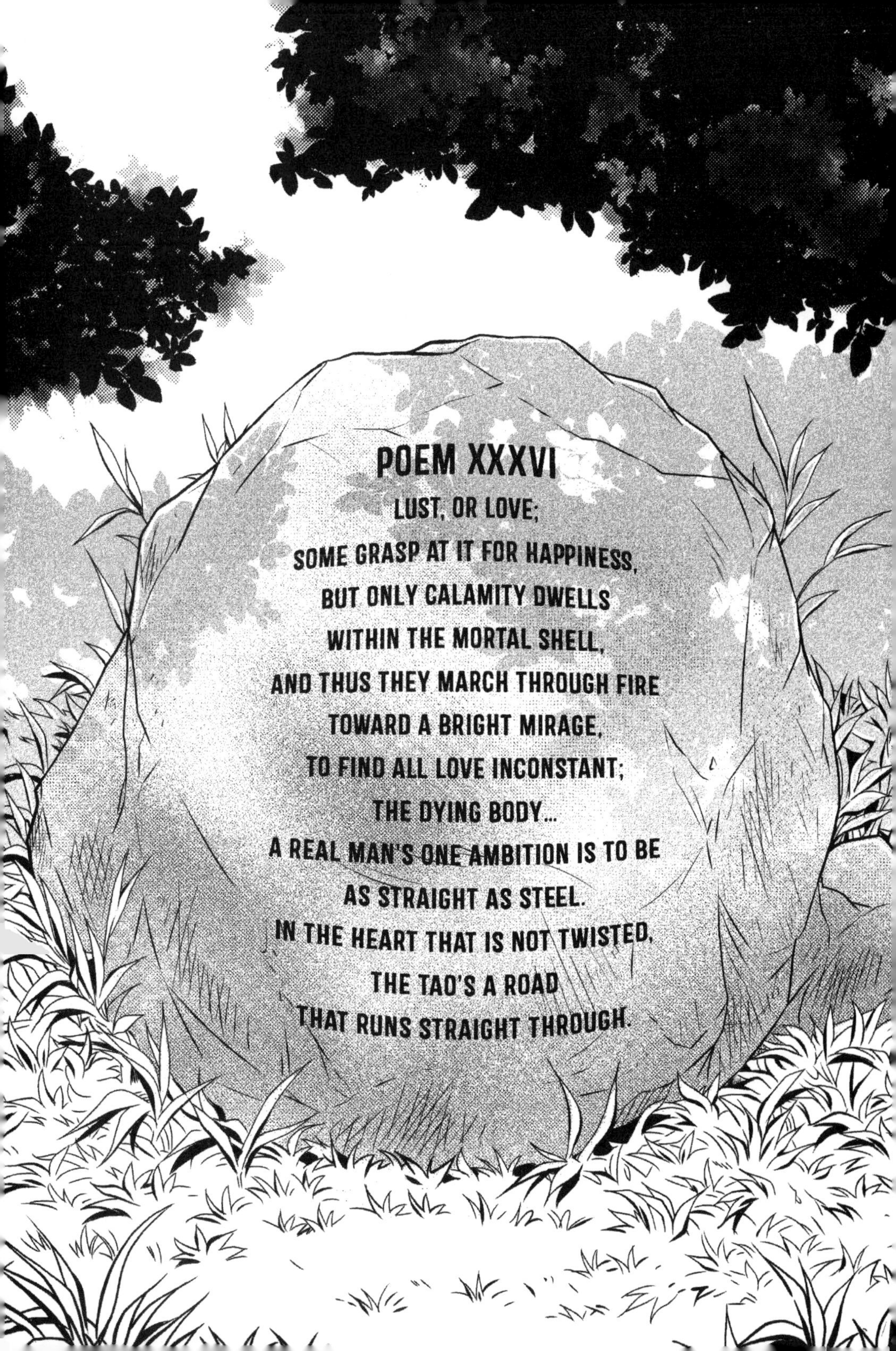
POEM XXXVI
LUST, OR LOVE;
SOME GRASP AT IT FOR HAPPINESS,
BUT ONLY CALAMITY DWELLS
WITHIN THE MORTAL SHELL,
AND THUS THEY MARCH THROUGH FIRE
TOWARD A BRIGHT MIRAGE,
TO FIND ALL LOVE INCONSTANT;
THE DYING BODY...
A REAL MAN'S ONE AMBITION IS TO BE
AS STRAIGHT AS STEEL.
IN THE HEART THAT IS NOT TWISTED,
THE TAO'S A ROAD
THAT RUNS STRAIGHT THROUGH.

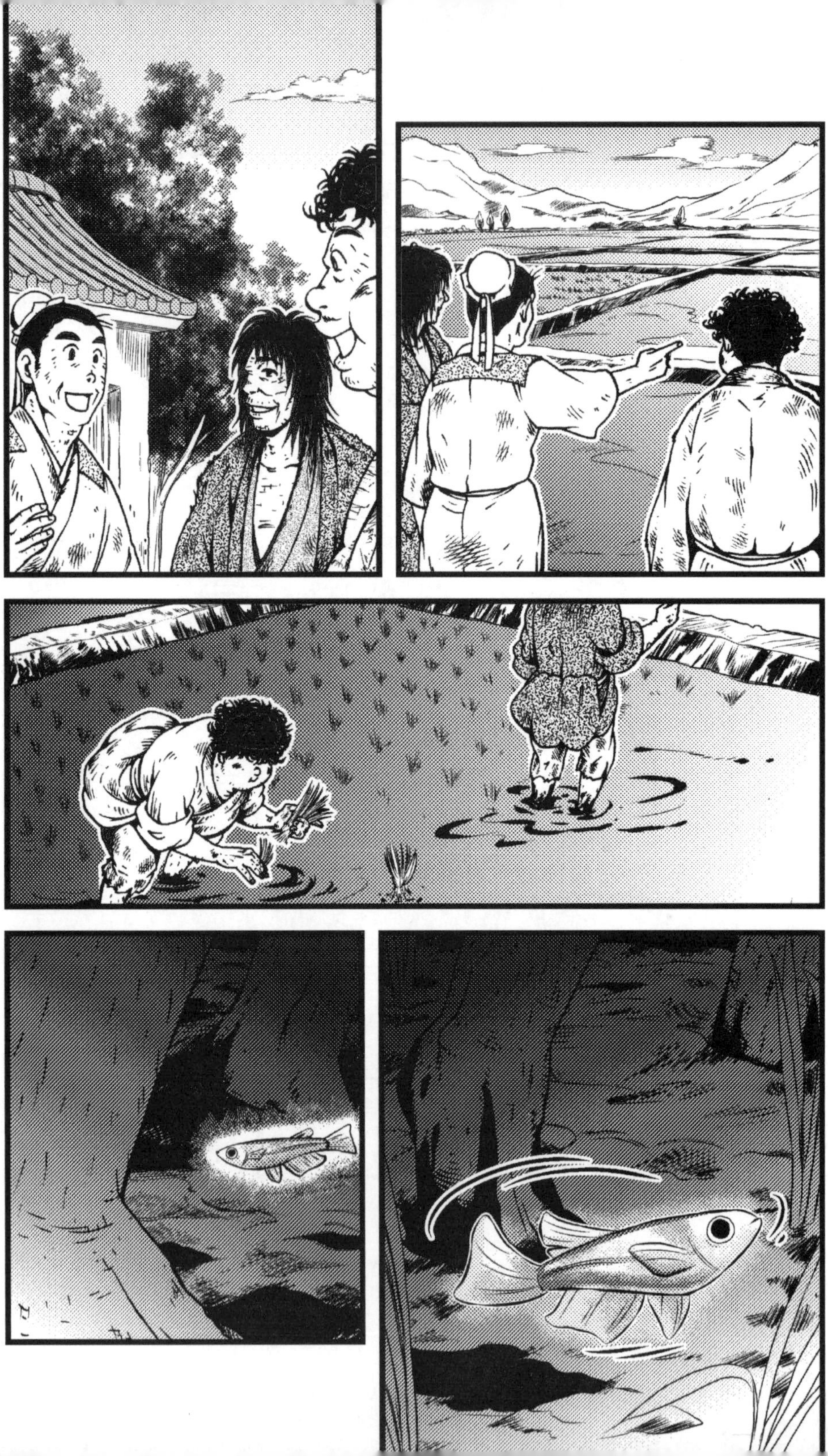

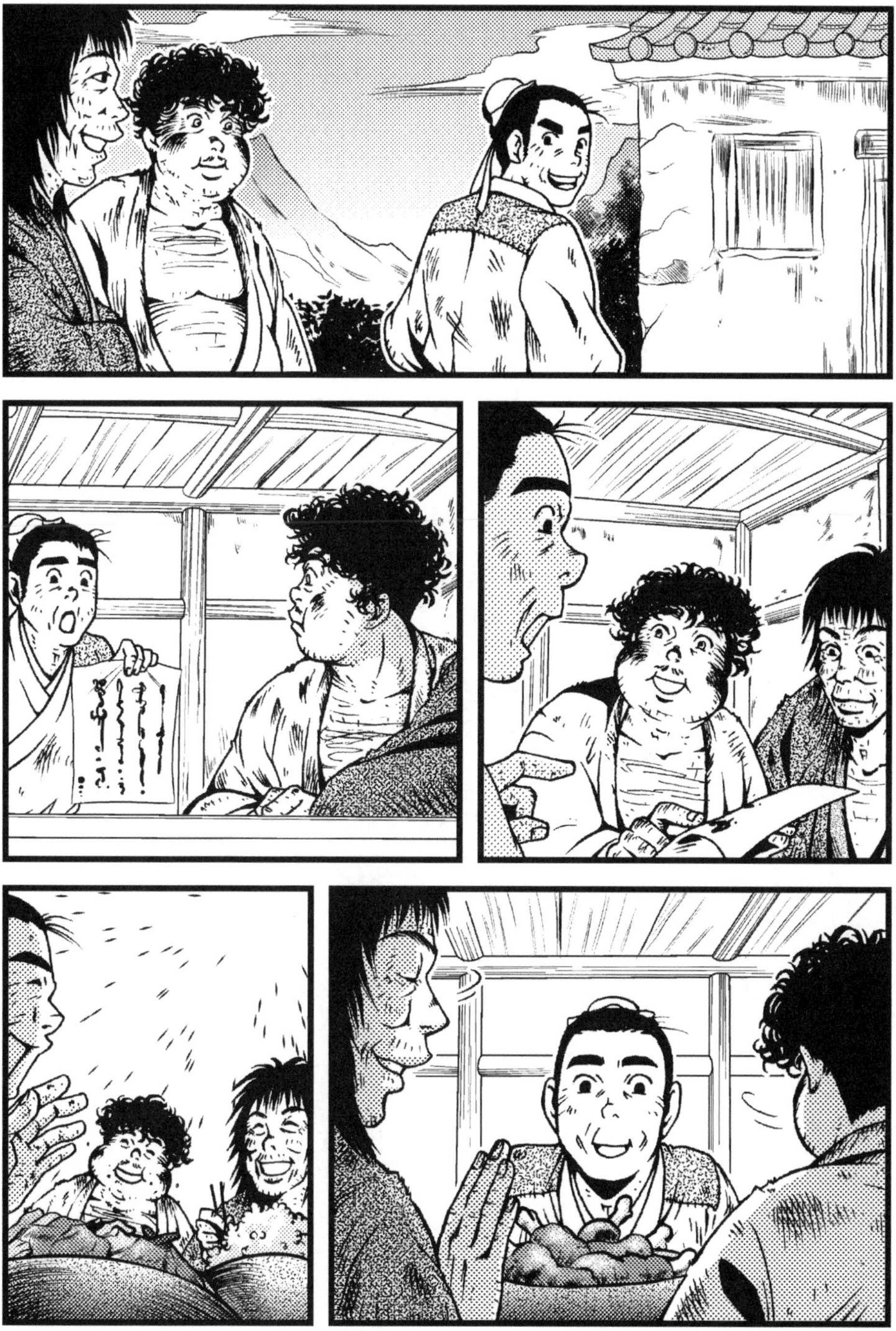

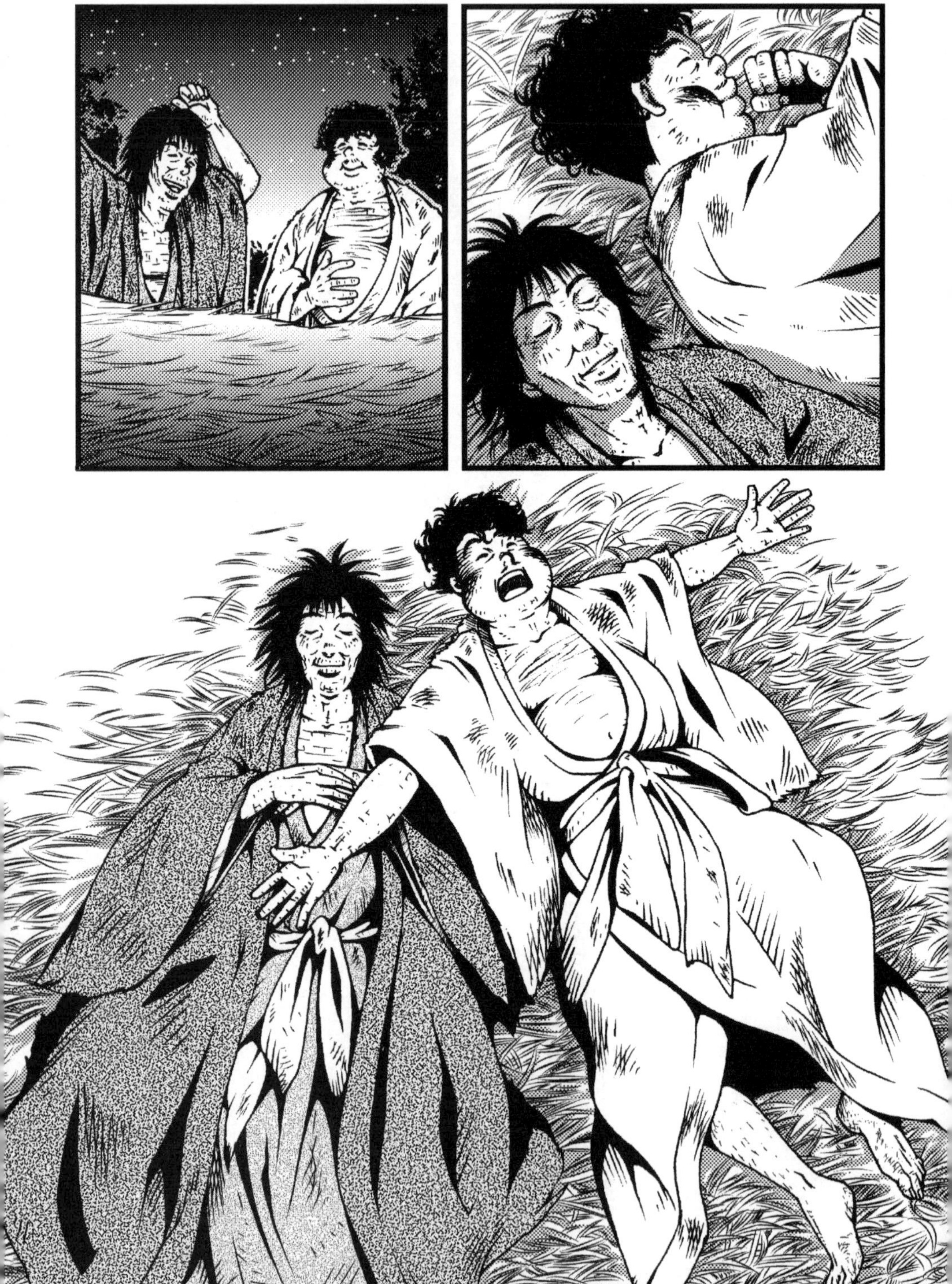

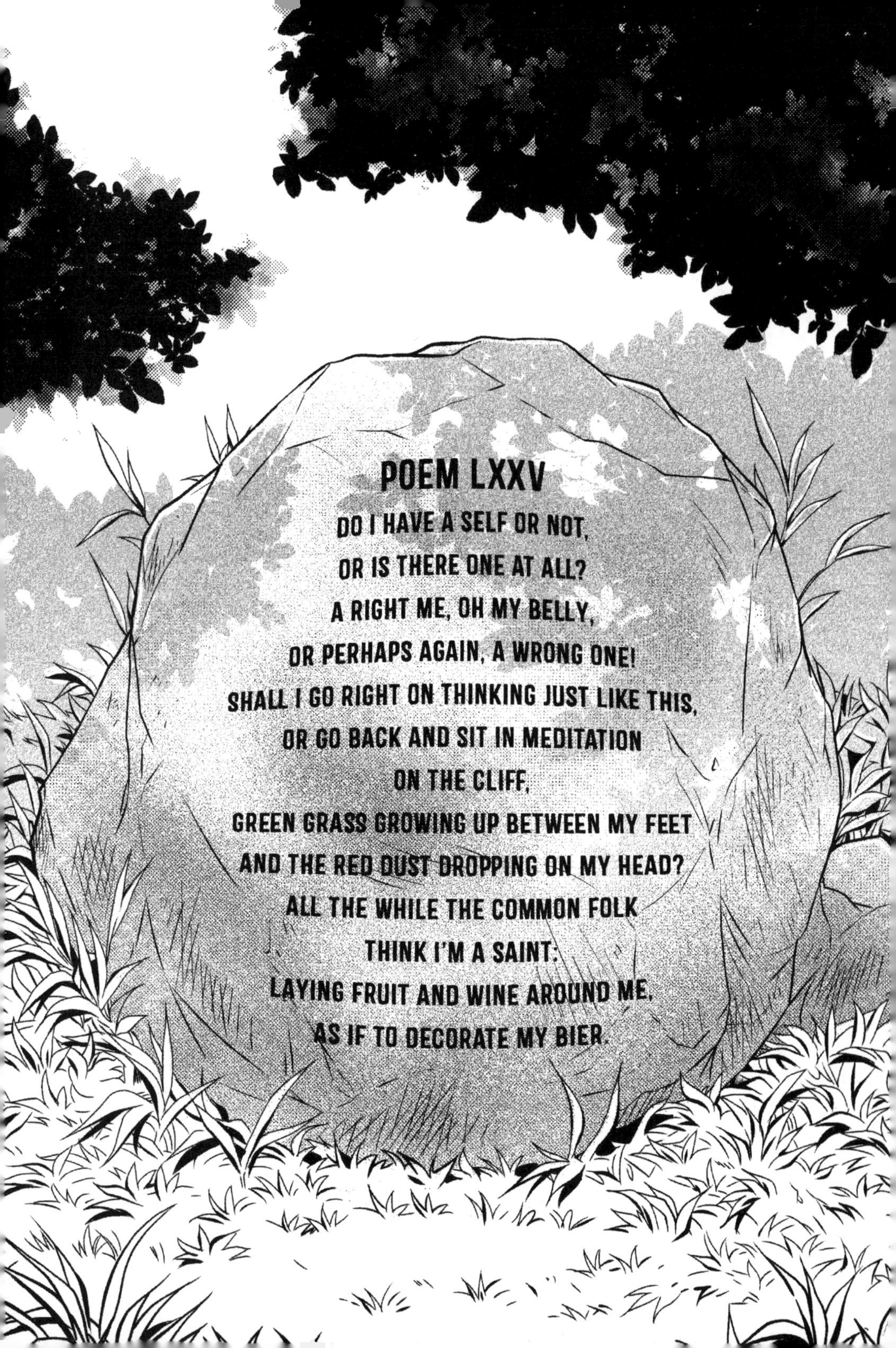
POEM LXXV
DO I HAVE A SELF OR NOT,
OR IS THERE ONE AT ALL?
A RIGHT ME, OH MY BELLY,
OR PERHAPS AGAIN, A WRONG ONE!
SHALL I GO RIGHT ON THINKING JUST LIKE THIS,
OR GO BACK AND SIT IN MEDITATION
ON THE CLIFF,
GREEN GRASS GROWING UP BETWEEN MY FEET
AND THE RED DUST DROPPING ON MY HEAD?
ALL THE WHILE THE COMMON FOLK
THINK I'M A SAINT:
LAYING FRUIT AND WINE AROUND ME,
AS IF TO DECORATE MY BIER.

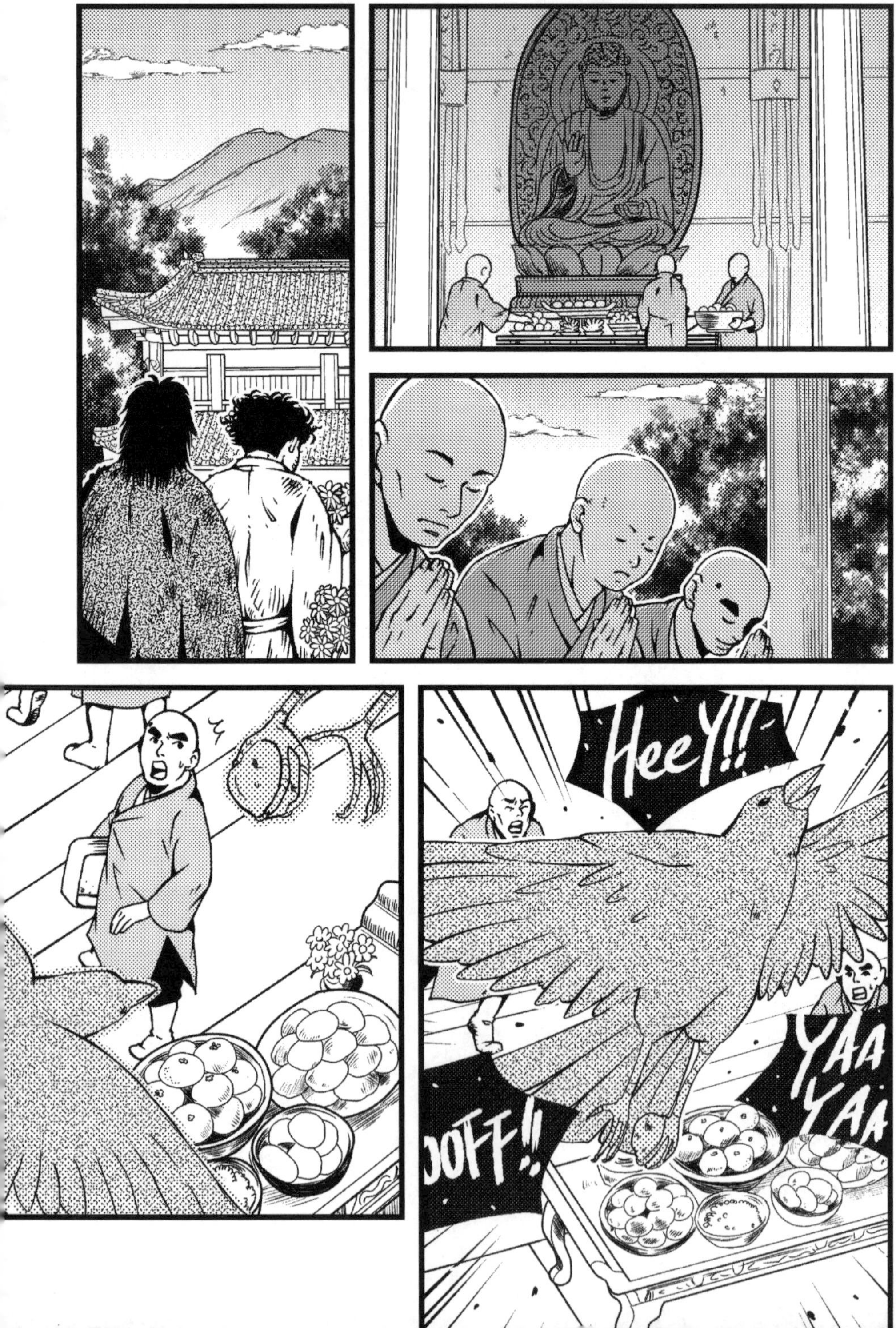
HeeY!!
YAA YAA
OFF!!

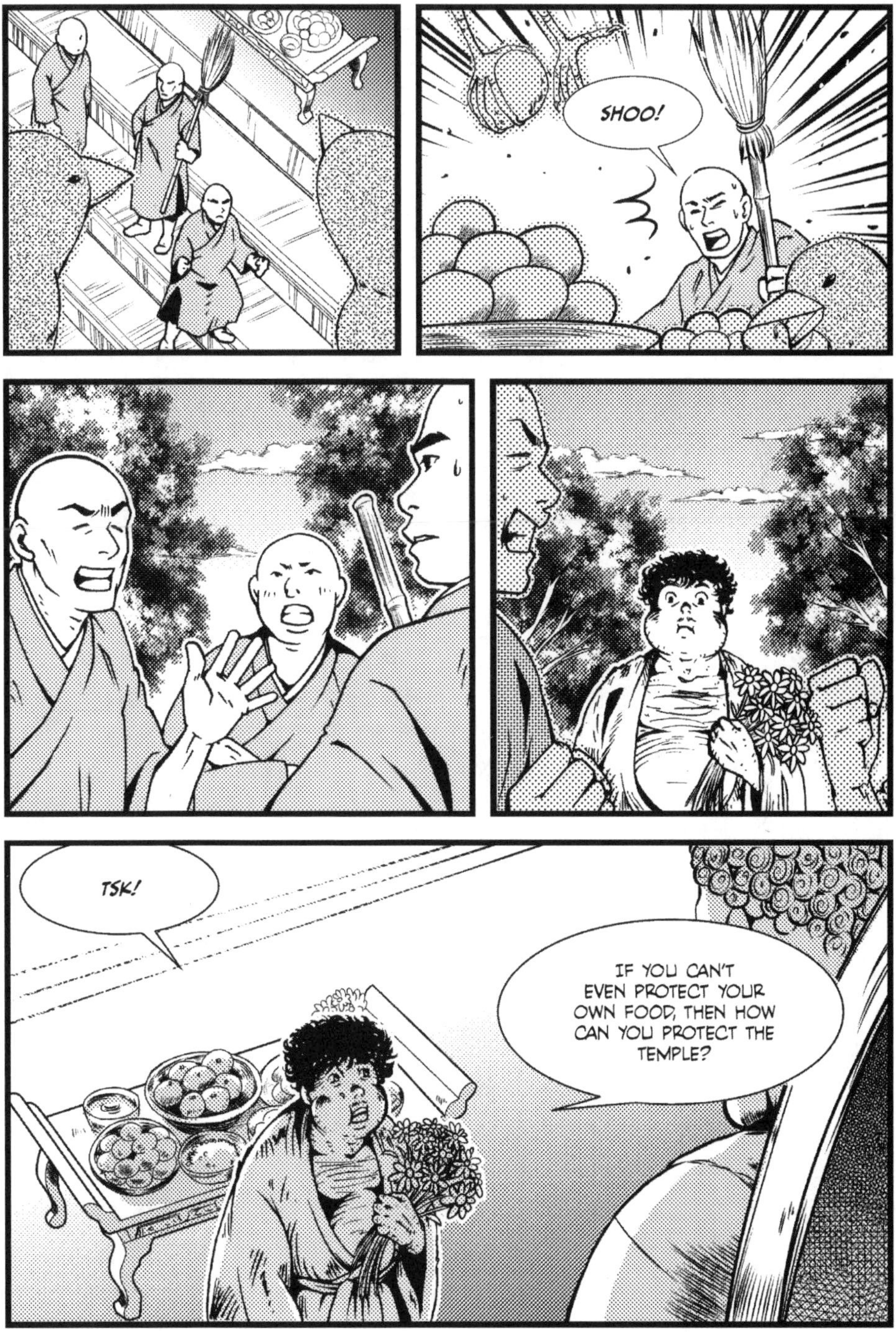
SHOO!
TSK!
IF YOU CAN'T EVEN PROTECT YOUR OWN FOOD, THEN HOW CAN YOU PROTECT THE TEMPLE?

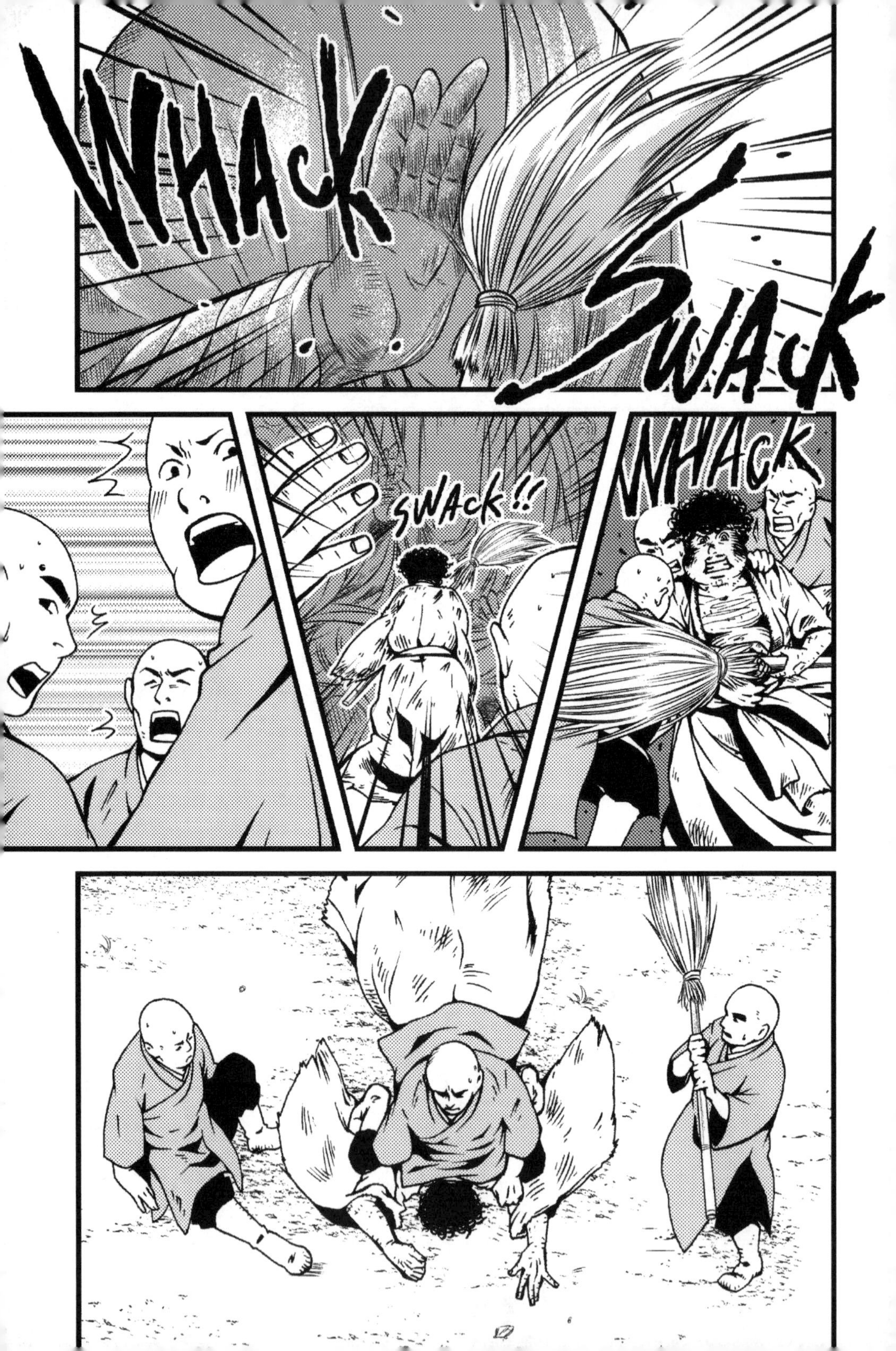
WHACK
SWACK
WHACK
SWACK!!

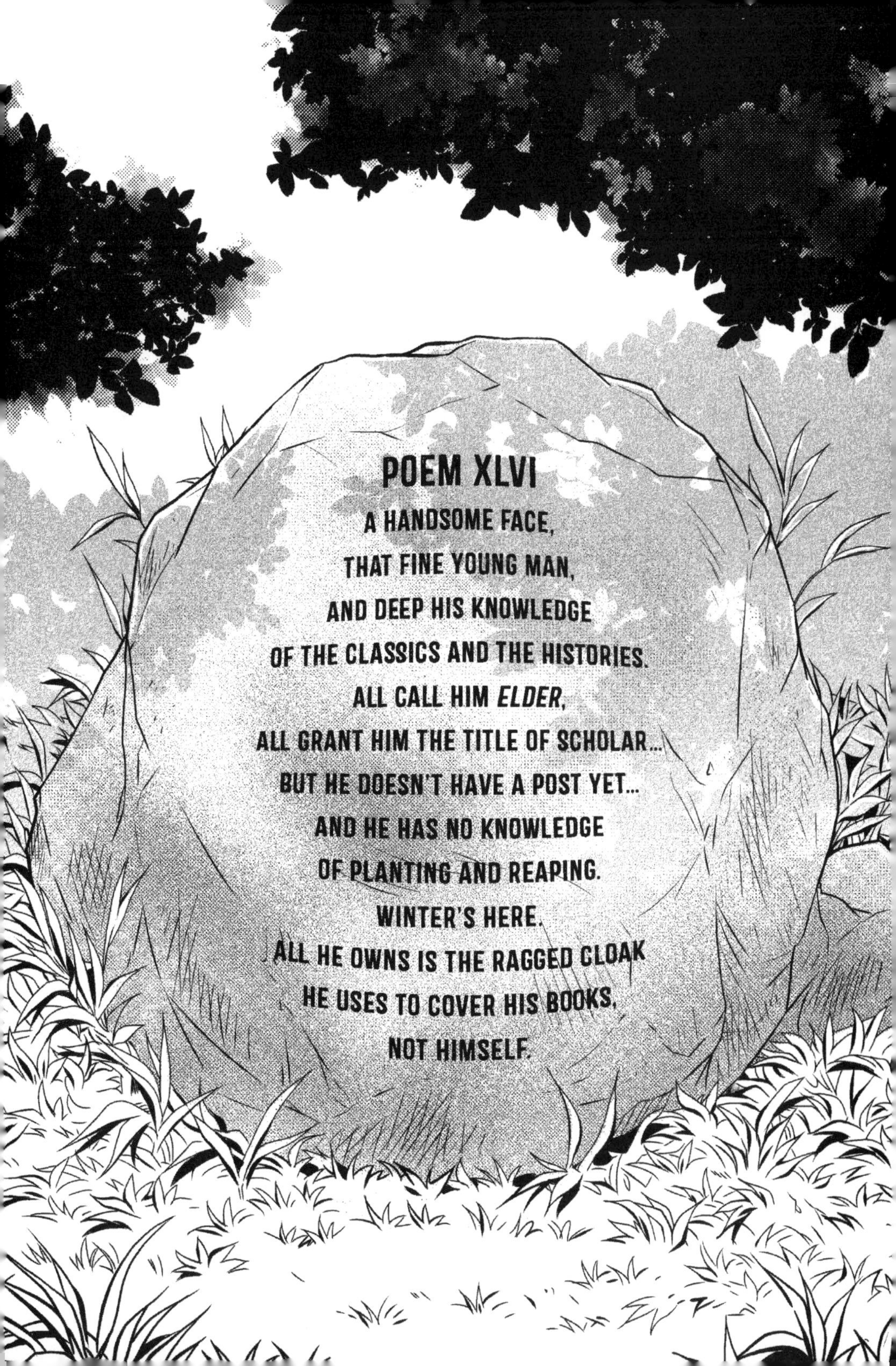
POEM XLVI
A HANDSOME FACE,
THAT FINE YOUNG MAN,
AND DEEP HIS KNOWLEDGE
OF THE CLASSICS AND THE HISTORIES.
ALL CALL HIM *ELDER*,
ALL GRANT HIM THE TITLE OF SCHOLAR...
BUT HE DOESN'T HAVE A POST YET...
AND HE HAS NO KNOWLEDGE
OF PLANTING AND REAPING.
WINTER'S HERE.
ALL HE OWNS IS THE RAGGED CLOAK
HE USES TO COVER HIS BOOKS,
NOT HIMSELF.

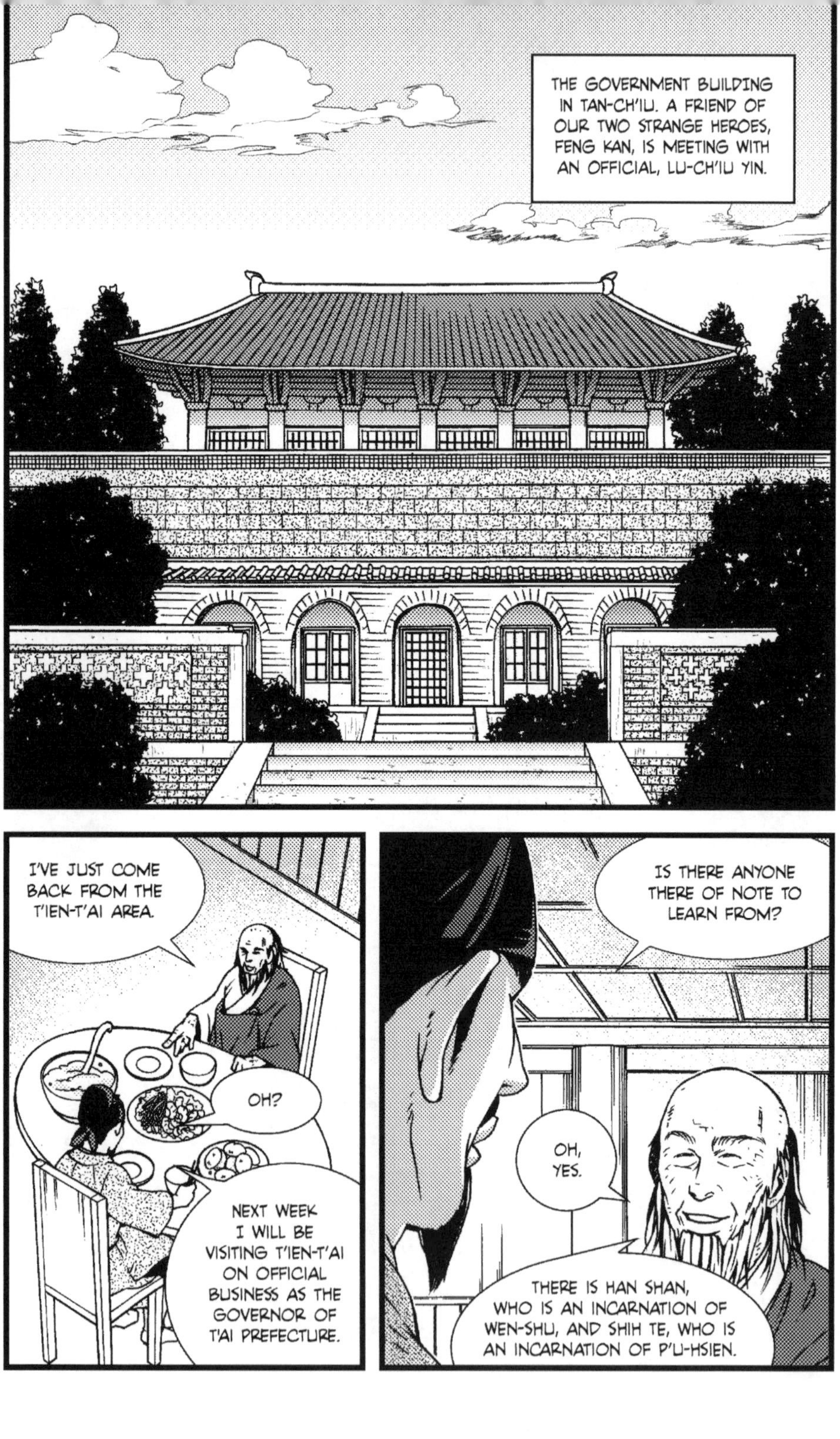
THE GOVERNMENT BUILDING IN TAN-CH'IU. A FRIEND OF OUR TWO STRANGE HEROES, FENG KAN, IS MEETING WITH AN OFFICIAL, LU-CH'IU YIN.
I'VE JUST COME BACK FROM THE T'IEN-T'AI AREA.
OH?
NEXT WEEK I WILL BE VISITING T'IEN-T'AI ON OFFICIAL BUSINESS AS THE GOVERNOR OF T'AI PREFECTURE.
IS THERE ANYONE THERE OF NOTE TO LEARN FROM?
OH, YES.
THERE IS HAN SHAN, WHO IS AN INCARNATION OF WEN-SHU, AND SHIH TE, WHO IS AN INCARNATION OF P'U-HSIEN.

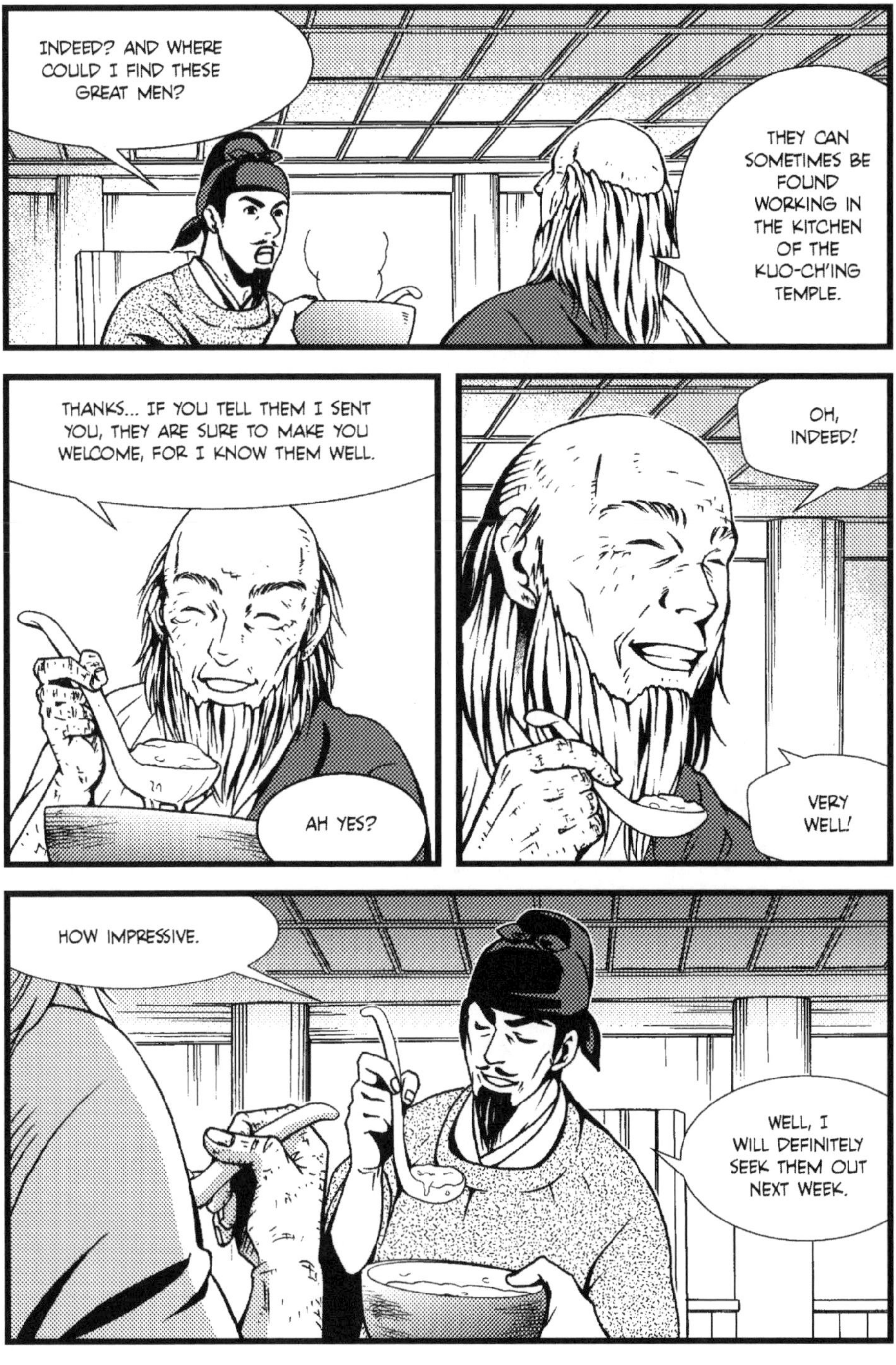
INDEED? AND WHERE COULD I FIND THESE GREAT MEN?
THEY CAN SOMETIMES BE FOUND WORKING IN THE KITCHEN OF THE KUO-CH'ING TEMPLE.
THANKS... IF YOU TELL THEM I SENT YOU, THEY ARE SURE TO MAKE YOU WELCOME, FOR I KNOW THEM WELL.
AH YES?
OH, INDEED!
VERY WELL!
HOW IMPRESSIVE.
WELL, I WILL DEFINITELY SEEK THEM OUT NEXT WEEK.

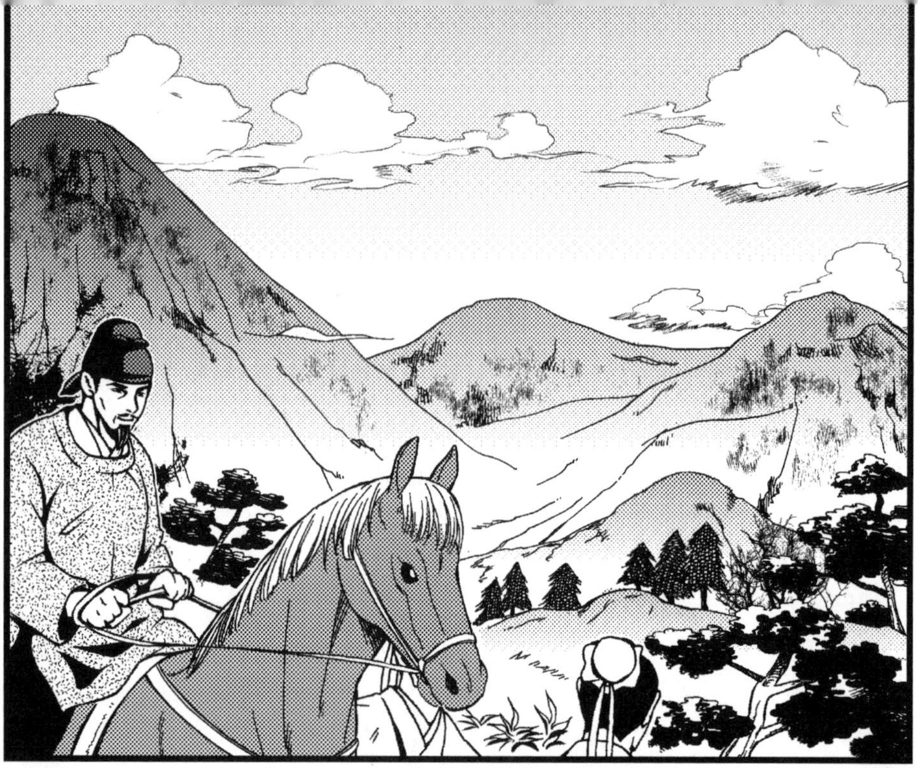

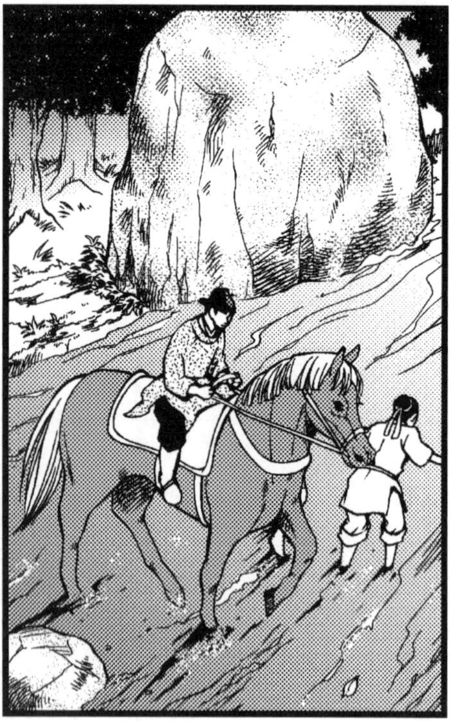

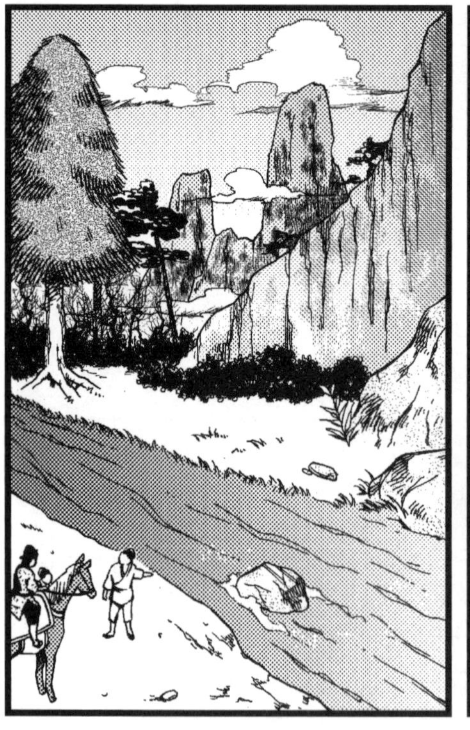

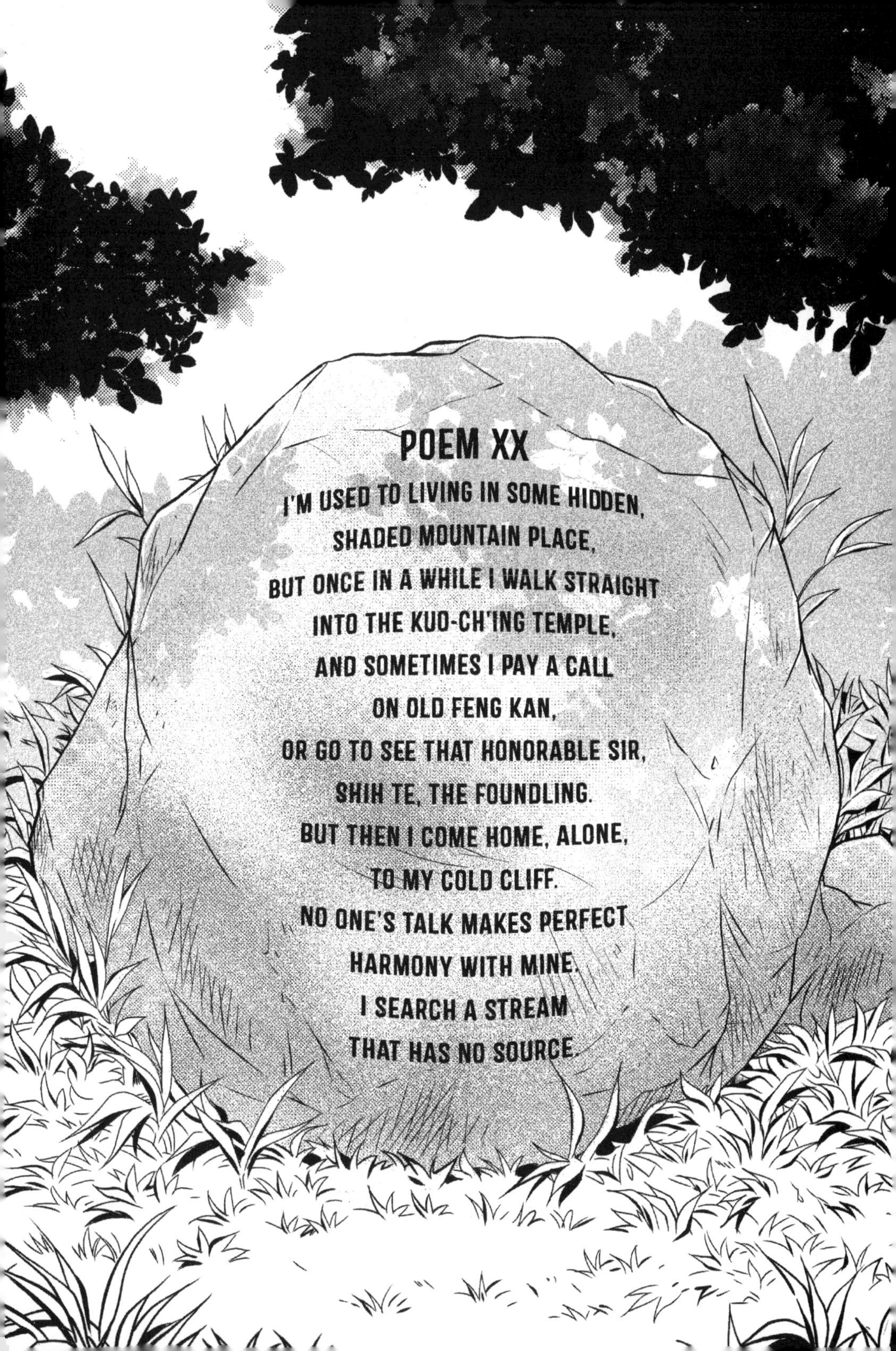
POEM XX
I'M USED TO LIVING IN SOME HIDDEN,
SHADED MOUNTAIN PLACE,
BUT ONCE IN A WHILE I WALK STRAIGHT
INTO THE KUO-CH'ING TEMPLE,
AND SOMETIMES I PAY A CALL
ON OLD FENG KAN,
OR GO TO SEE THAT HONORABLE SIR,
SHIH TE, THE FOUNDLING.
BUT THEN I COME HOME, ALONE,
TO MY COLD CLIFF.
NO ONE'S TALK MAKES PERFECT
HARMONY WITH MINE.
I SEARCH A STREAM
THAT HAS NO SOURCE.

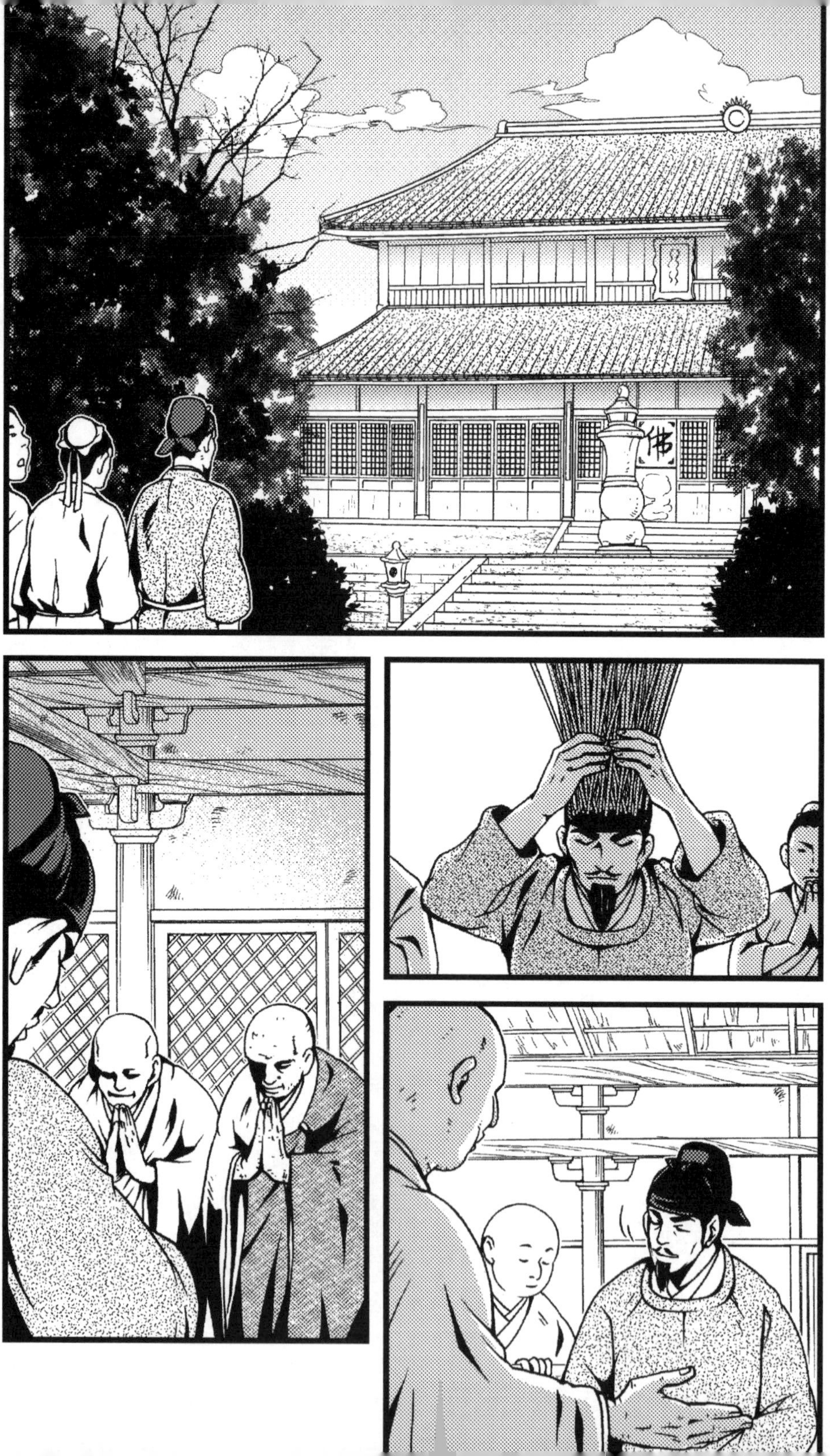
佛

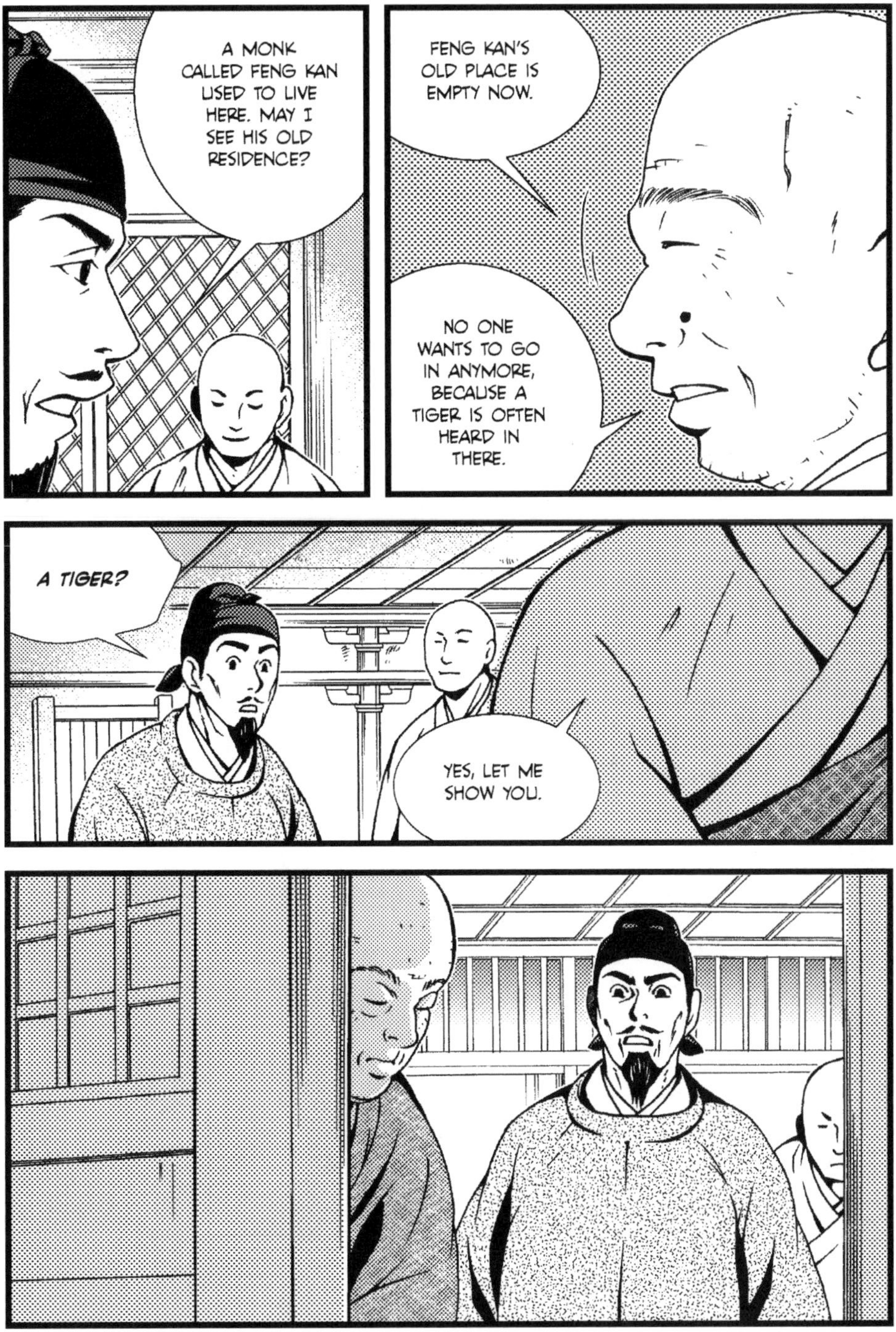
A MONK CALLED FENG KAN USED TO LIVE HERE. MAY I SEE HIS OLD RESIDENCE?
FENG KAN'S OLD PLACE IS EMPTY NOW.
NO ONE WANTS TO GO IN ANYMORE, BECAUSE A TIGER IS OFTEN HEARD IN THERE.
A TIGER?
YES, LET ME SHOW YOU.

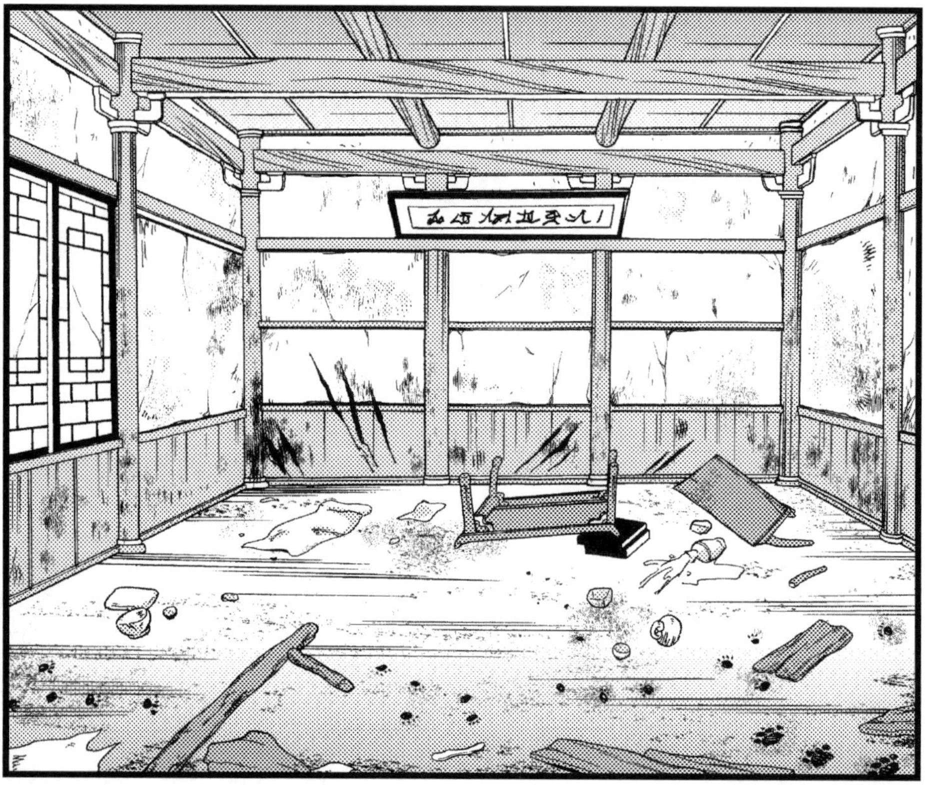
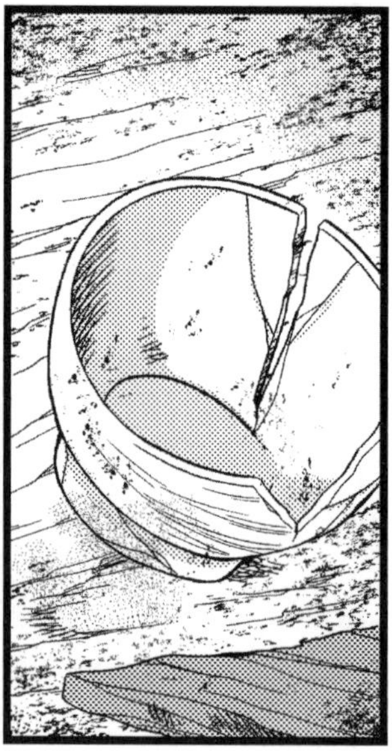
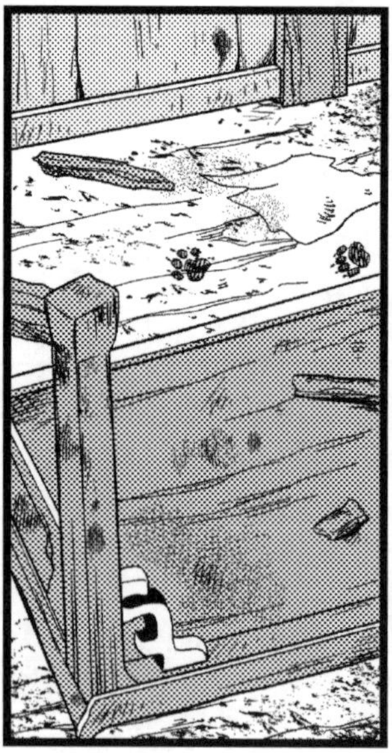
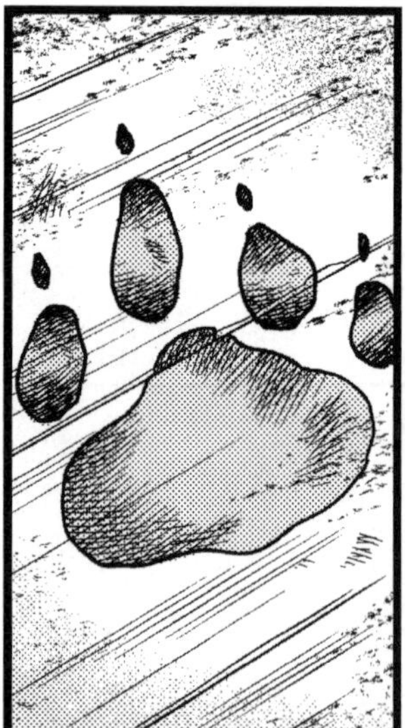

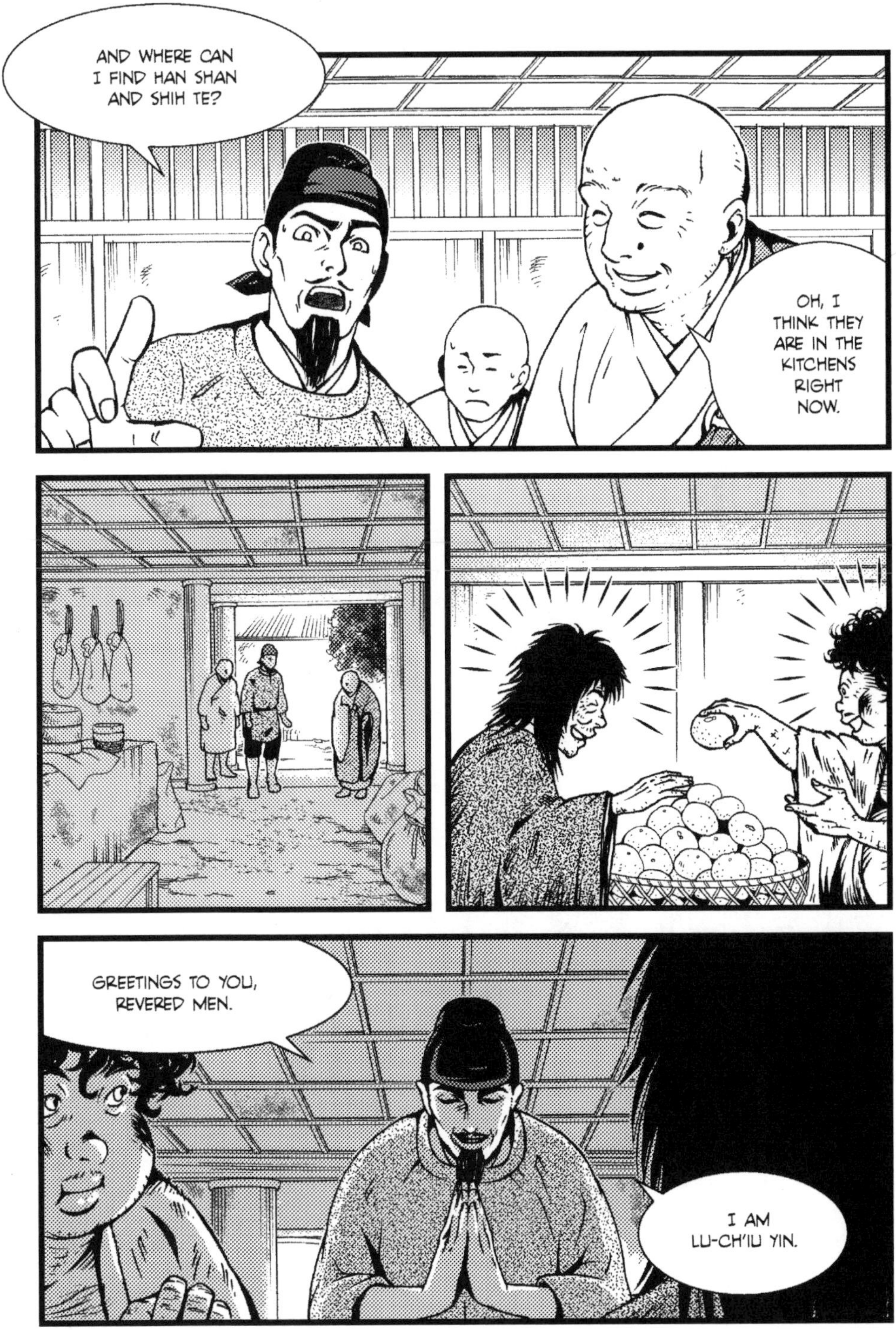
AND WHERE CAN I FIND HAN SHAN AND SHIH TE?
OH, I THINK THEY ARE IN THE KITCHENS RIGHT NOW.
GREETINGS TO YOU, REVERED MEN.
I AM LU-CH'IU YIN.

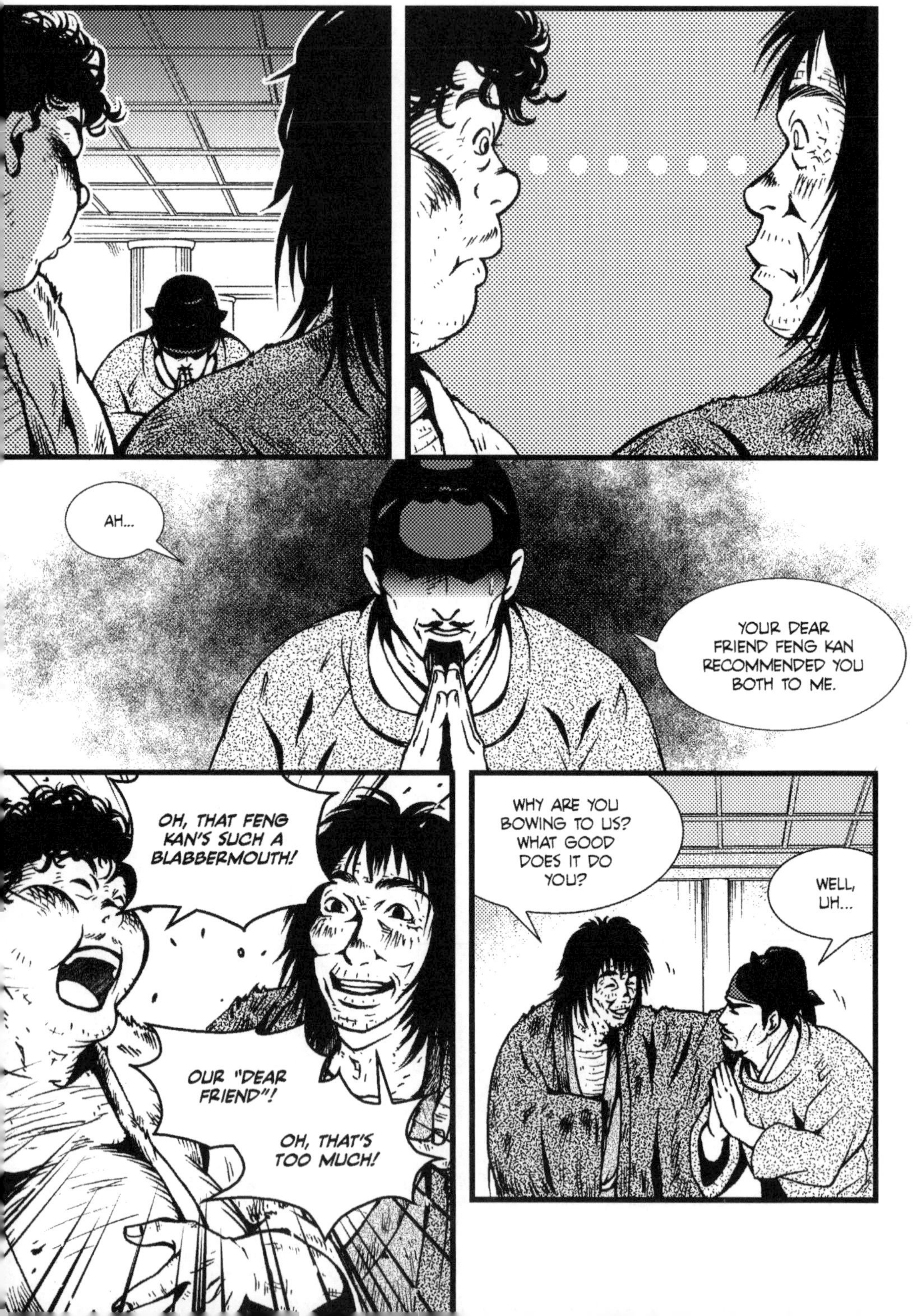
......
AH...
YOUR DEAR FRIEND FENG KAN RECOMMENDED YOU BOTH TO ME.
OH, THAT FENG KAN'S SUCH A BLABBERMOUTH!
OUR "DEAR FRIEND"!
OH, THAT'S TOO MUCH!
WHY ARE YOU BOWING TO US? WHAT GOOD DOES IT DO YOU?
WELL, UH...

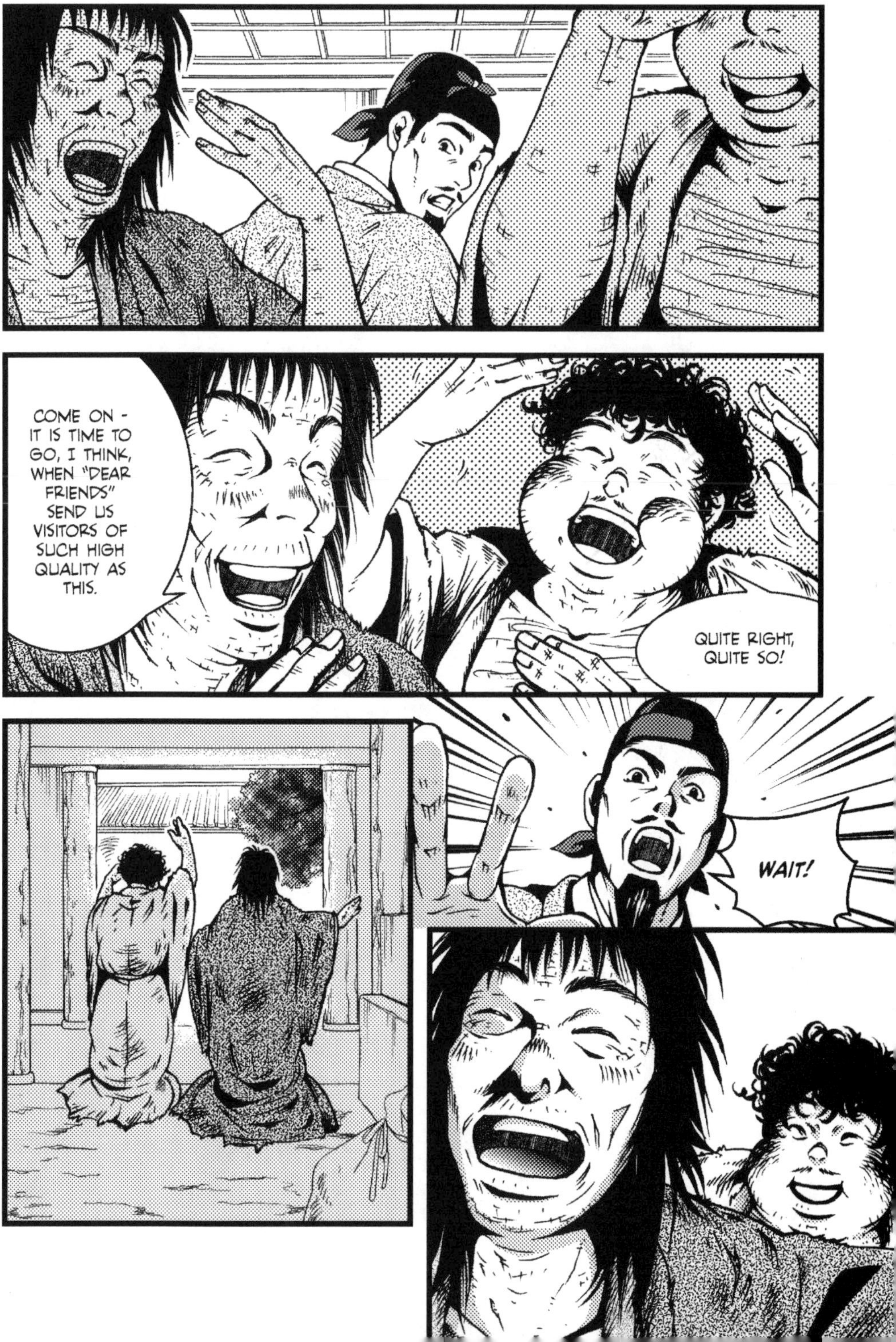
COME ON - IT IS TIME TO GO, I THINK, WHEN "DEAR FRIENDS" SEND US VISITORS OF SUCH HIGH QUALITY AS THIS.
QUITE RIGHT, QUITE SO!
WAIT!

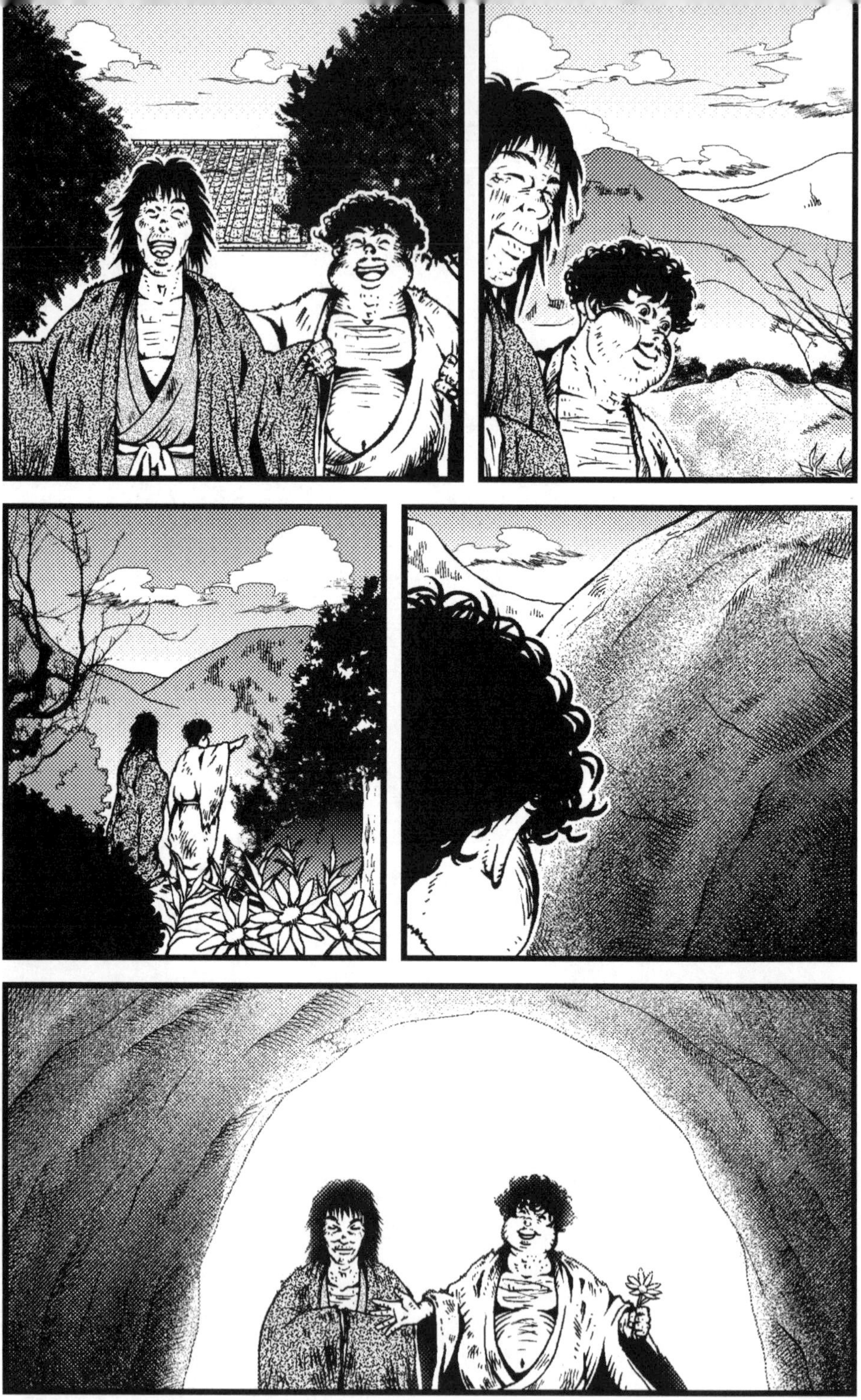

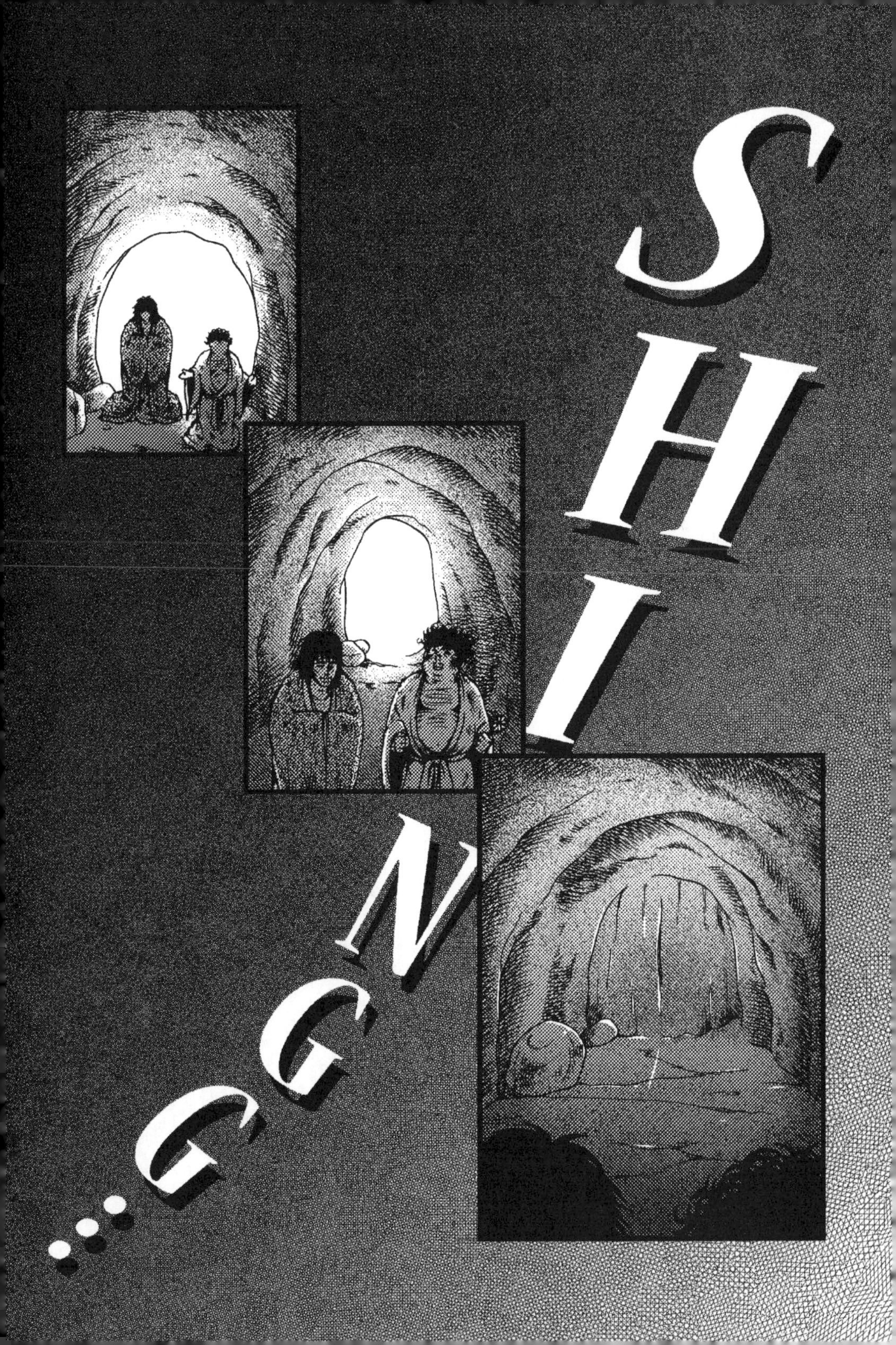
SHINGG…

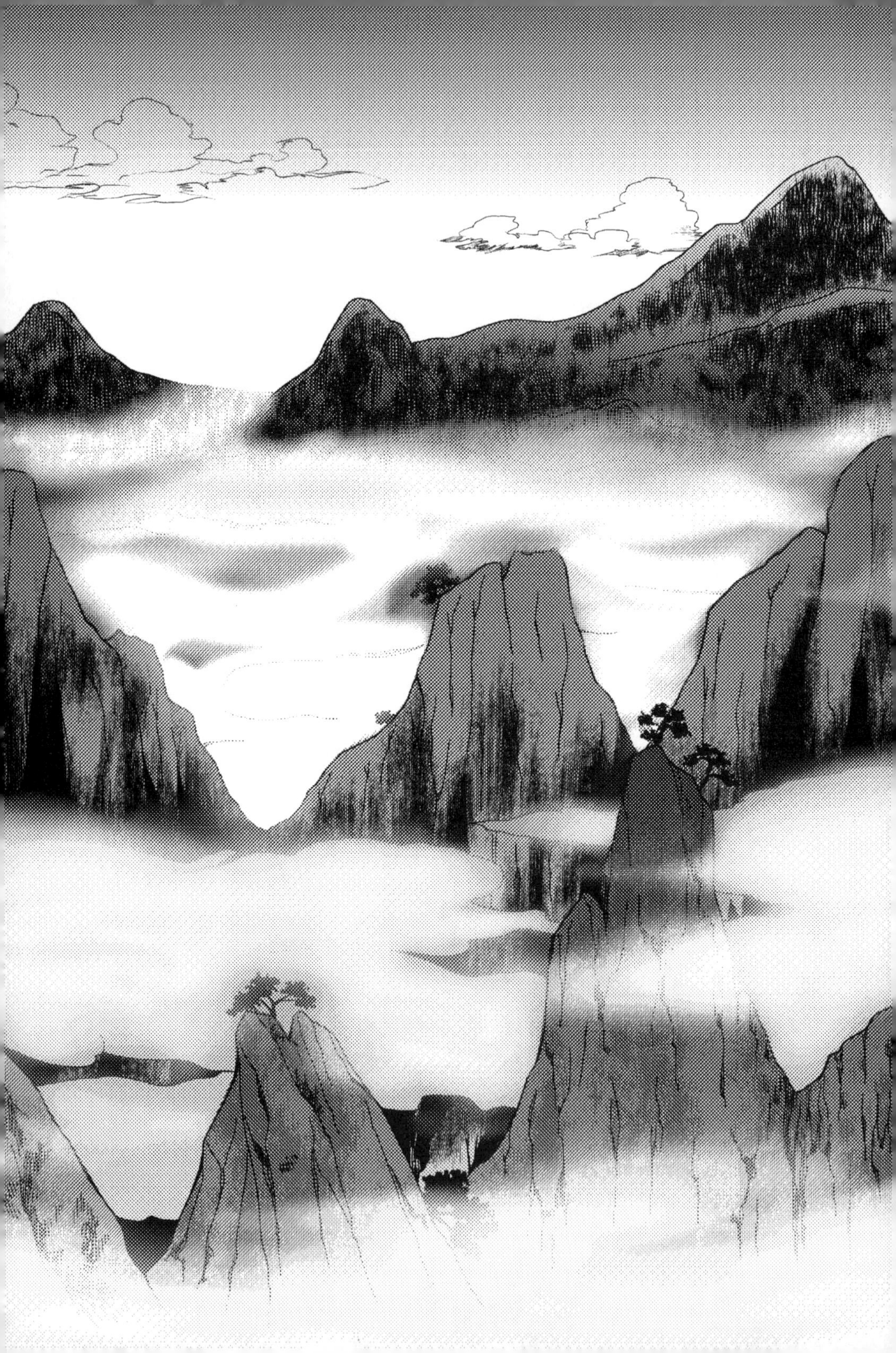

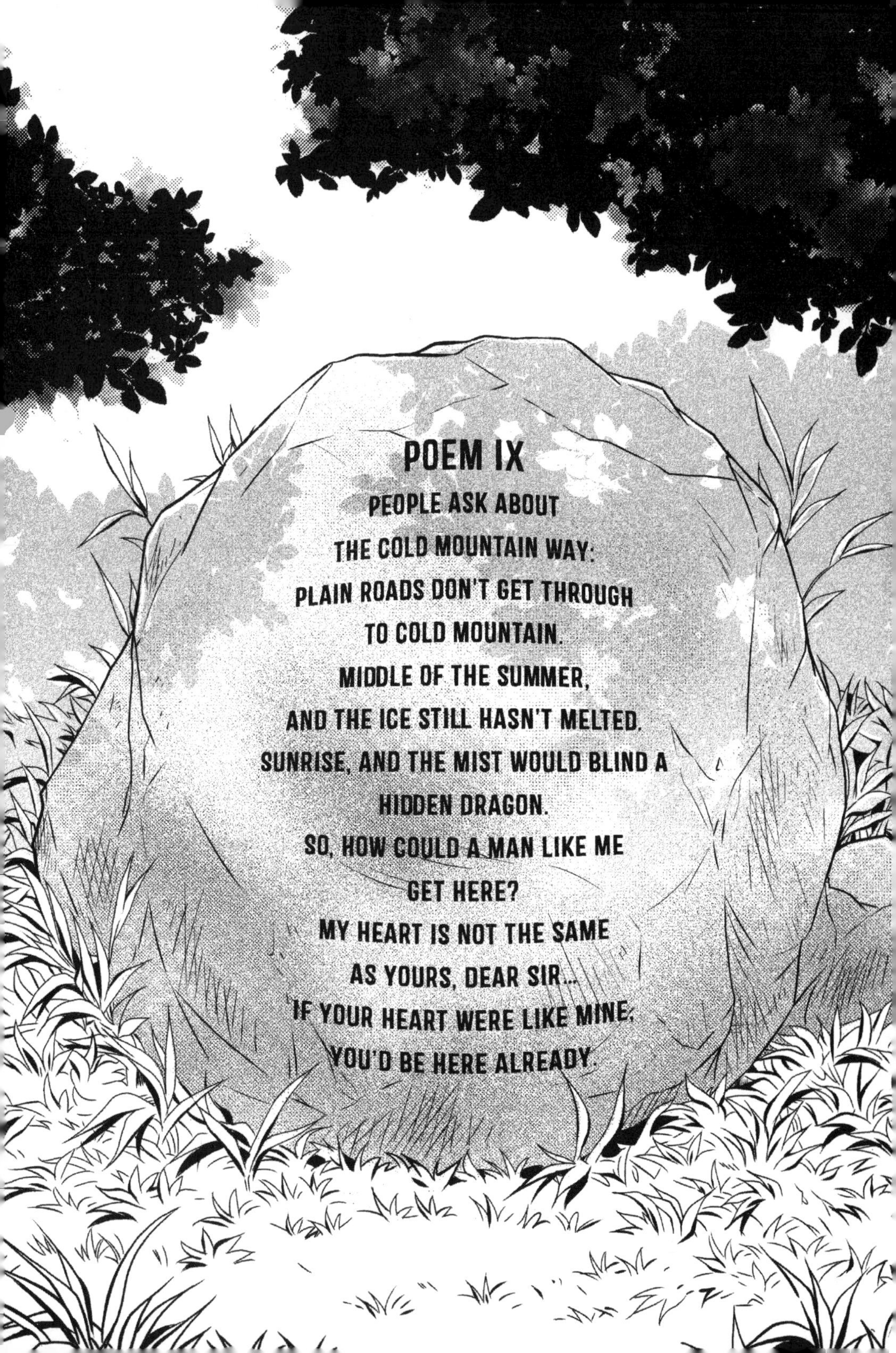
POEM IX
PEOPLE ASK ABOUT
THE COLD MOUNTAIN WAY:
PLAIN ROADS DON'T GET THROUGH
TO COLD MOUNTAIN.
MIDDLE OF THE SUMMER,
AND THE ICE STILL HASN'T MELTED.
SUNRISE, AND THE MIST WOULD BLIND A
HIDDEN DRAGON.
SO, HOW COULD A MAN LIKE ME
GET HERE?
MY HEART IS NOT THE SAME
AS YOURS, DEAR SIR...
IF YOUR HEART WERE LIKE MINE,
YOU'D BE HERE ALREADY.

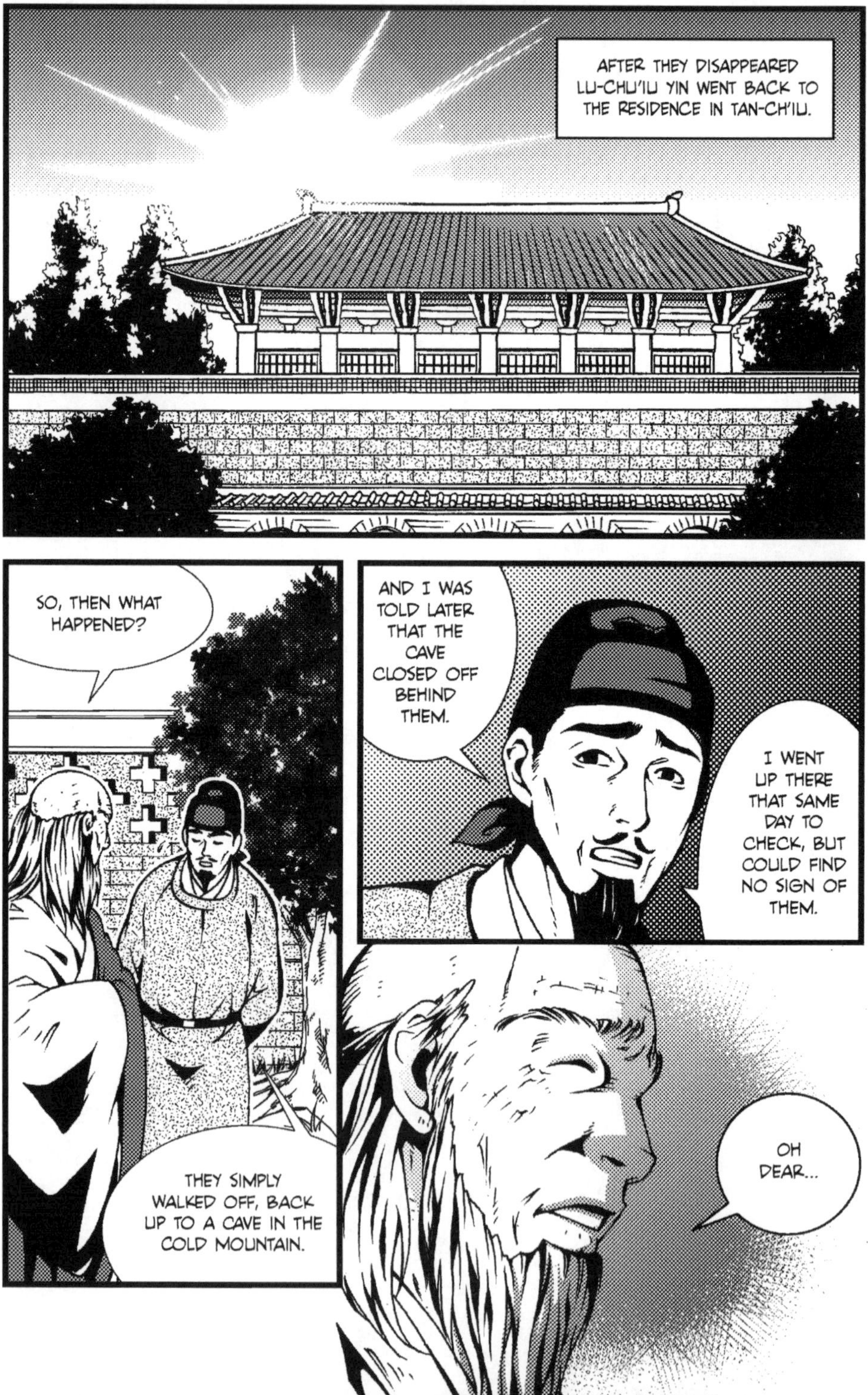
AFTER THEY DISAPPEARED LU-CHU'IU YIN WENT BACK TO THE RESIDENCE IN TAN-CH'IU.
SO, THEN WHAT HAPPENED?
THEY SIMPLY WALKED OFF, BACK UP TO A CAVE IN THE COLD MOUNTAIN.
AND I WAS TOLD LATER THAT THE CAVE CLOSED OFF BEHIND THEM.
I WENT UP THERE THAT SAME DAY TO CHECK, BUT COULD FIND NO SIGN OF THEM.
OH DEAR...

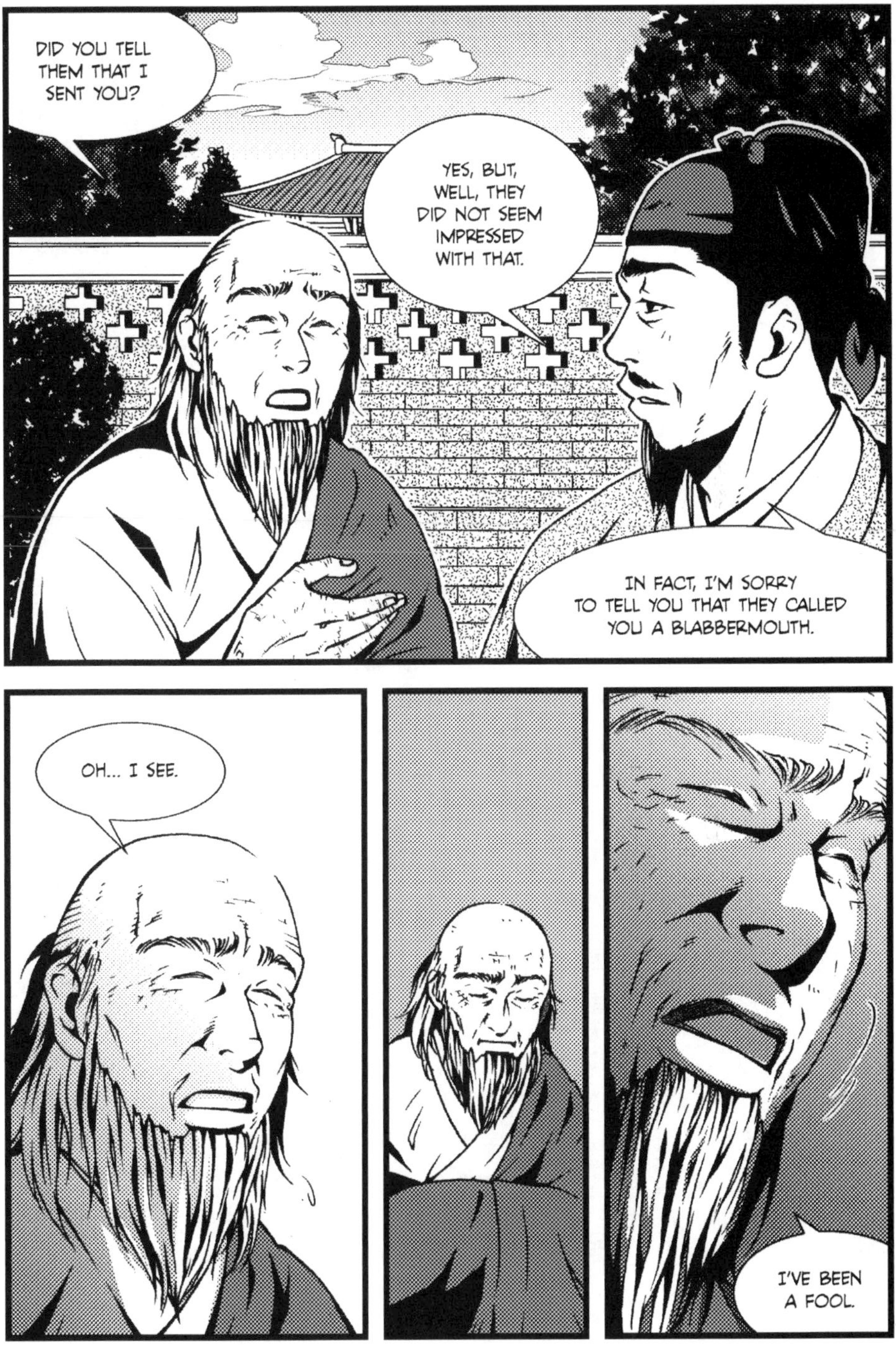
DID YOU TELL THEM THAT I SENT YOU?
YES, BUT, WELL, THEY DID NOT SEEM IMPRESSED WITH THAT.
IN FACT, I'M SORRY TO TELL YOU THAT THEY CALLED YOU A BLABBERMOUTH.
OH... I SEE.
I'VE BEEN A FOOL.

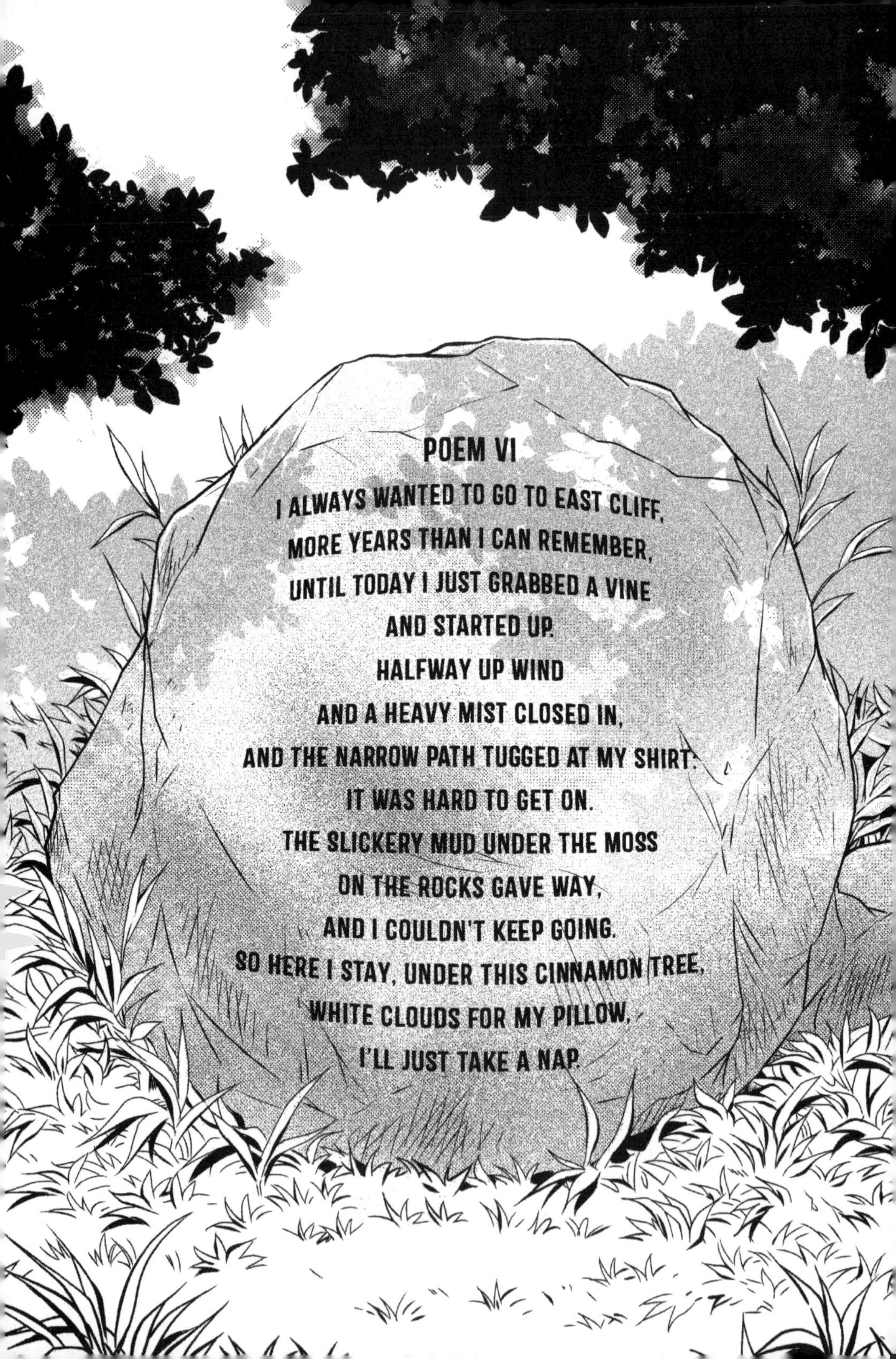
POEM VI
I ALWAYS WANTED TO GO TO EAST CLIFF,
MORE YEARS THAN I CAN REMEMBER,
UNTIL TODAY I JUST GRABBED A VINE
AND STARTED UP.
HALFWAY UP WIND
AND A HEAVY MIST CLOSED IN,
AND THE NARROW PATH TUGGED AT MY SHIRT:
IT WAS HARD TO GET ON.
THE SLICKERY MUD UNDER THE MOSS
ON THE ROCKS GAVE WAY,
AND I COULDN'T KEEP GOING.
SO HERE I STAY, UNDER THIS CINNAMON TREE,
WHITE CLOUDS FOR MY PILLOW,
I'LL JUST TAKE A NAP.

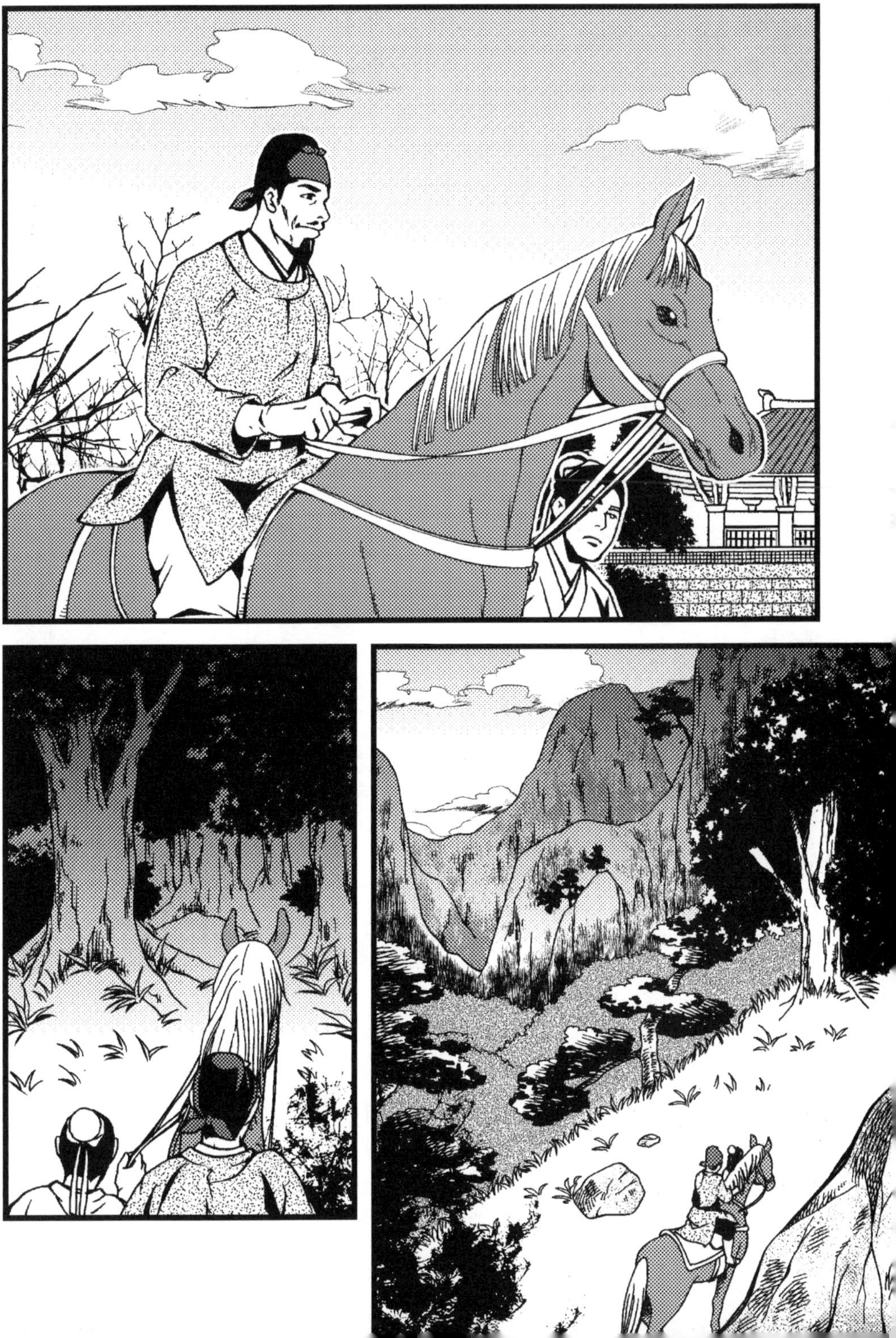

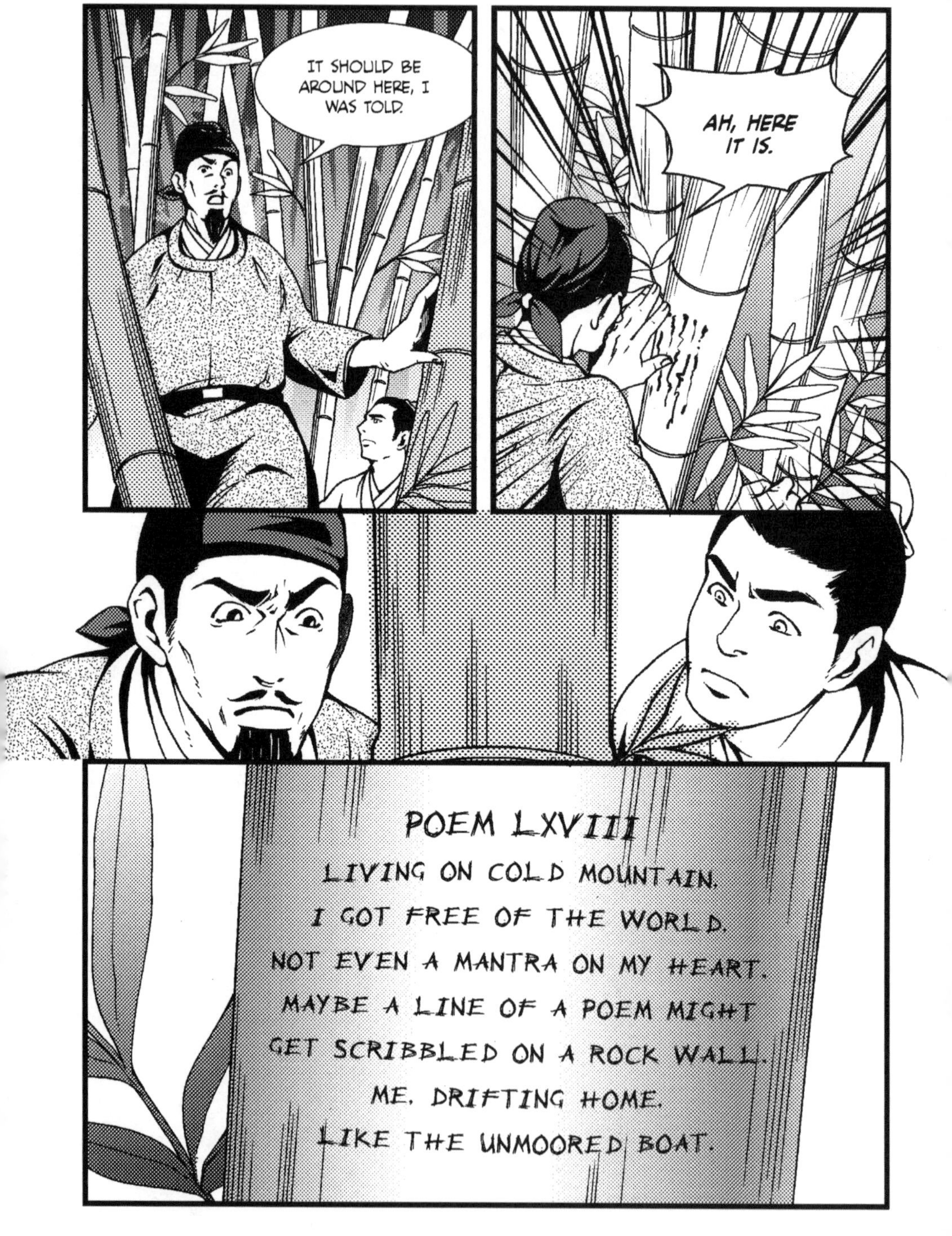
IT SHOULD BE AROUND HERE, I WAS TOLD.
AH, HERE IT IS.
POEM LXVIII
LIVING ON COLD MOUNTAIN,
I GOT FREE OF THE WORLD.
NOT EVEN A MANTRA ON MY HEART.
MAYBE A LINE OF A POEM MIGHT
GET SCRIBBLED ON A ROCK WALL.
ME, DRIFTING HOME,
LIKE THE UNMOORED BOAT.

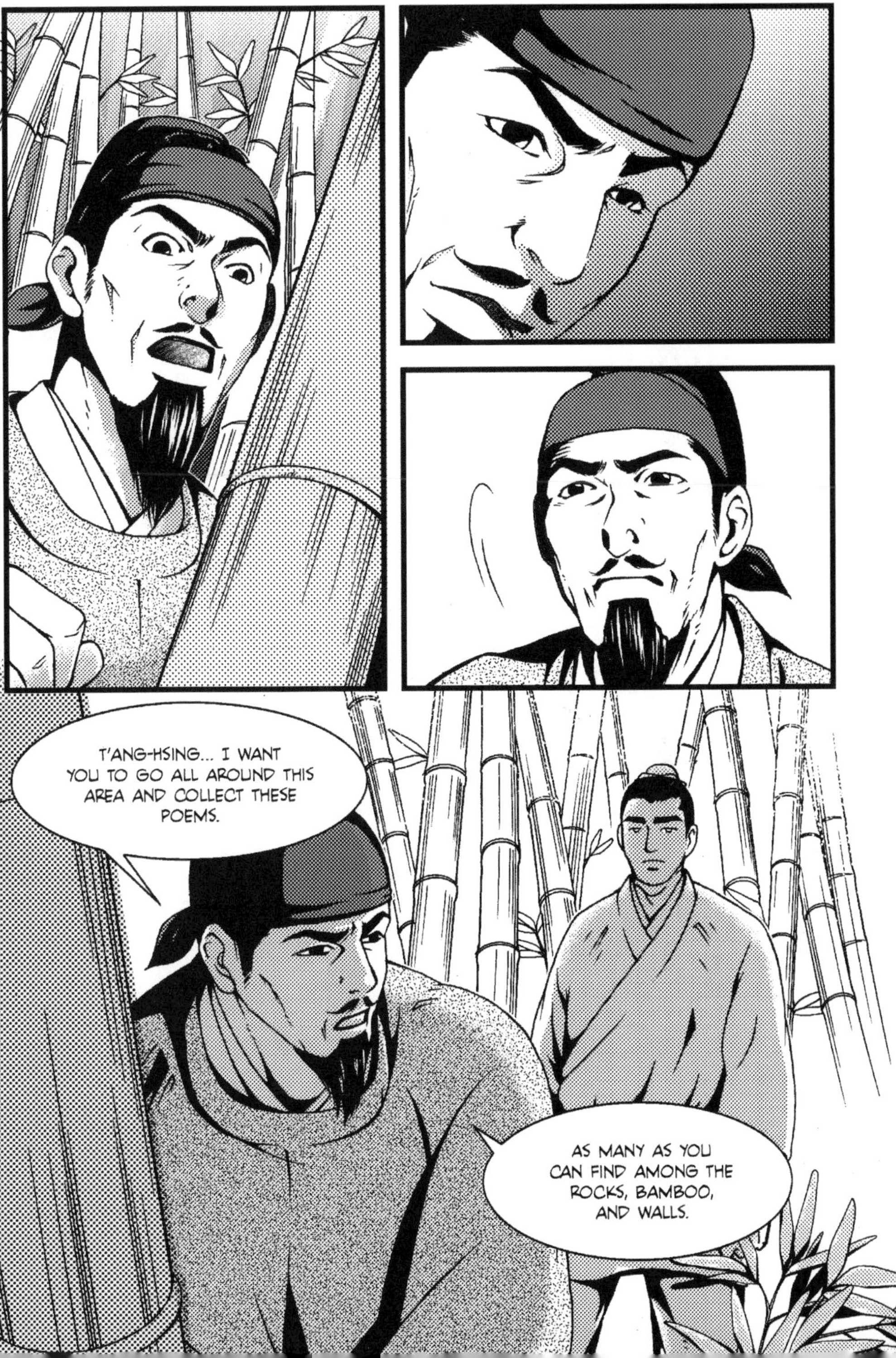
T'ANG-HSING... I WANT YOU TO GO ALL AROUND THIS AREA AND COLLECT THESE POEMS.
AS MANY AS YOU CAN FIND AMONG THE ROCKS, BAMBOO, AND WALLS.

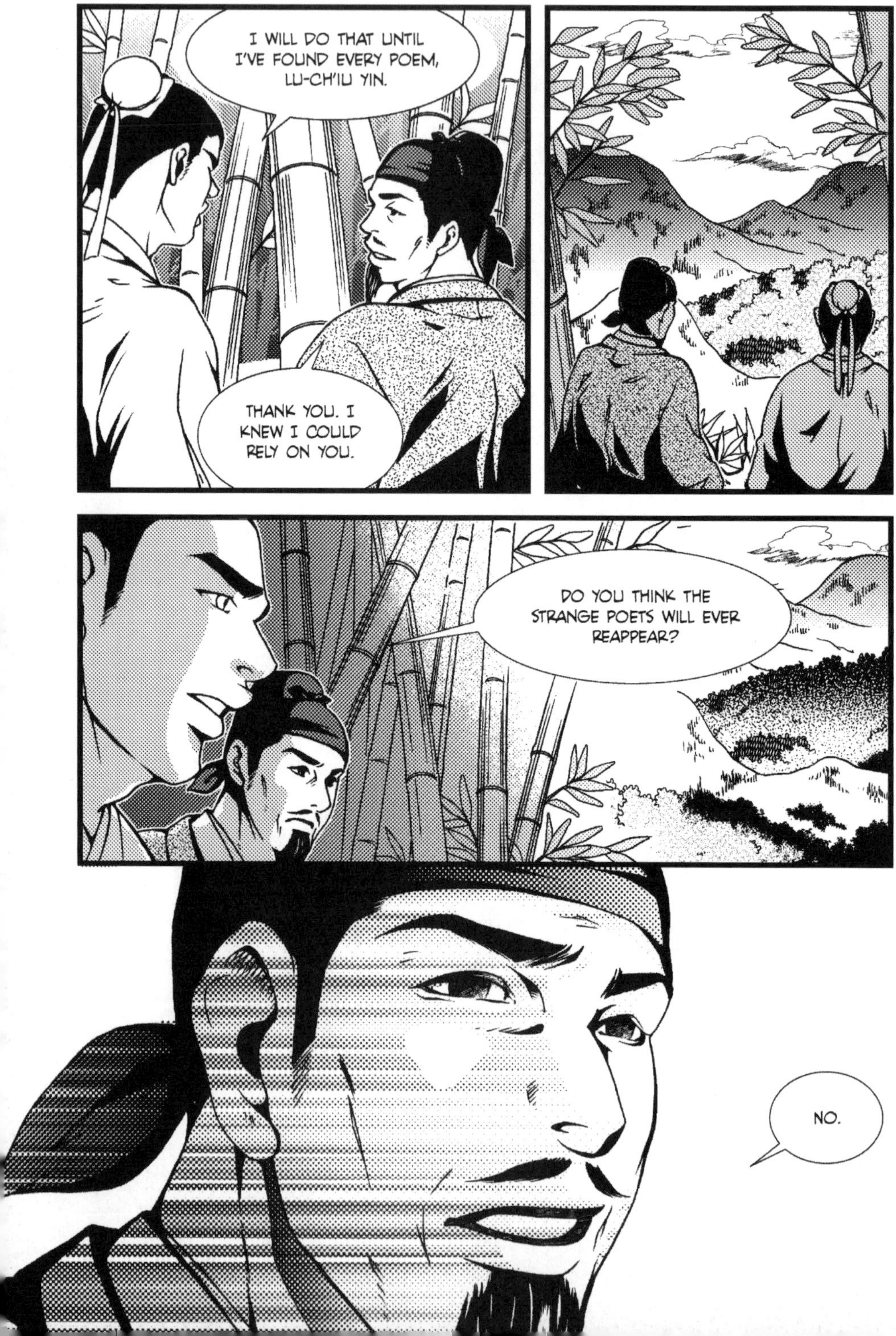
I WILL DO THAT UNTIL I'VE FOUND EVERY POEM, LU-CH'IU YIN.
THANK YOU. I KNEW I COULD RELY ON YOU.
DO YOU THINK THE STRANGE POETS WILL EVER REAPPEAR?
NO.

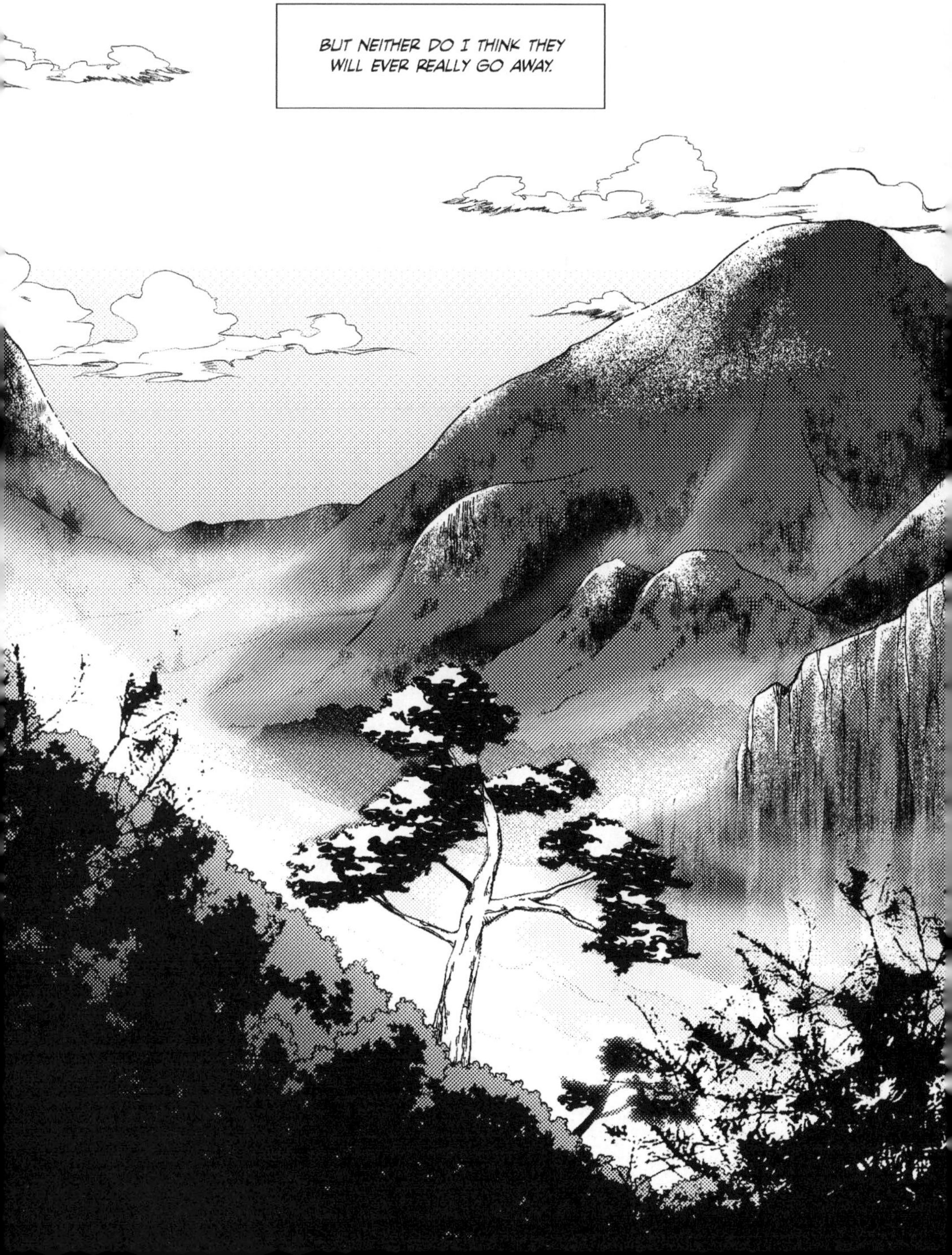
BUT NEITHER DO I THINK THEY WILL EVER REALLY GO AWAY.

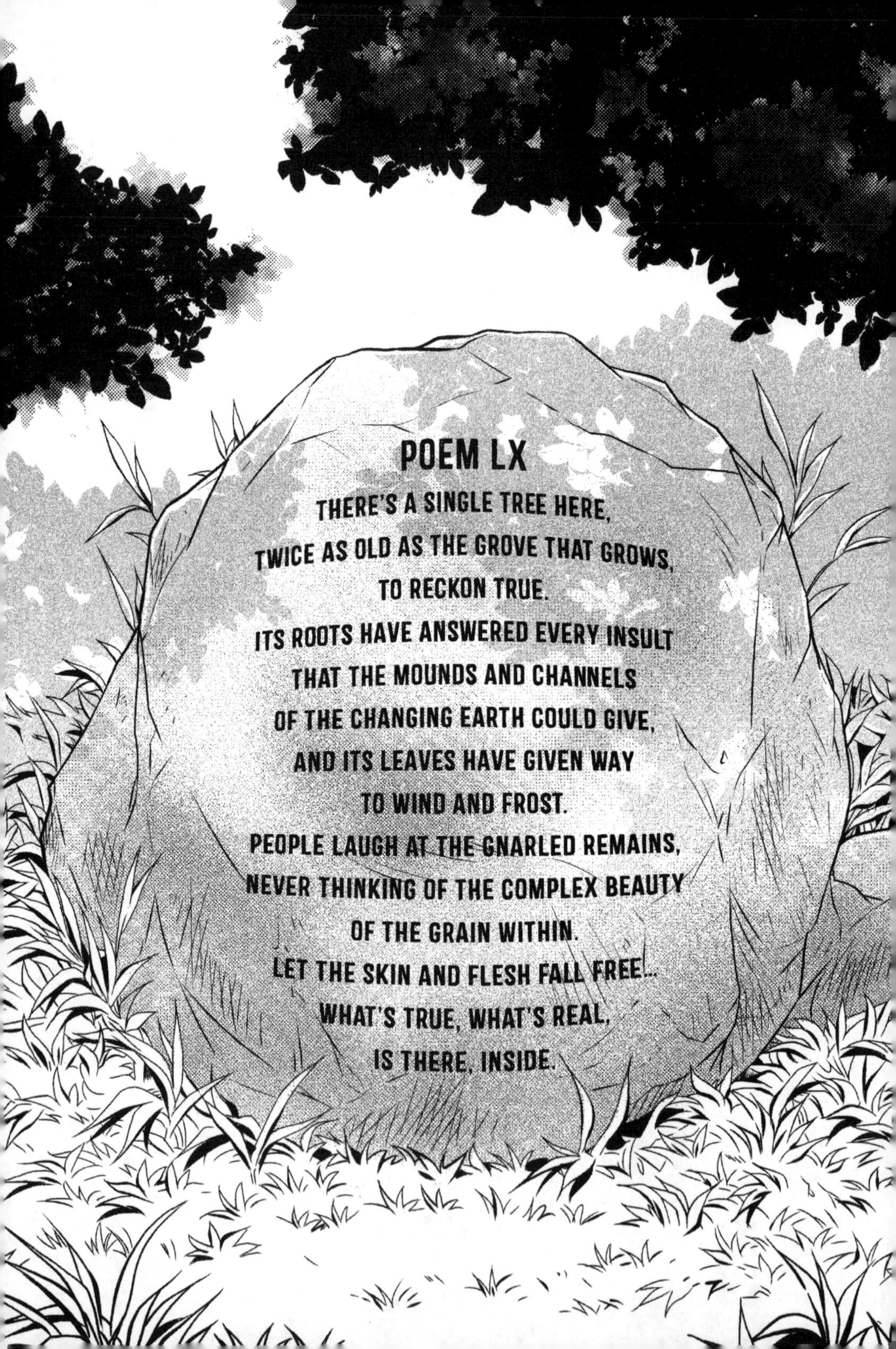
POEM LX
THERE'S A SINGLE TREE HERE,
TWICE AS OLD AS THE GROVE THAT GROWS,
TO RECKON TRUE.
ITS ROOTS HAVE ANSWERED EVERY INSULT
THAT THE MOUNDS AND CHANNELS
OF THE CHANGING EARTH COULD GIVE,
AND ITS LEAVES HAVE GIVEN WAY
TO WIND AND FROST.
PEOPLE LAUGH AT THE GNARLED REMAINS,
NEVER THINKING OF THE COMPLEX BEAUTY
OF THE GRAIN WITHIN.
LET THE SKIN AND FLESH FALL FREE...
WHAT'S TRUE, WHAT'S REAL,
IS THERE, INSIDE.

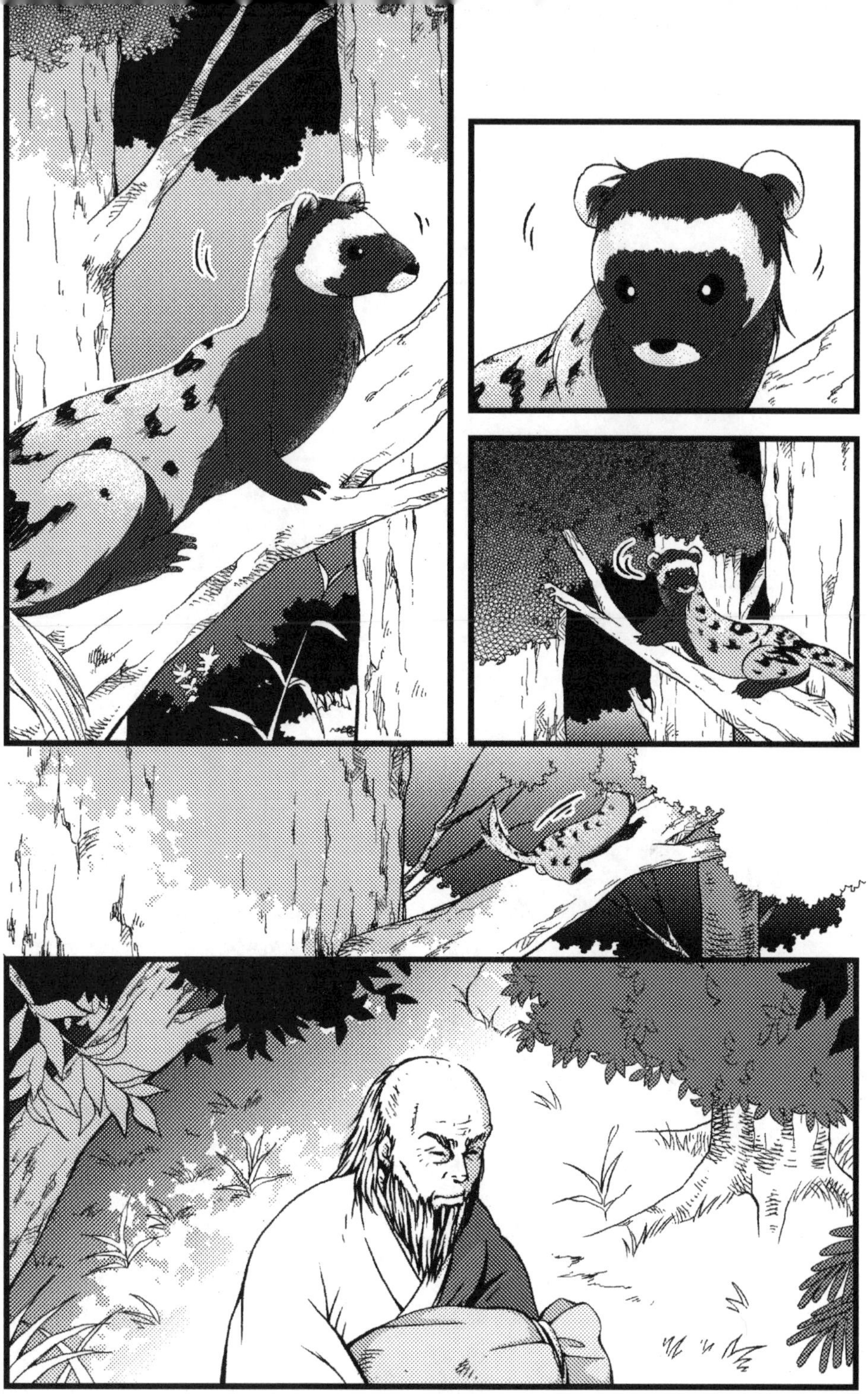

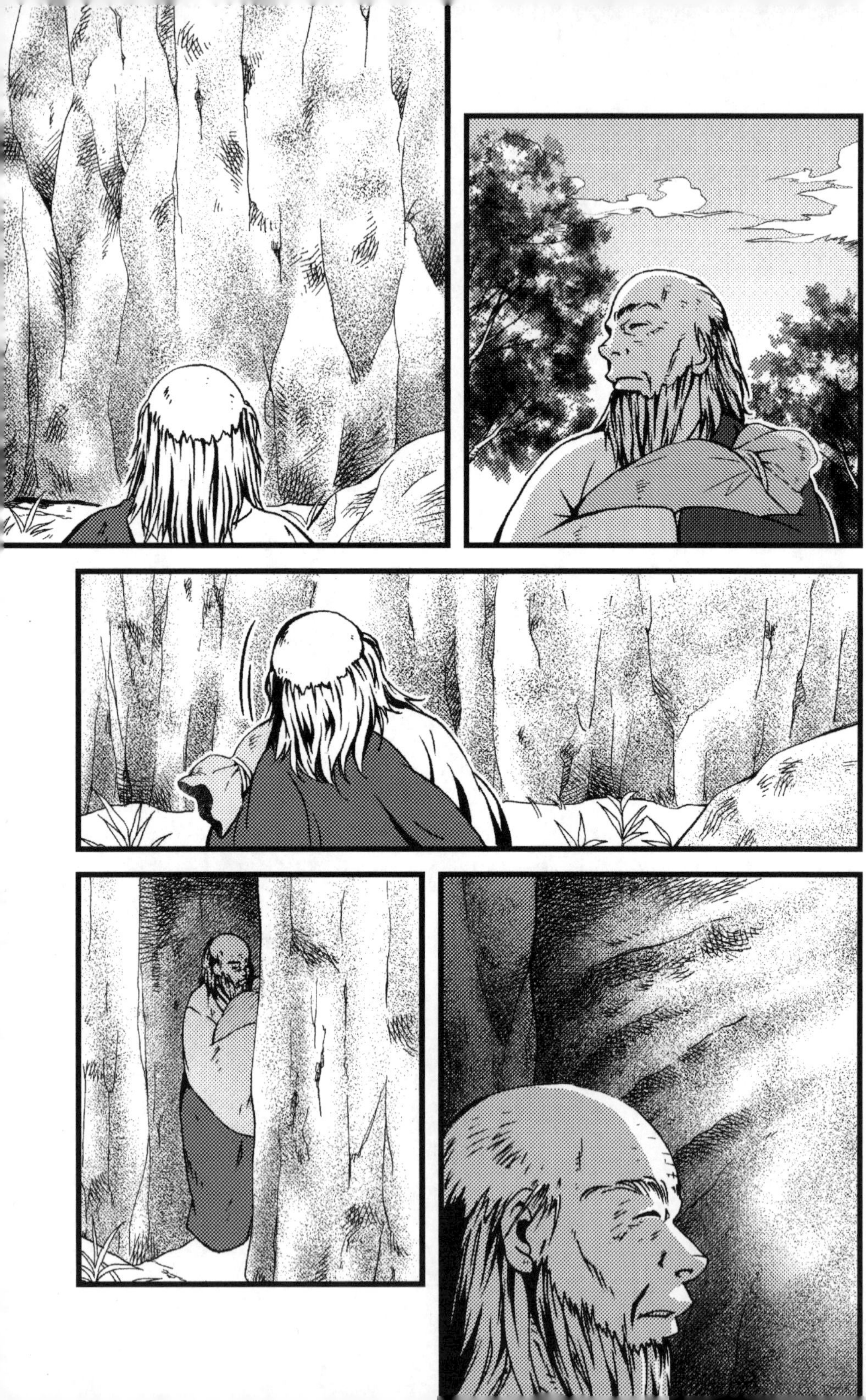

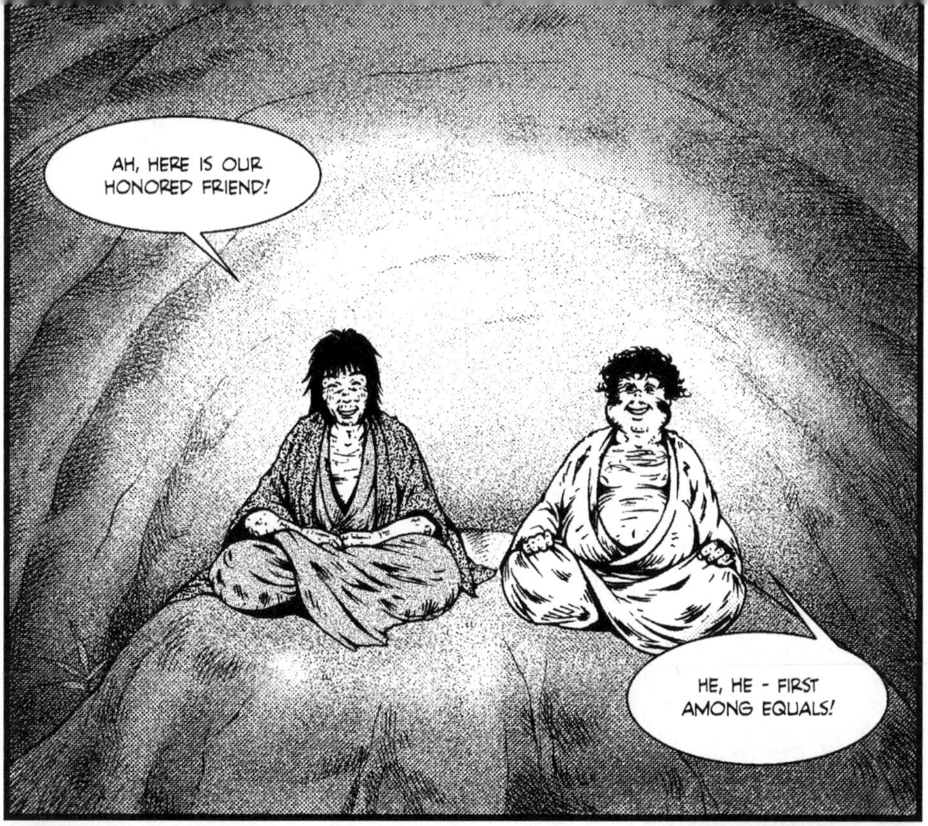
AH, HERE IS OUR HONORED FRIEND!
HE, HE - FIRST AMONG EQUALS!
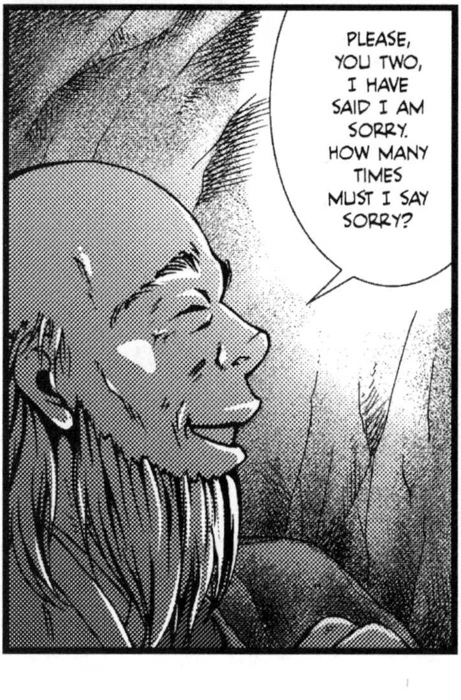
PLEASE, YOU TWO, I HAVE SAID I AM SORRY. HOW MANY TIMES MUST I SAY SORRY?
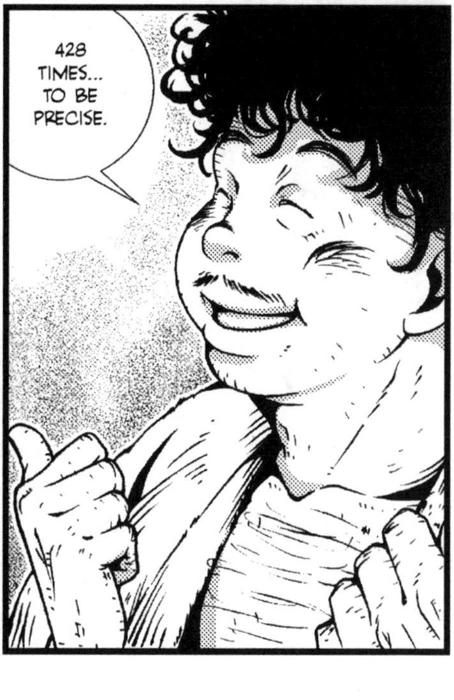
428 TIMES... TO BE PRECISE.

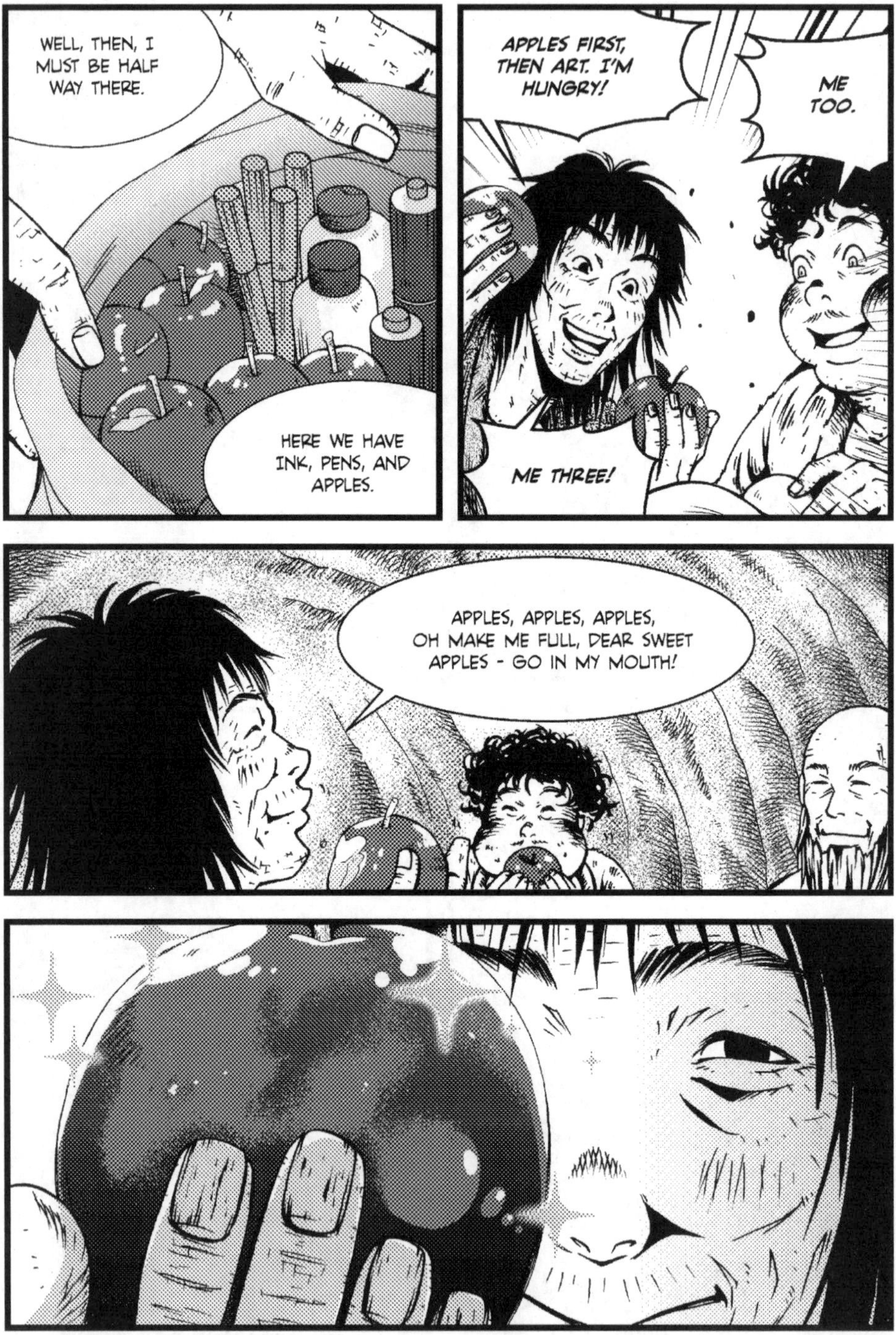
WELL, THEN, I MUST BE HALF WAY THERE.
HERE WE HAVE INK, PENS, AND APPLES.
APPLES FIRST, THEN ART. I'M HUNGRY!
ME TOO.
ME THREE!
APPLES, APPLES, APPLES, OH MAKE ME FULL, DEAR SWEET APPLES - GO IN MY MOUTH!

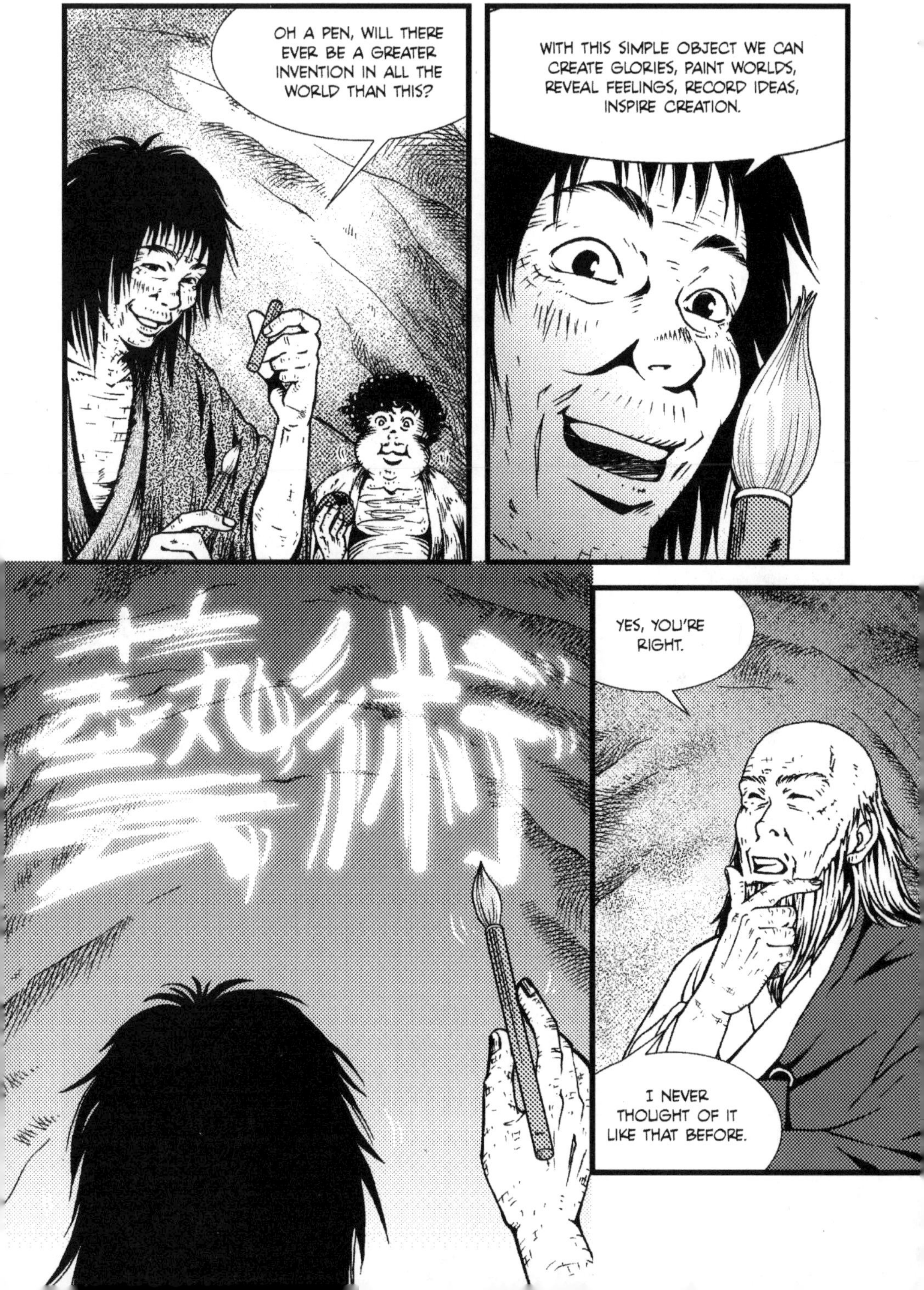
OH A PEN, WILL THERE EVER BE A GREATER INVENTION IN ALL THE WORLD THAN THIS?
WITH THIS SIMPLE OBJECT WE CAN CREATE GLORIES, PAINT WORLDS, REVEAL FEELINGS, RECORD IDEAS, INSPIRE CREATION.
YES, YOU'RE RIGHT.
I NEVER THOUGHT OF IT LIKE THAT BEFORE.

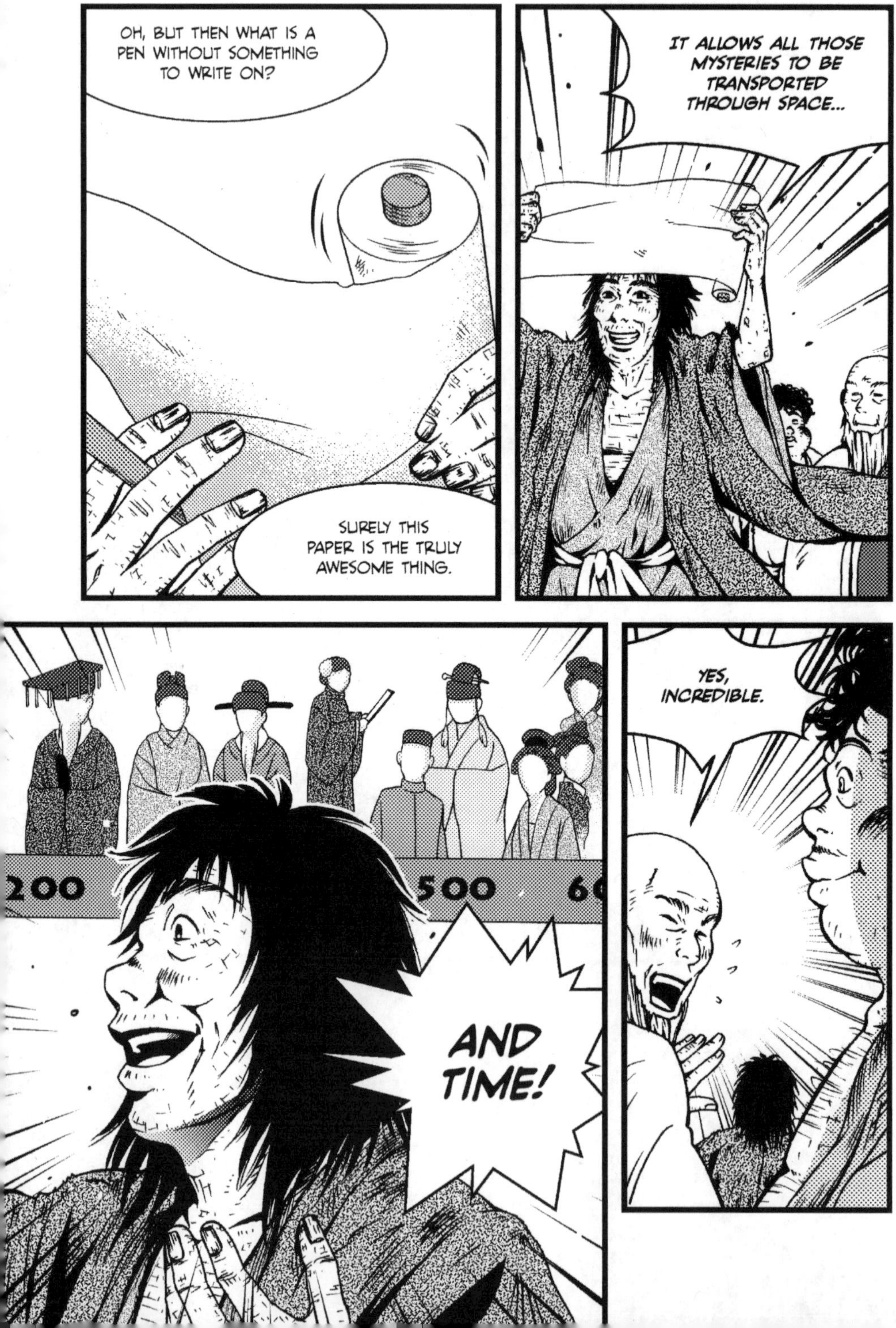
OH, BUT THEN WHAT IS A PEN WITHOUT SOMETHING TO WRITE ON?
SURELY THIS PAPER IS THE TRULY AWESOME THING.
IT ALLOWS ALL THOSE MYSTERIES TO BE TRANSPORTED THROUGH SPACE...
200
500
AND TIME!
YES, INCREDIBLE.

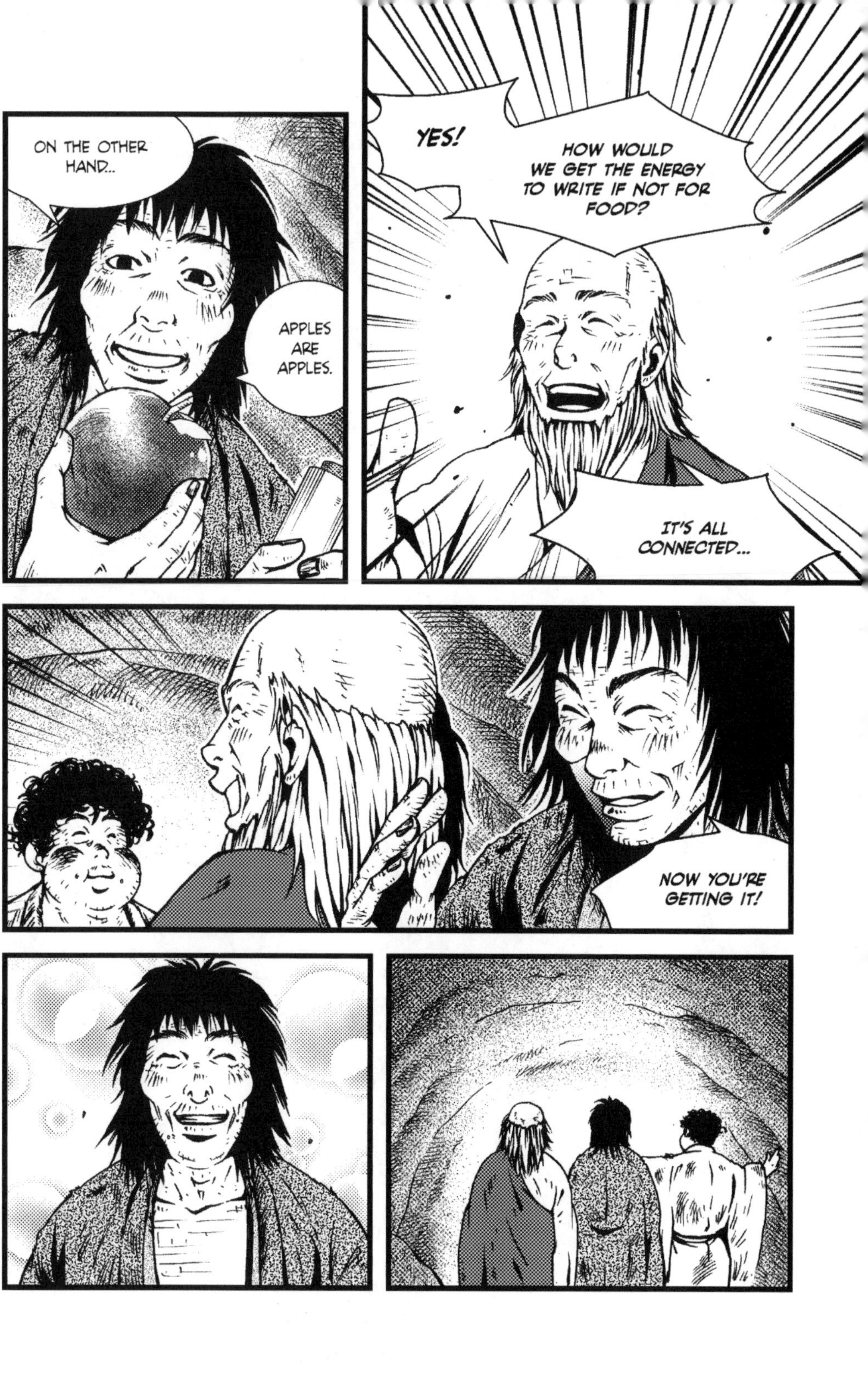
ON THE OTHER HAND...
APPLES ARE APPLES.
YES!
HOW WOULD WE GET THE ENERGY TO WRITE IF NOT FOR FOOD?
IT'S ALL CONNECTED...
NOW YOU'RE GETTING IT!

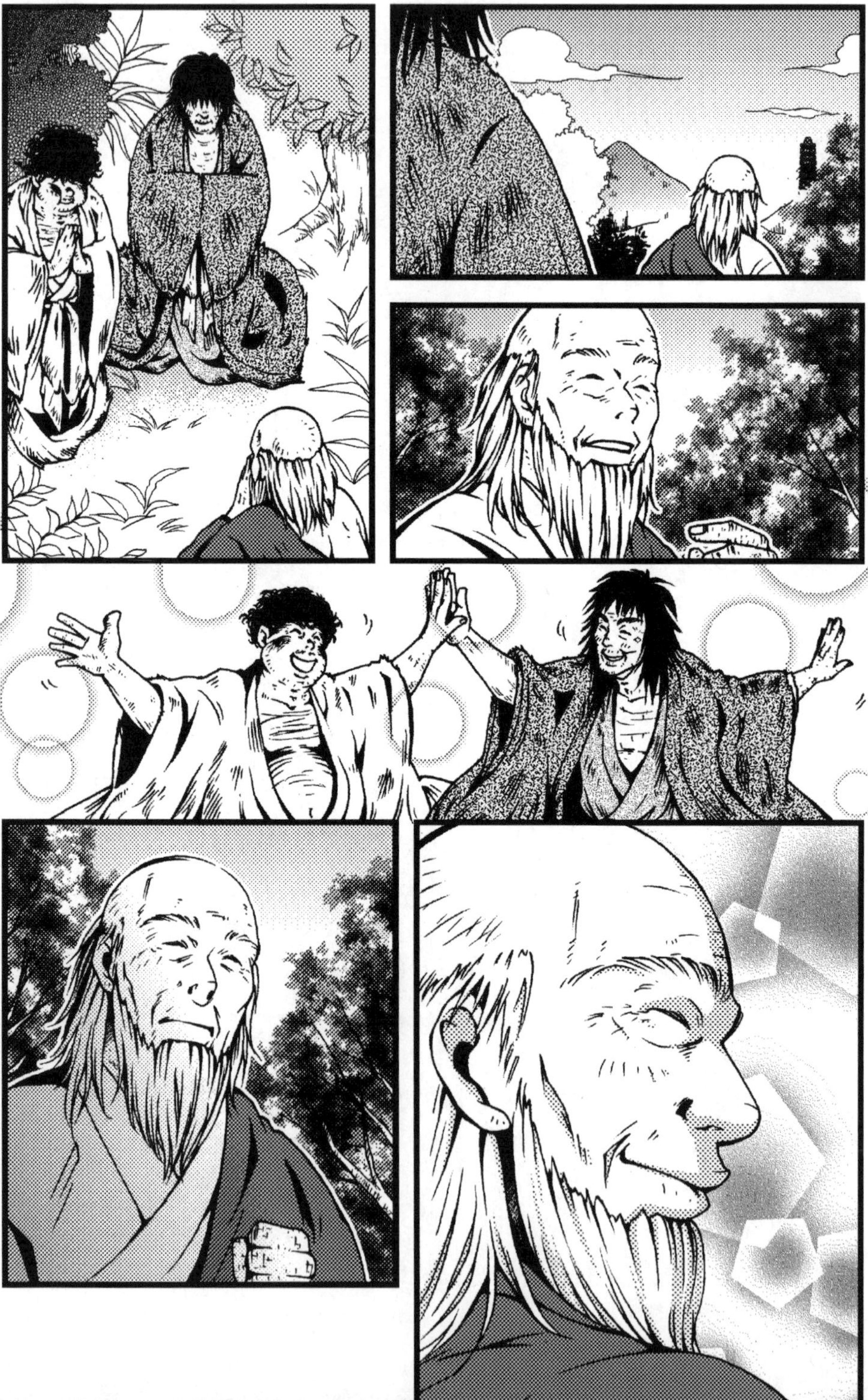

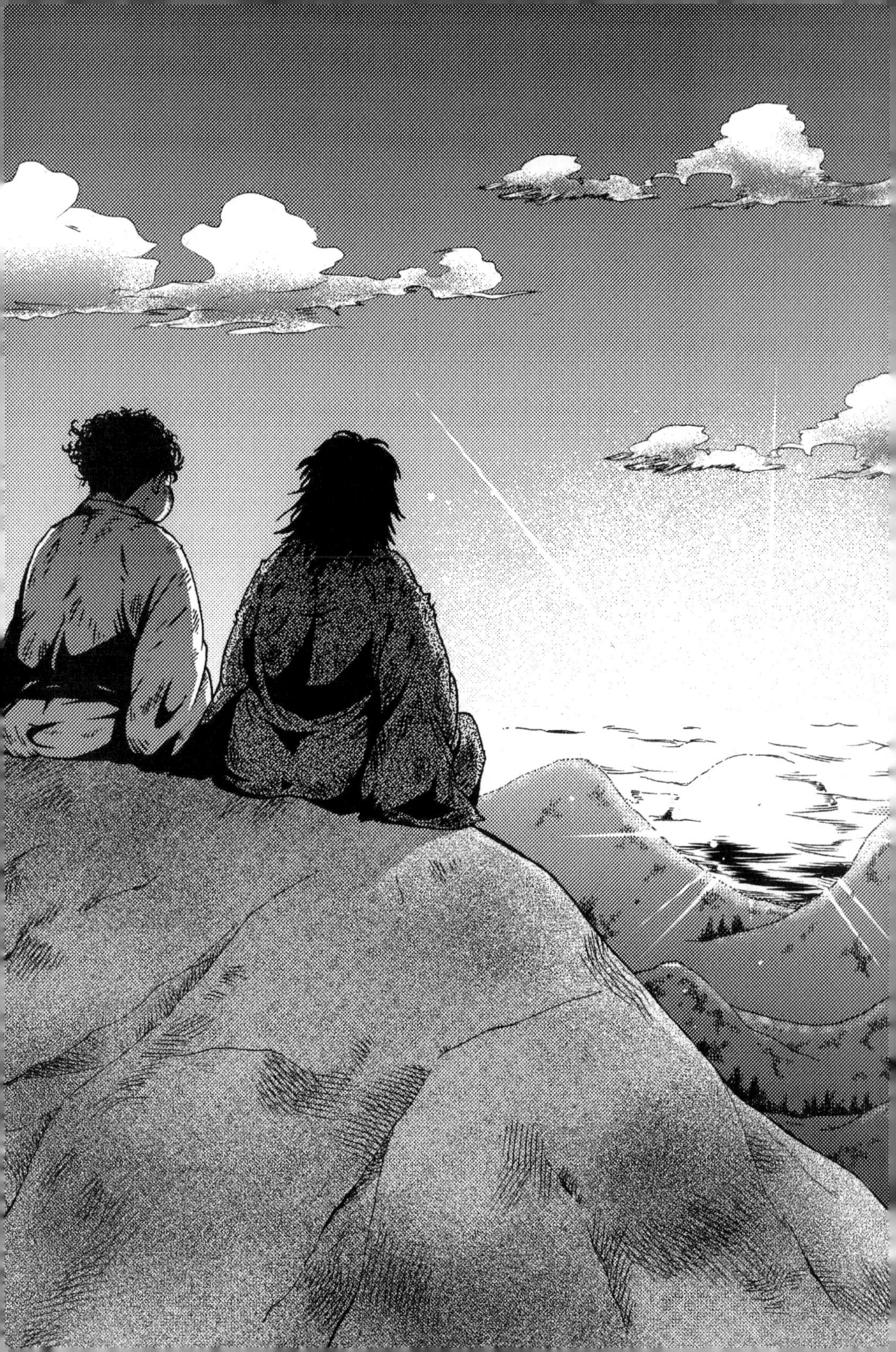

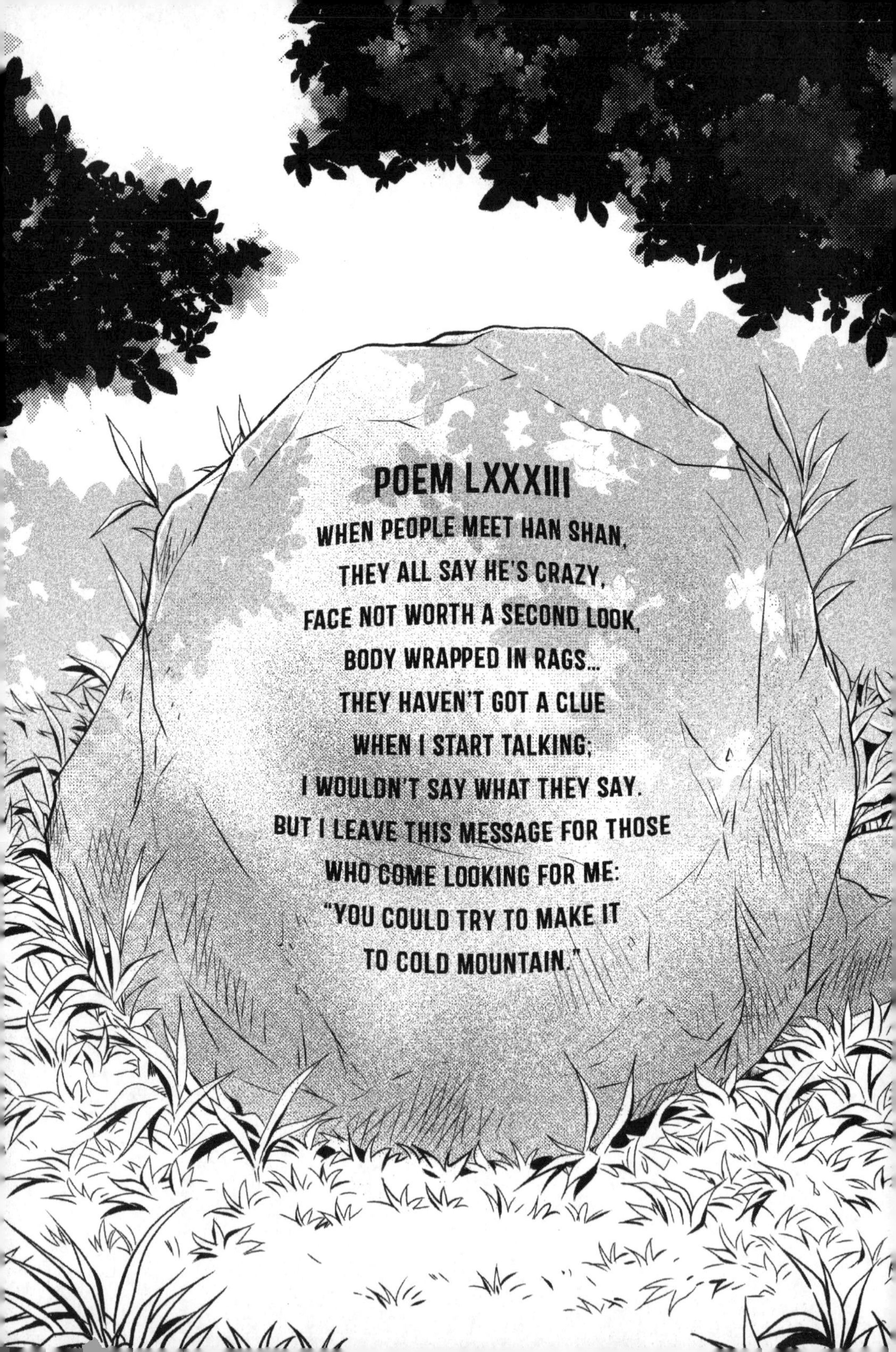
POEM LXXXIII
WHEN PEOPLE MEET HAN SHAN,
THEY ALL SAY HE'S CRAZY,
FACE NOT WORTH A SECOND LOOK,
BODY WRAPPED IN RAGS...
THEY HAVEN'T GOT A CLUE
WHEN I START TALKING;
I WOULDN'T SAY WHAT THEY SAY.
BUT I LEAVE THIS MESSAGE FOR THOSE
WHO COME LOOKING FOR ME:
"YOU COULD TRY TO MAKE IT
TO COLD MOUNTAIN."

PART 3

HAN SHAN - POEM VII

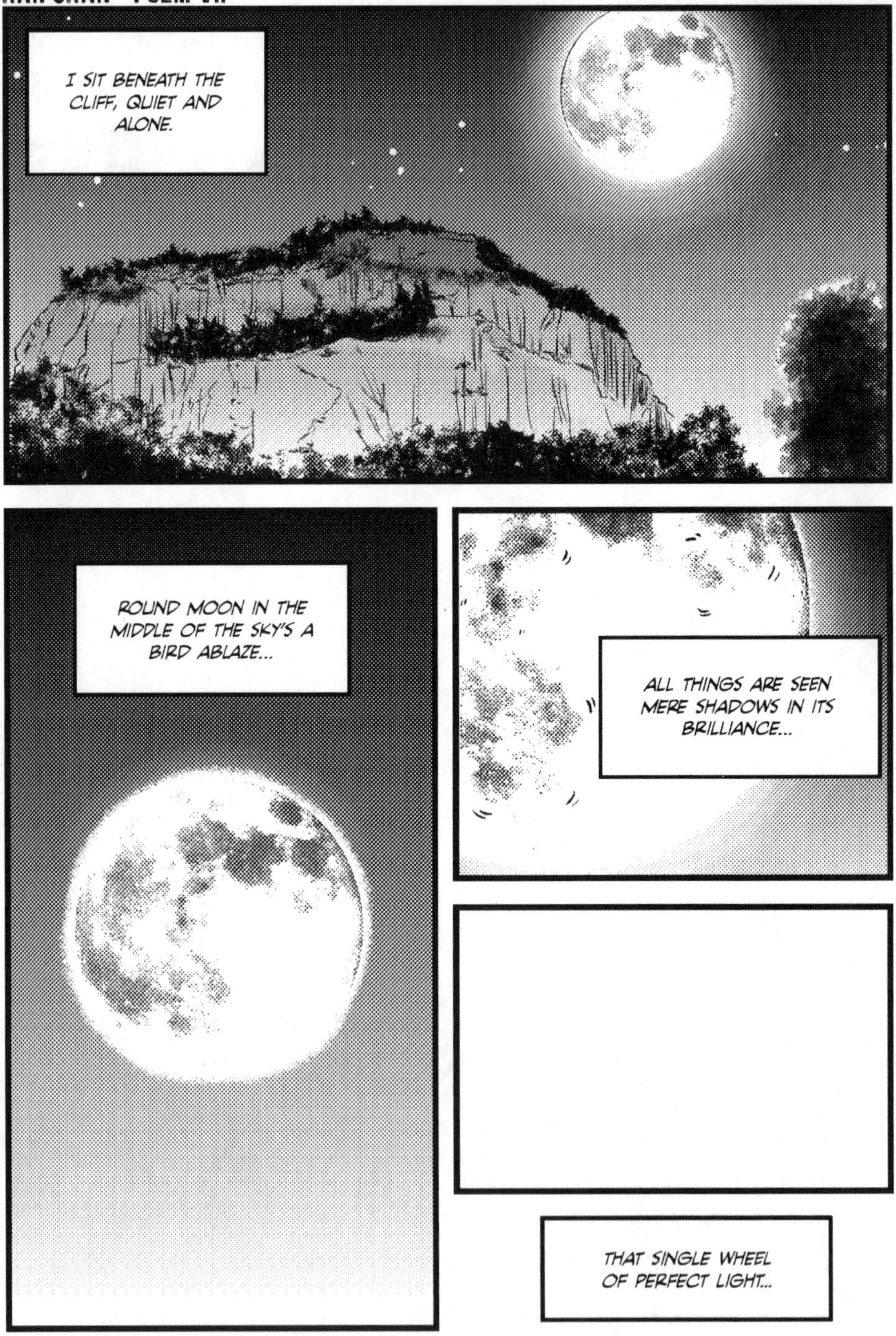
I SIT BENEATH THE CLIFF, QUIET AND ALONE.
ROUND MOON IN THE MIDDLE OF THE SKY'S A BIRD ABLAZE...
ALL THINGS ARE SEEN MERE SHADOWS IN ITS BRILLIANCE...
THAT SINGLE WHEEL OF PERFECT LIGHT...

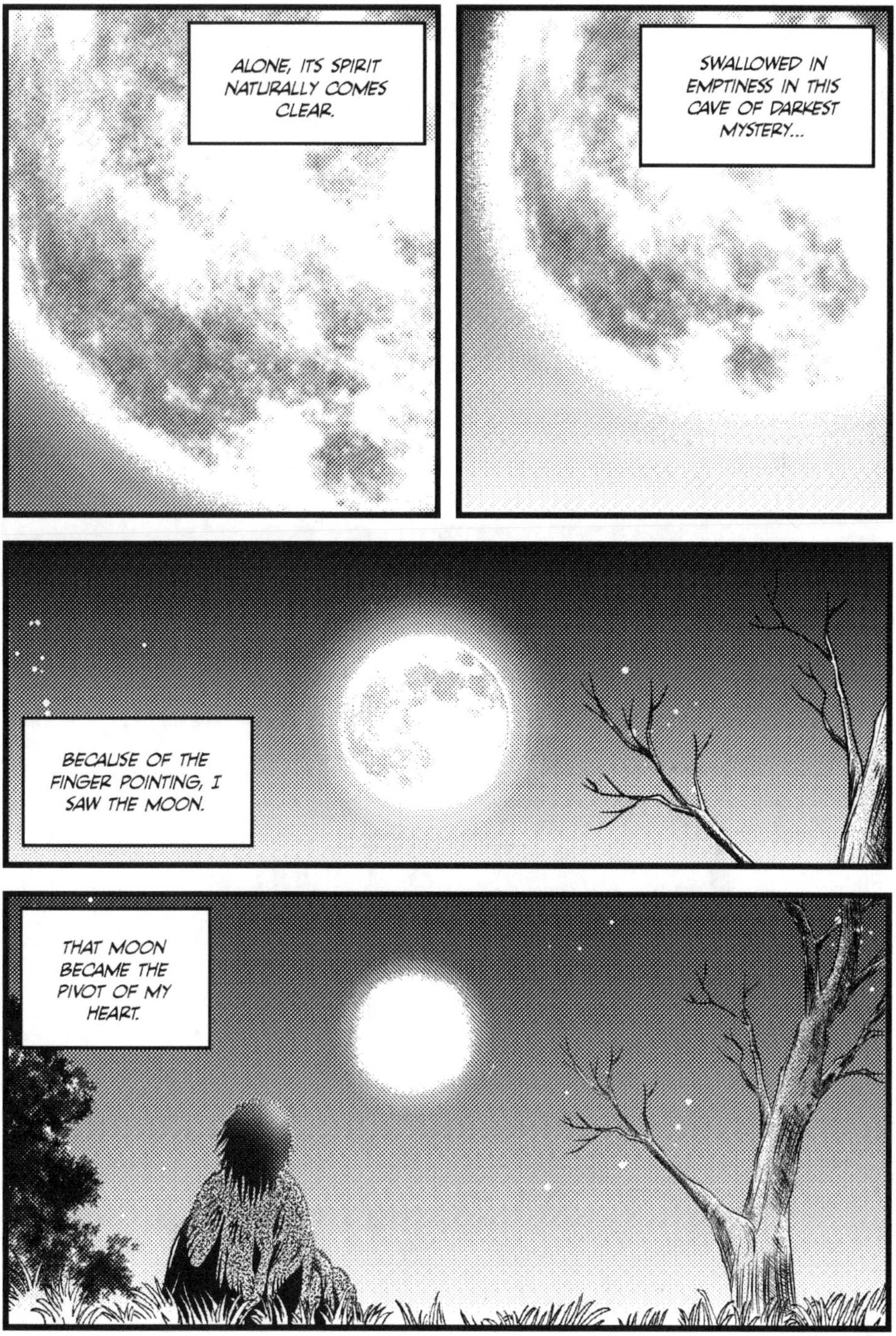
SWALLOWED IN EMPTINESS IN THIS CAVE OF DARKEST MYSTERY...
ALONE, ITS SPIRIT NATURALLY COMES CLEAR.
BECAUSE OF THE FINGER POINTING, I SAW THE MOON.
THAT MOON BECAME THE PIVOT OF MY HEART.

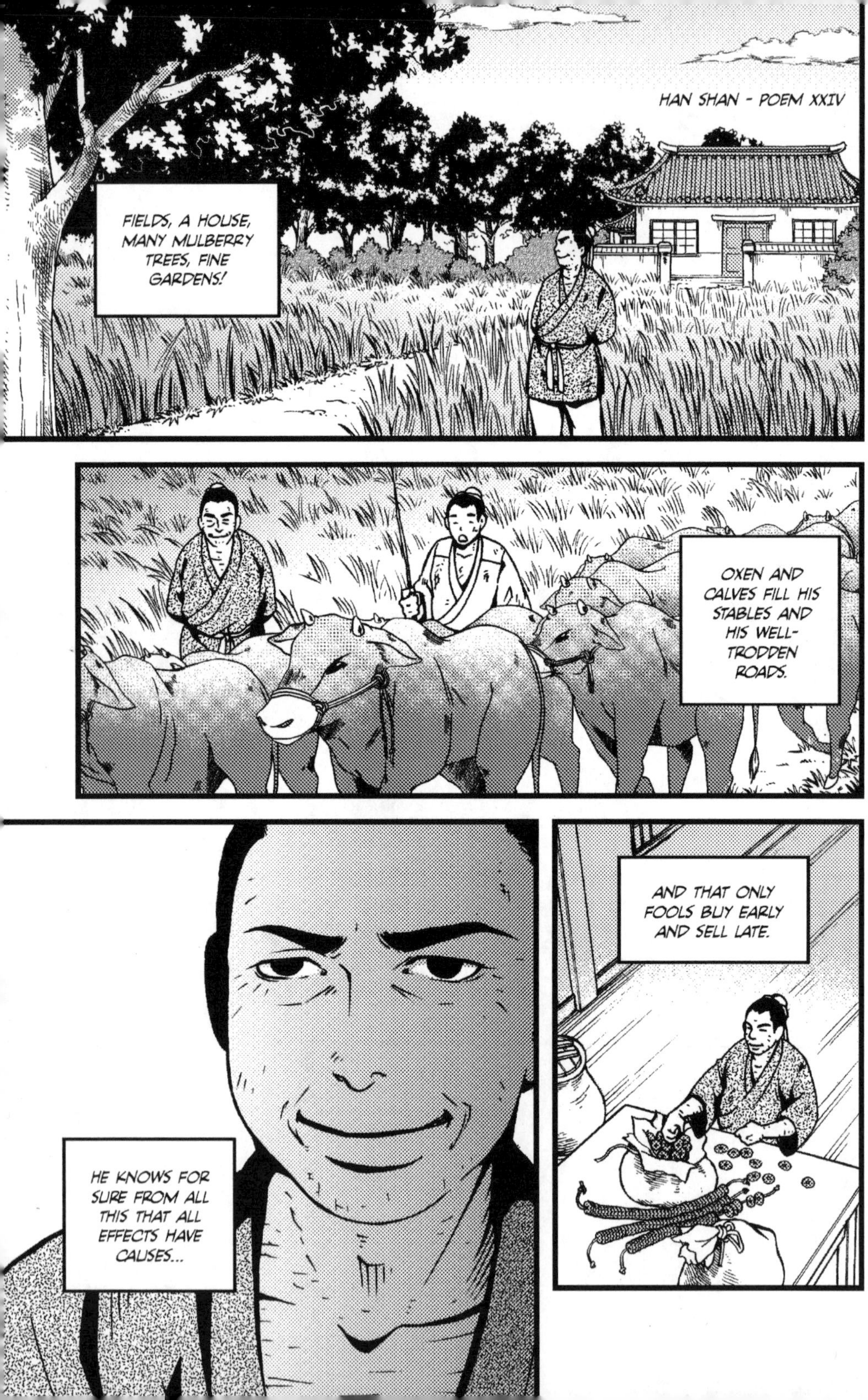
HAN SHAN - POEM XXIV
FIELDS, A HOUSE, MANY MULBERRY TREES, FINE GARDENS!
OXEN AND CALVES FILL HIS STABLES AND HIS WELL-TRODDEN ROADS.
HE KNOWS FOR SURE FROM ALL THIS THAT ALL EFFECTS HAVE CAUSES...
AND THAT ONLY FOOLS BUY EARLY AND SELL LATE.

HAN SHAN - POEM XXV

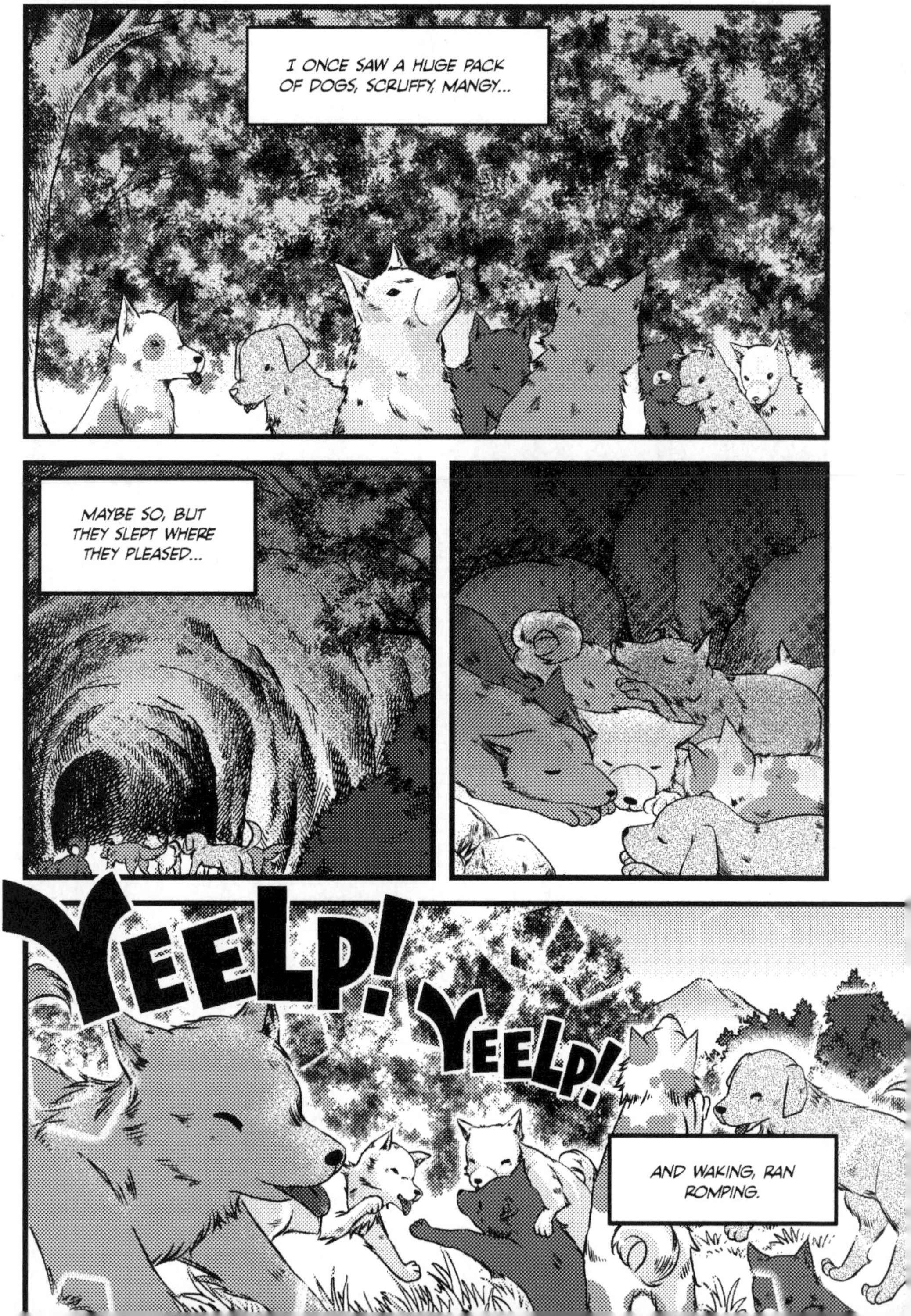
I ONCE SAW A HUGE PACK OF DOGS, SCRUFFY, MANGY...
MAYBE SO, BUT THEY SLEPT WHERE THEY PLEASED...
YEELP!
YEELP!
AND WAKING, RAN ROMPING.

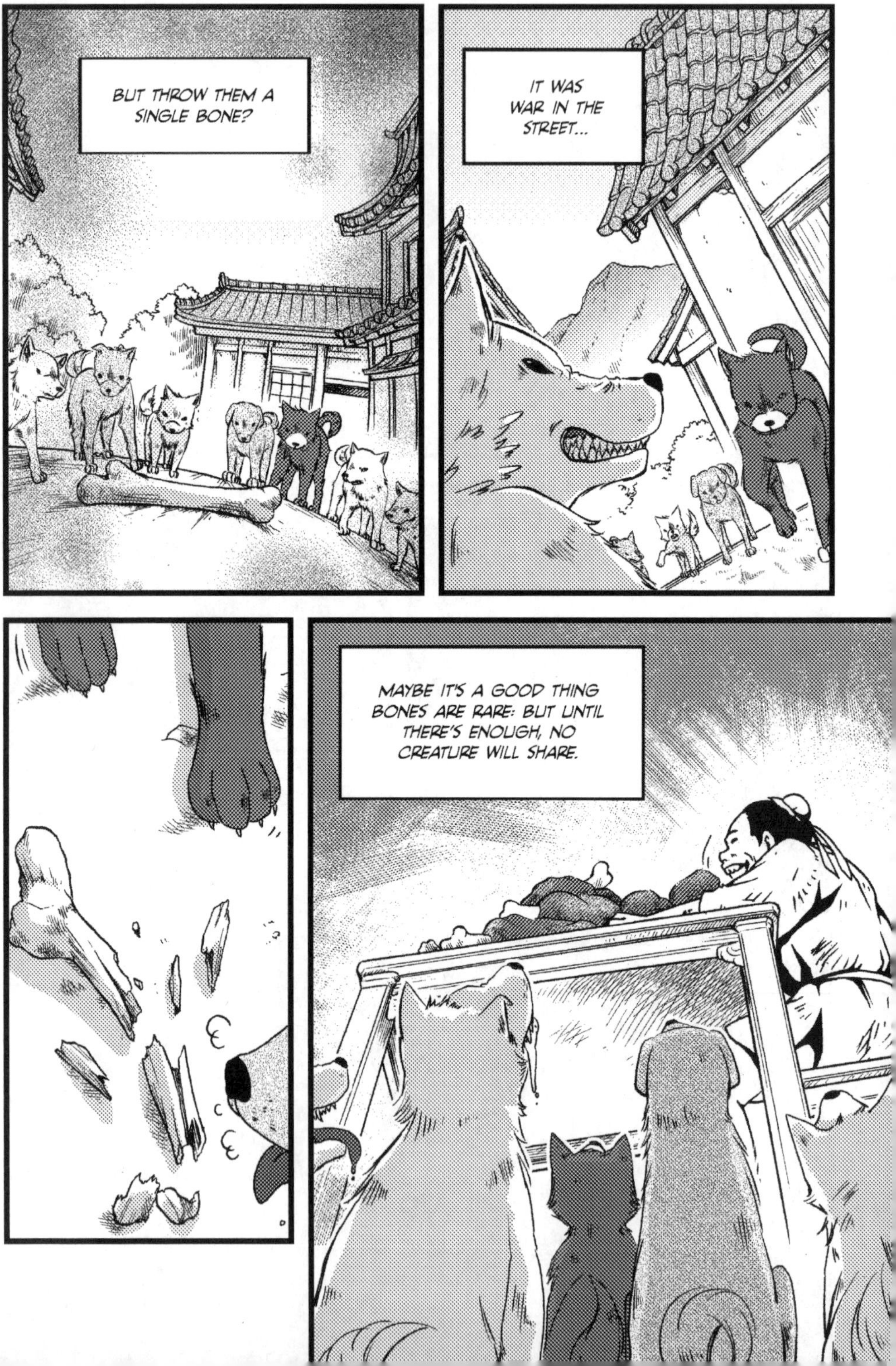
BUT THROW THEM A SINGLE BONE?
IT WAS WAR IN THE STREET...
MAYBE IT'S A GOOD THING BONES ARE RARE: BUT UNTIL THERE'S ENOUGH, NO CREATURE WILL SHARE.

HAN SHAN - POEM XXXII

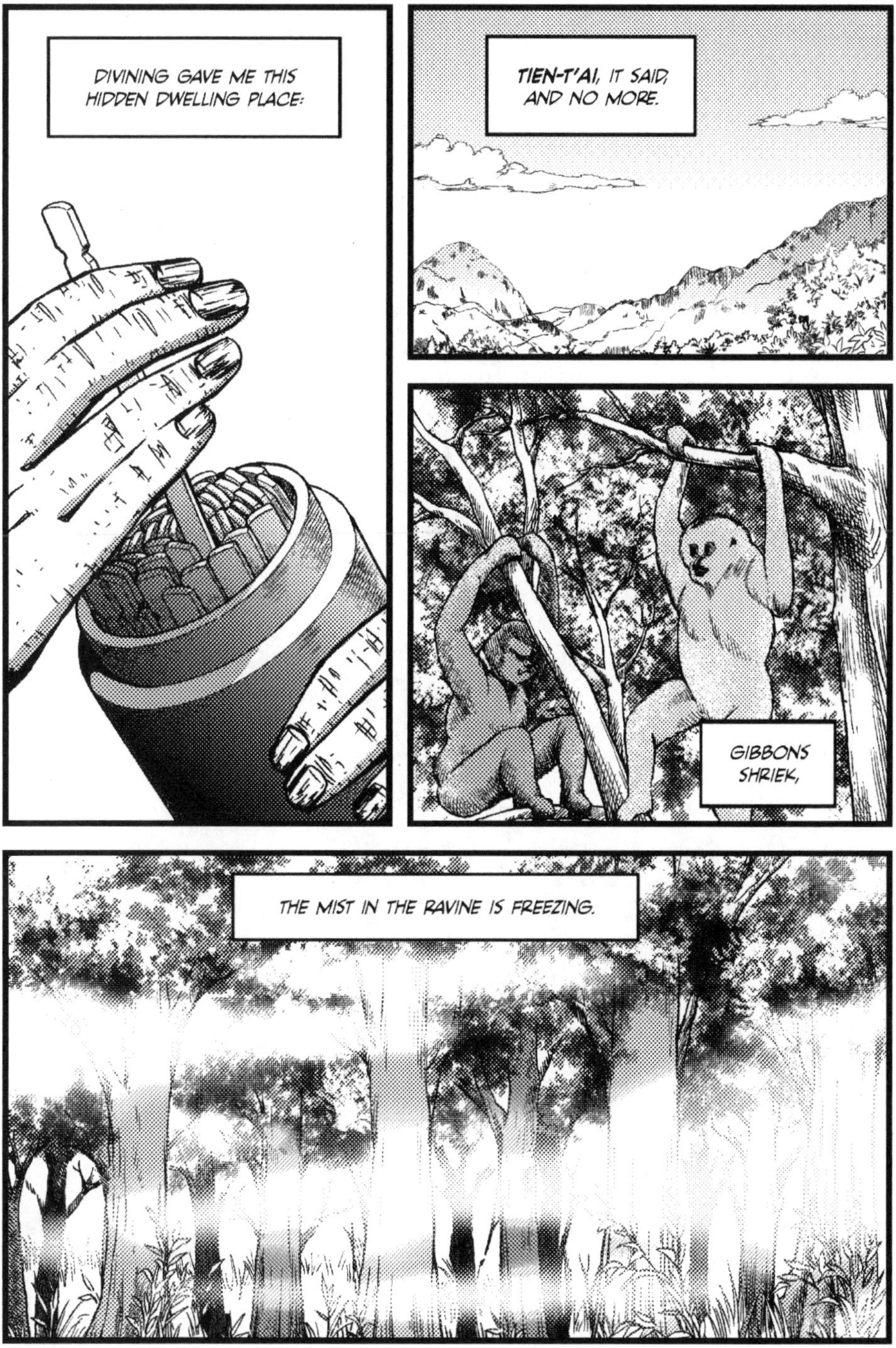
DIVINING GAVE ME THIS HIDDEN DWELLING PLACE:
TIEN-T'AI, IT SAID, AND NO MORE.
GIBBONS SHRIEK,
THE MIST IN THE RAVINE IS FREEZING.

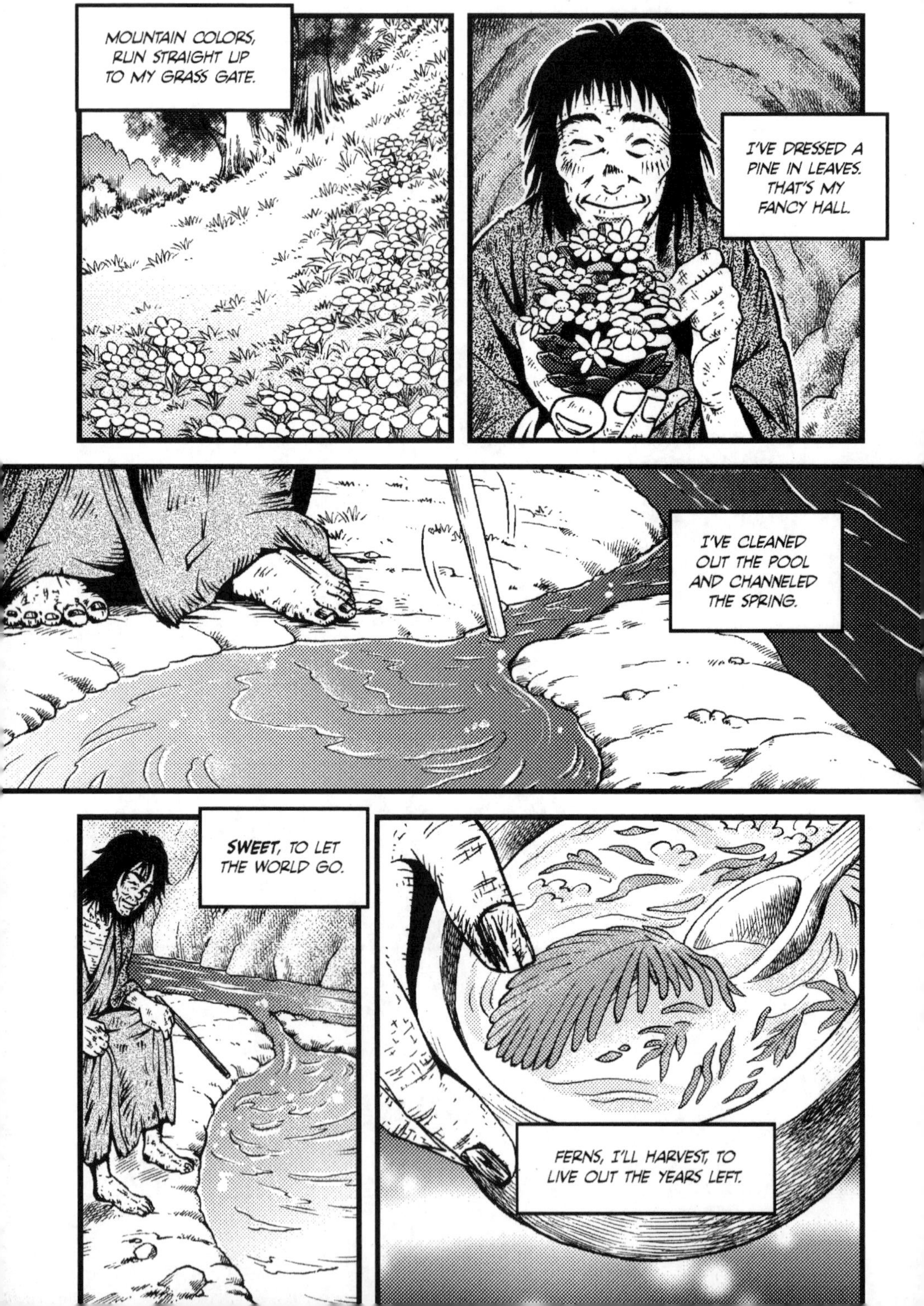
MOUNTAIN COLORS, RUN STRAIGHT UP TO MY GRASS GATE.
I'VE DRESSED A PINE IN LEAVES. THAT'S MY FANCY HALL.
I'VE CLEANED OUT THE POOL AND CHANNELED THE SPRING.
SWEET, TO LET THE WORLD GO.
FERNS, I'LL HARVEST, TO LIVE OUT THE YEARS LEFT.

HAN SHAN - POEM XL

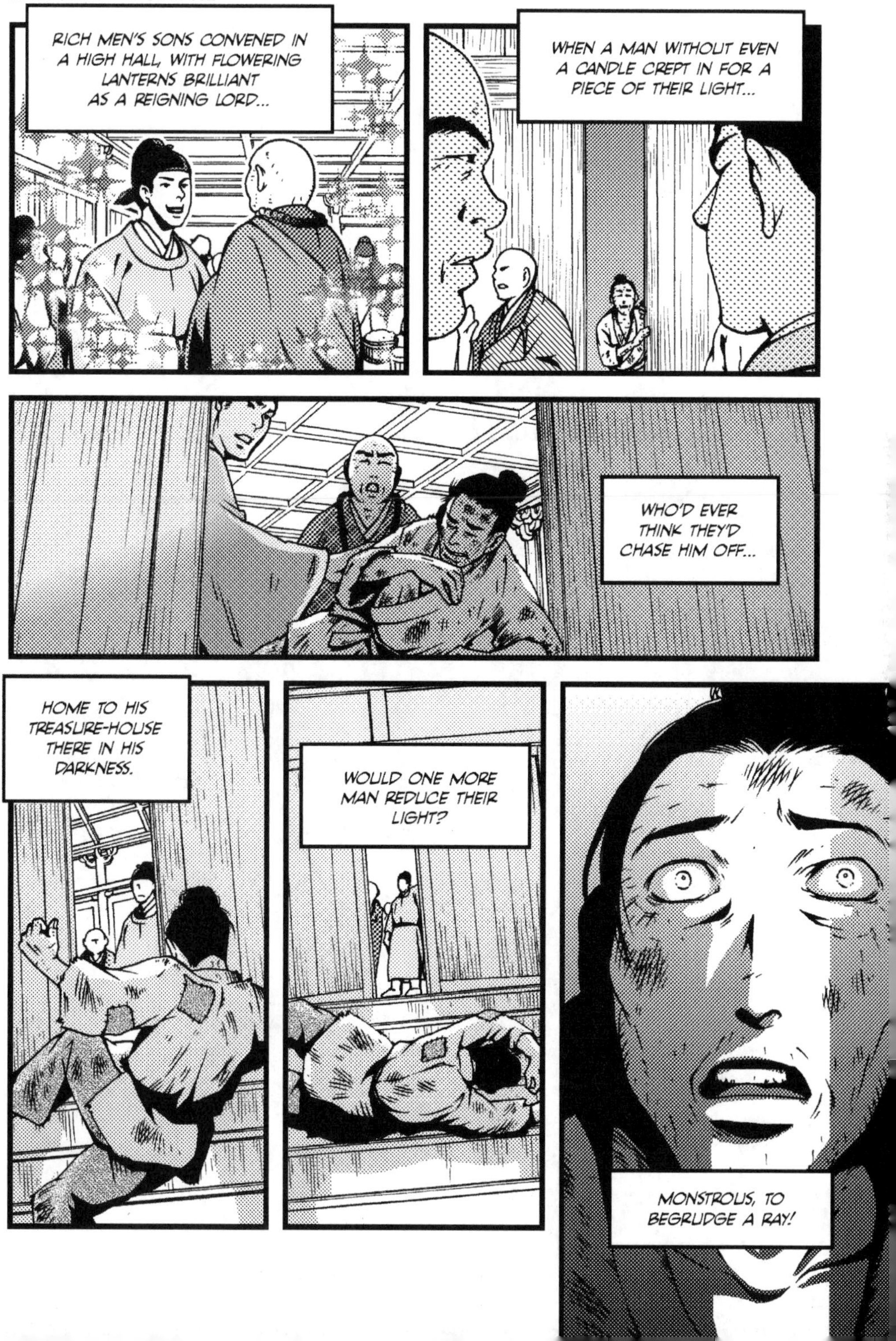

RICH MEN'S SONS CONVENED IN A HIGH HALL, WITH FLOWERING LANTERNS BRILLIANT AS A REIGNING LORD...
WHEN A MAN WITHOUT EVEN A CANDLE CREPT IN FOR A PIECE OF THEIR LIGHT...
WHO'D EVER THINK THEY'D CHASE HIM OFF...
HOME TO HIS TREASURE-HOUSE THERE IN HIS DARKNESS.
WOULD ONE MORE MAN REDUCE THEIR LIGHT?
MONSTROUS, TO BEGRUDGE A RAY!

HAN SHAN - POEM XLV

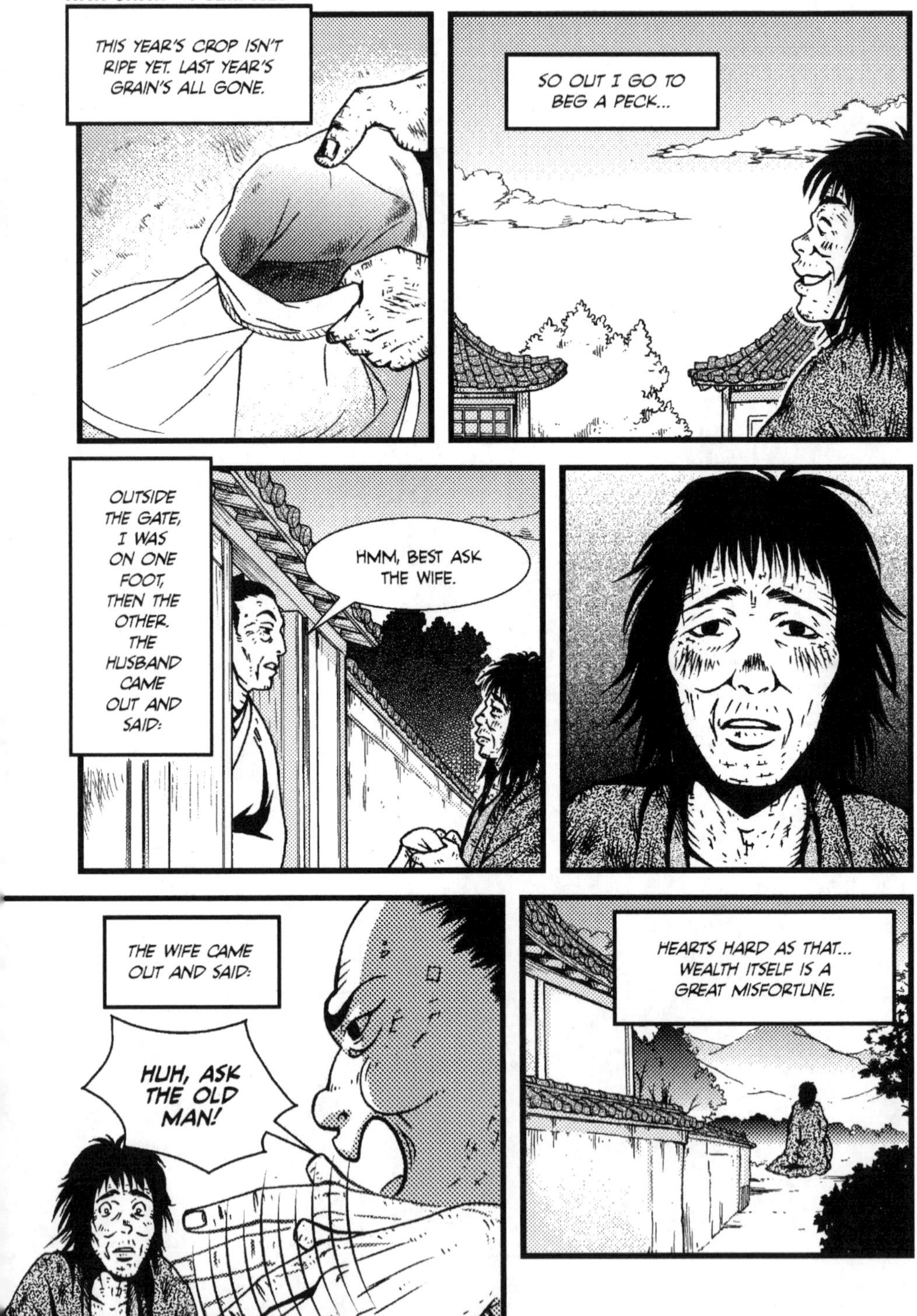
THIS YEAR'S CROP ISN'T RIPE YET. LAST YEAR'S GRAIN'S ALL GONE.
SO OUT I GO TO BEG A PECK...
OUTSIDE THE GATE, I WAS ON ONE FOOT, THEN THE OTHER. THE HUSBAND CAME OUT AND SAID:
HMM, BEST ASK THE WIFE.
THE WIFE CAME OUT AND SAID:
HUH, ASK THE OLD MAN!
HEARTS HARD AS THAT... WEALTH ITSELF IS A GREAT MISFORTUNE.

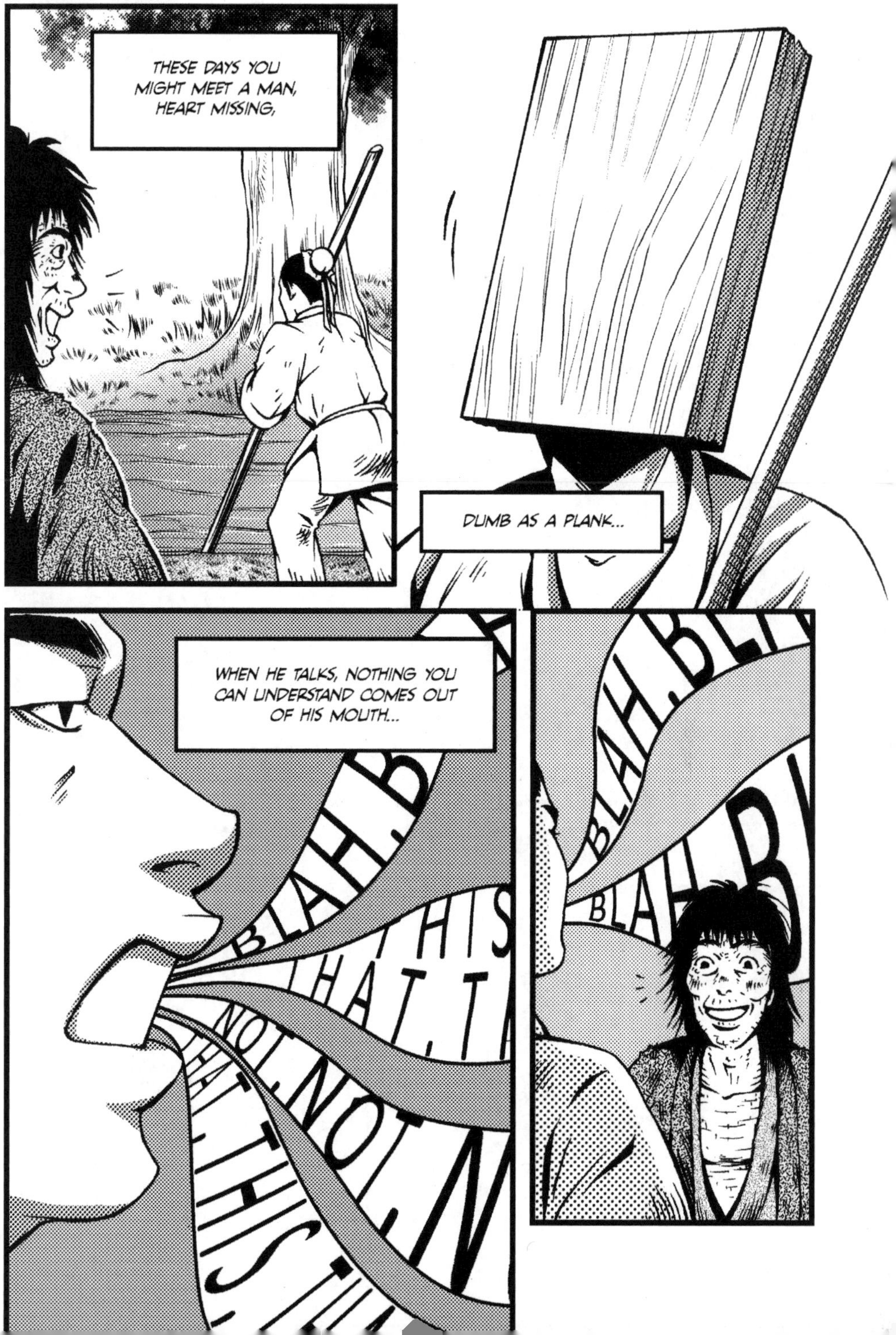
THESE DAYS YOU MIGHT MEET A MAN, HEART MISSING,
DUMB AS A PLANK...
WHEN HE TALKS, NOTHING YOU CAN UNDERSTAND COMES OUT OF HIS MOUTH...
BLAH.
THIS
THAT.
NOT.NOT.
THAT
THIS
BLAH.
BLAH

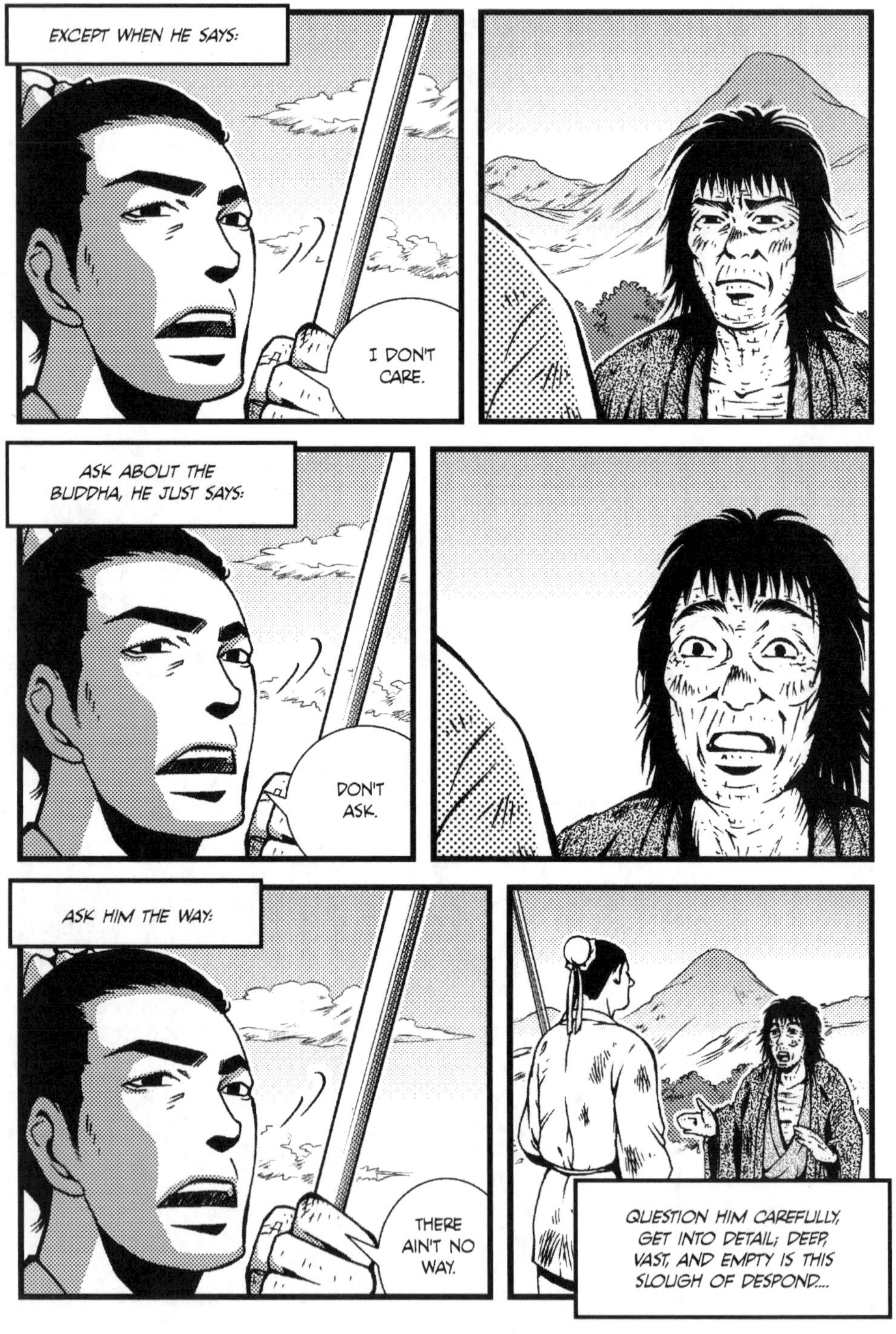
EXCEPT WHEN HE SAYS:
I DON'T CARE.
ASK ABOUT THE BUDDHA, HE JUST SAYS:
DON'T ASK.
ASK HIM THE WAY:
THERE AIN'T NO WAY.
QUESTION HIM CAREFULLY, GET INTO DETAIL; DEEP, VAST, AND EMPTY IS THIS SLOUGH OF DESPOND....

HAN SHAN - POEM LXVI

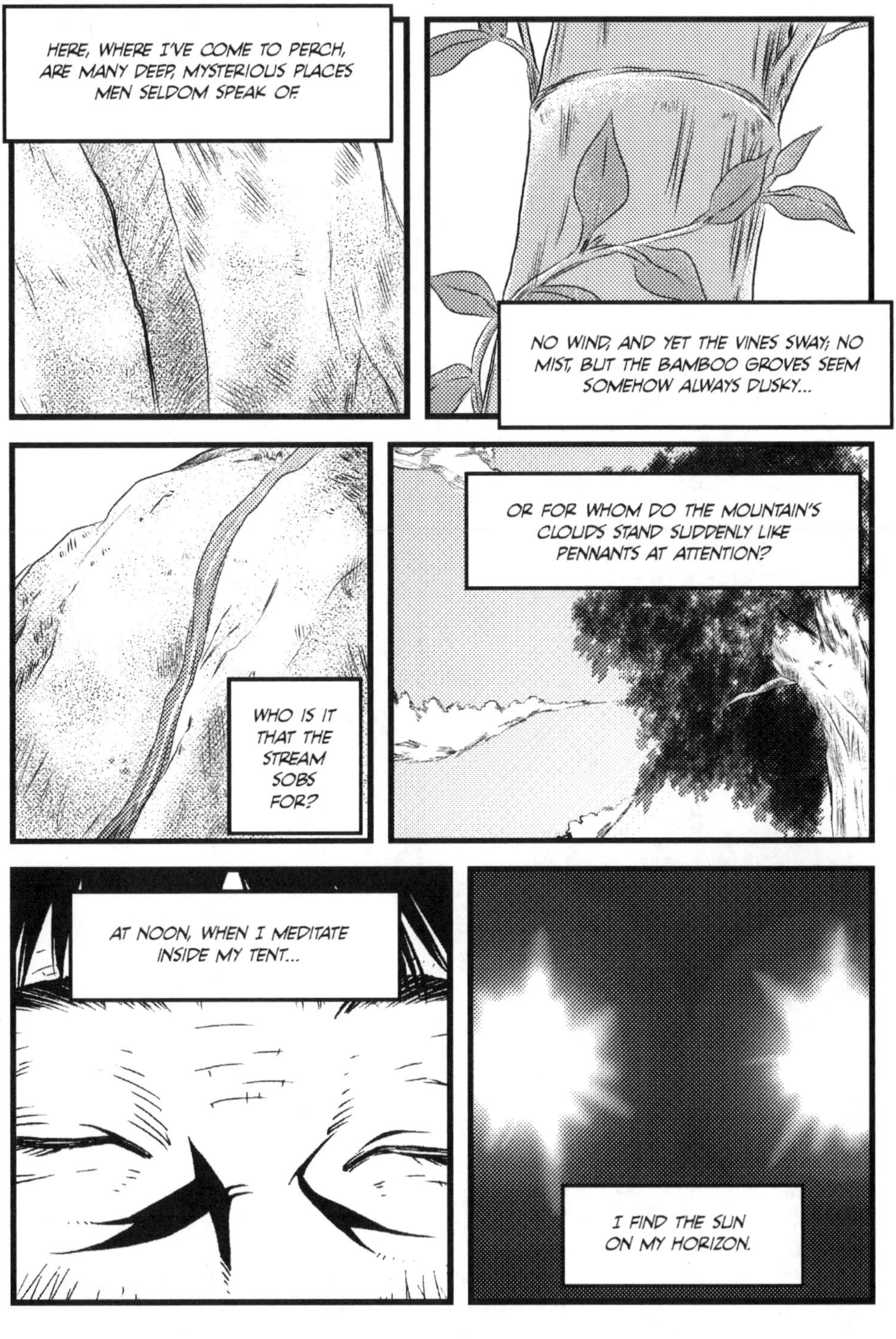
HERE, WHERE I'VE COME TO PERCH, ARE MANY DEEP, MYSTERIOUS PLACES MEN SELDOM SPEAK OF.
NO WIND, AND YET THE VINES SWAY; NO MIST, BUT THE BAMBOO GROVES SEEM SOMEHOW ALWAYS DUSKY...
WHO IS IT THAT THE STREAM SOBS FOR?
OR FOR WHOM DO THE MOUNTAIN'S CLOUDS STAND SUDDENLY LIKE PENNANTS AT ATTENTION?
AT NOON, WHEN I MEDITATE INSIDE MY TENT...
I FIND THE SUN ON MY HORIZON.

HAN SHAN - POEM LXIX

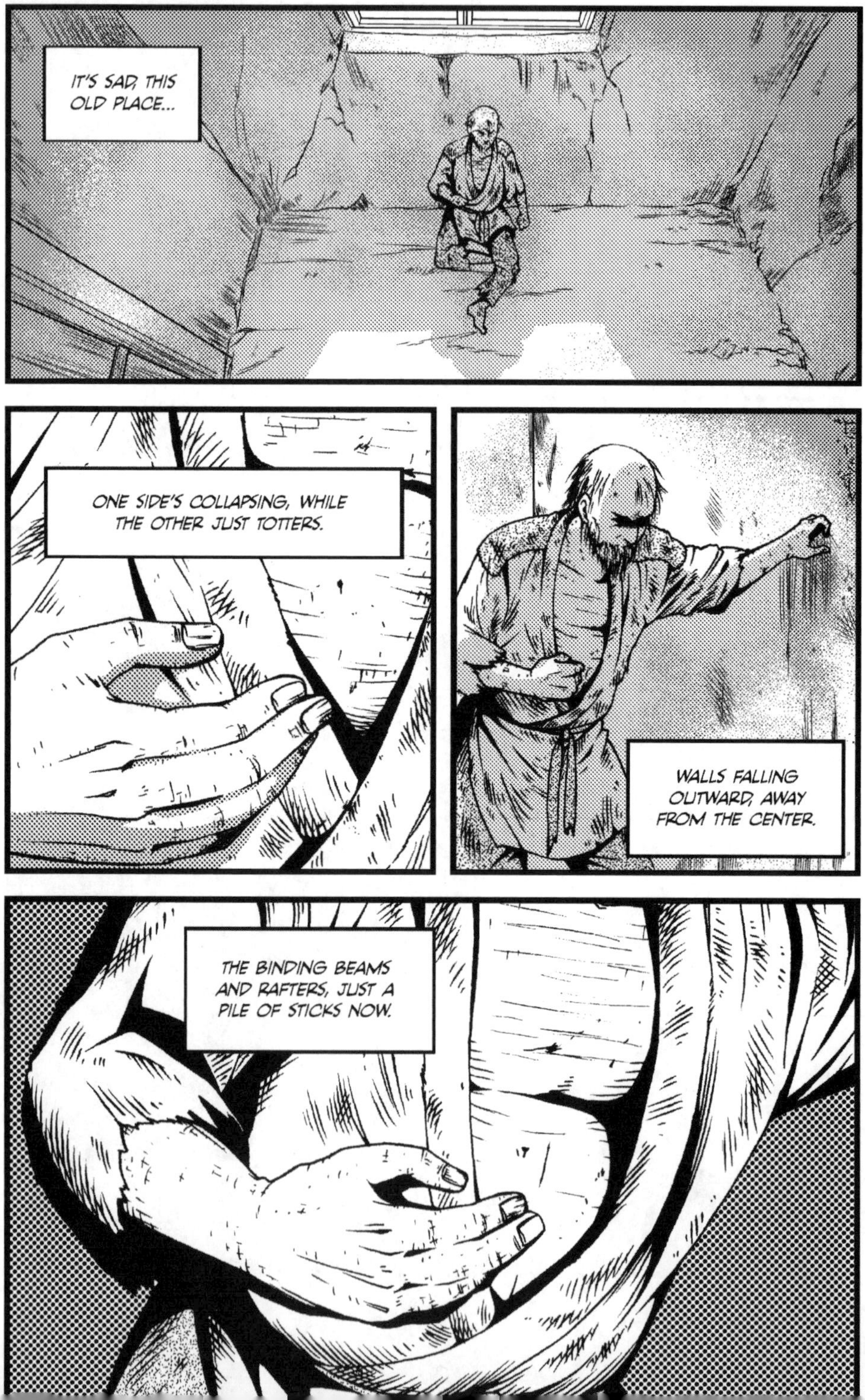
IT'S SAD, THIS OLD PLACE...
ONE SIDE'S COLLAPSING, WHILE THE OTHER JUST TOTTERS.
WALLS FALLING OUTWARD, AWAY FROM THE CENTER.
THE BINDING BEAMS AND RAFTERS, JUST A PILE OF STICKS NOW.

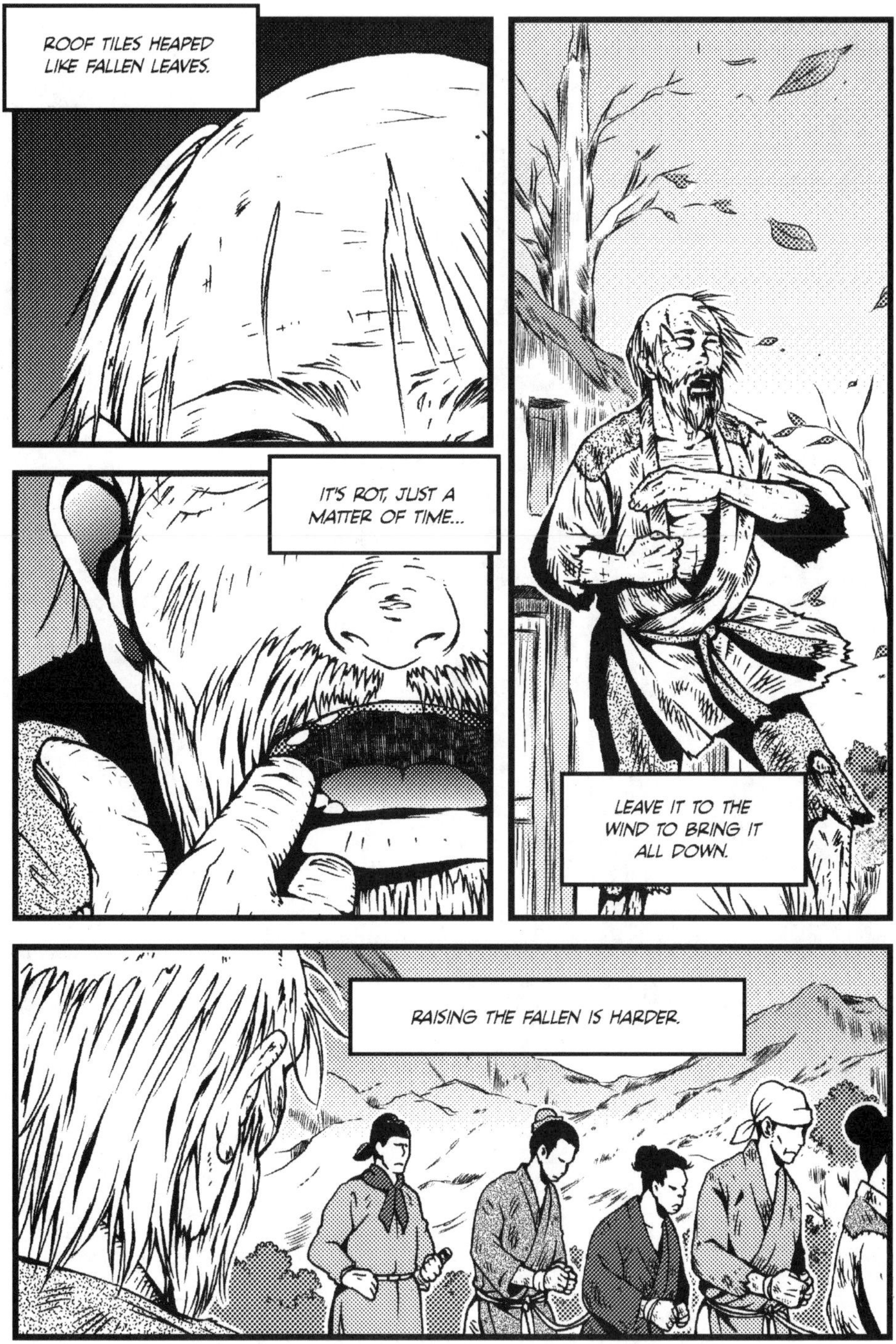
ROOF TILES HEAPED LIKE FALLEN LEAVES.
IT'S ROT, JUST A MATTER OF TIME...
LEAVE IT TO THE WIND TO BRING IT ALL DOWN.
RAISING THE FALLEN IS HARDER.

HAN SHAN - POEM LXXII

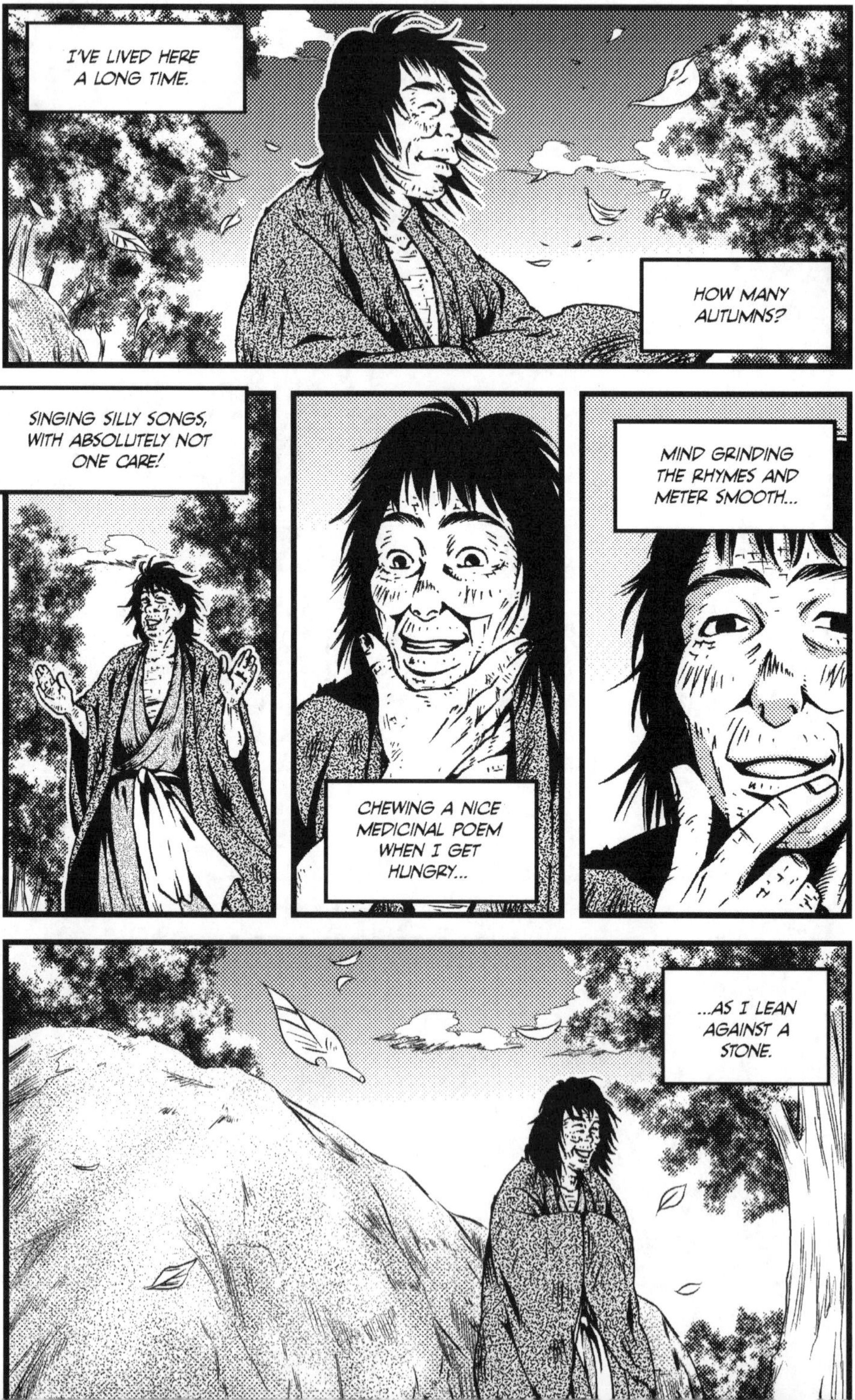
I'VE LIVED HERE A LONG TIME.
HOW MANY AUTUMNS?
SINGING SILLY SONGS, WITH ABSOLUTELY NOT ONE CARE!
CHEWING A NICE MEDICINAL POEM WHEN I GET HUNGRY...
MIND GRINDING THE RHYMES AND METER SMOOTH...
...AS I LEAN AGAINST A STONE.

HAN SHAN - POEM LXXXVIII

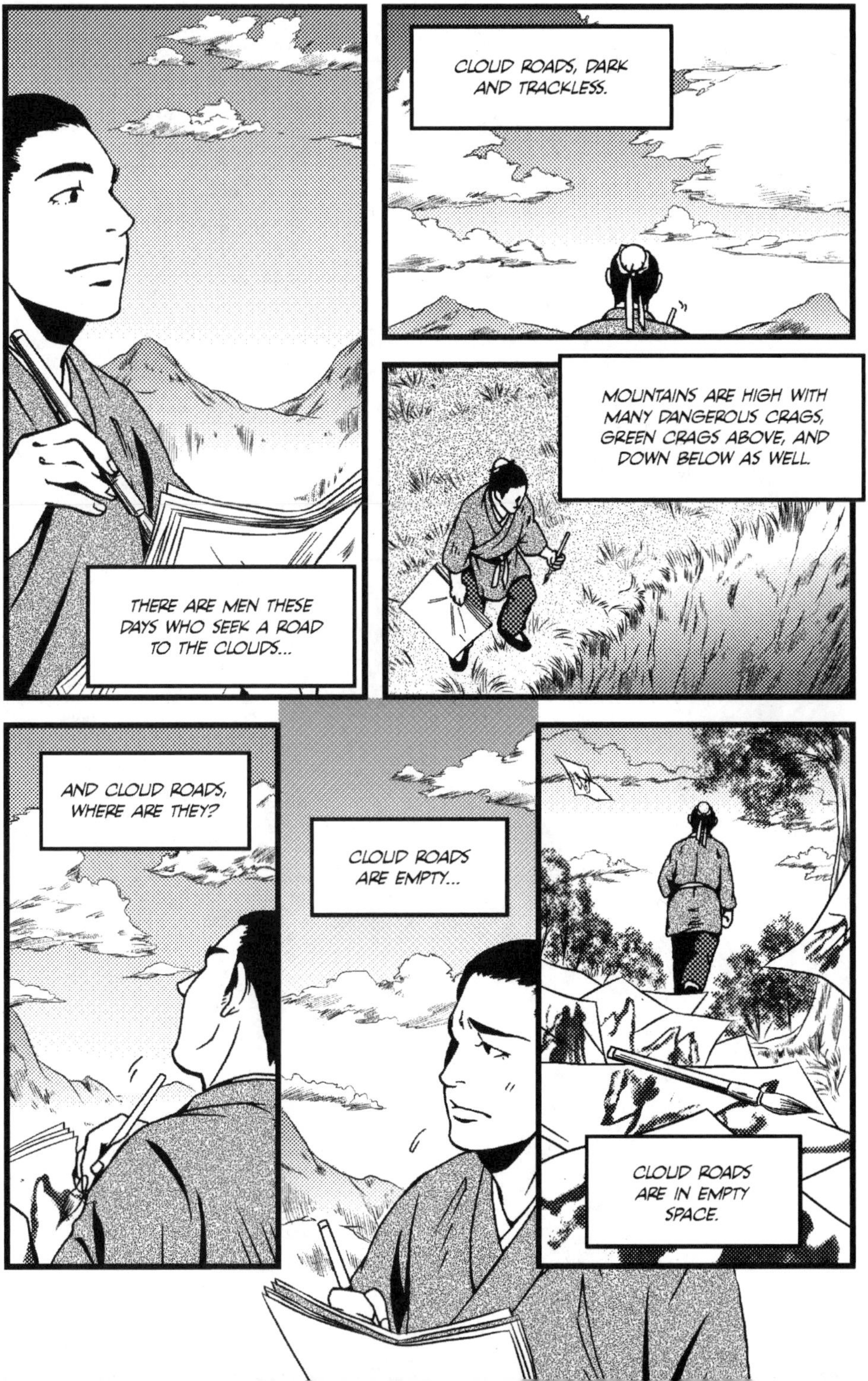
THERE ARE MEN THESE DAYS WHO SEEK A ROAD TO THE CLOUDS...
CLOUD ROADS, DARK AND TRACKLESS.
MOUNTAINS ARE HIGH WITH MANY DANGEROUS CRAGS, GREEN CRAGS ABOVE, AND DOWN BELOW AS WELL.
AND CLOUD ROADS, WHERE ARE THEY?
CLOUD ROADS ARE EMPTY...
CLOUD ROADS ARE IN EMPTY SPACE.

HAN SHAN - POEM LXXXV

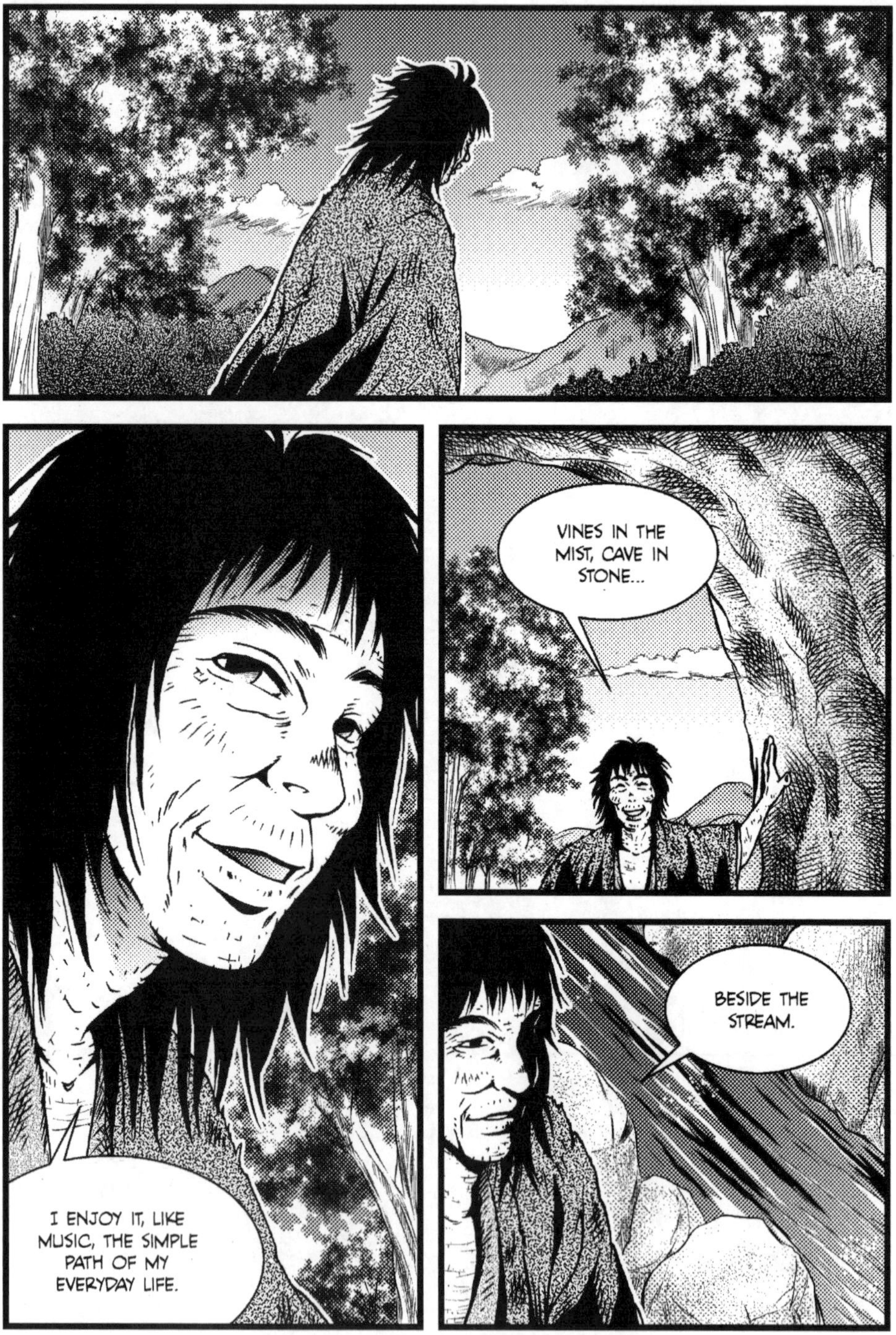
VINES IN THE MIST, CAVE IN STONE...
BESIDE THE STREAM.
I ENJOY IT, LIKE MUSIC, THE SIMPLE PATH OF MY EVERYDAY LIFE.

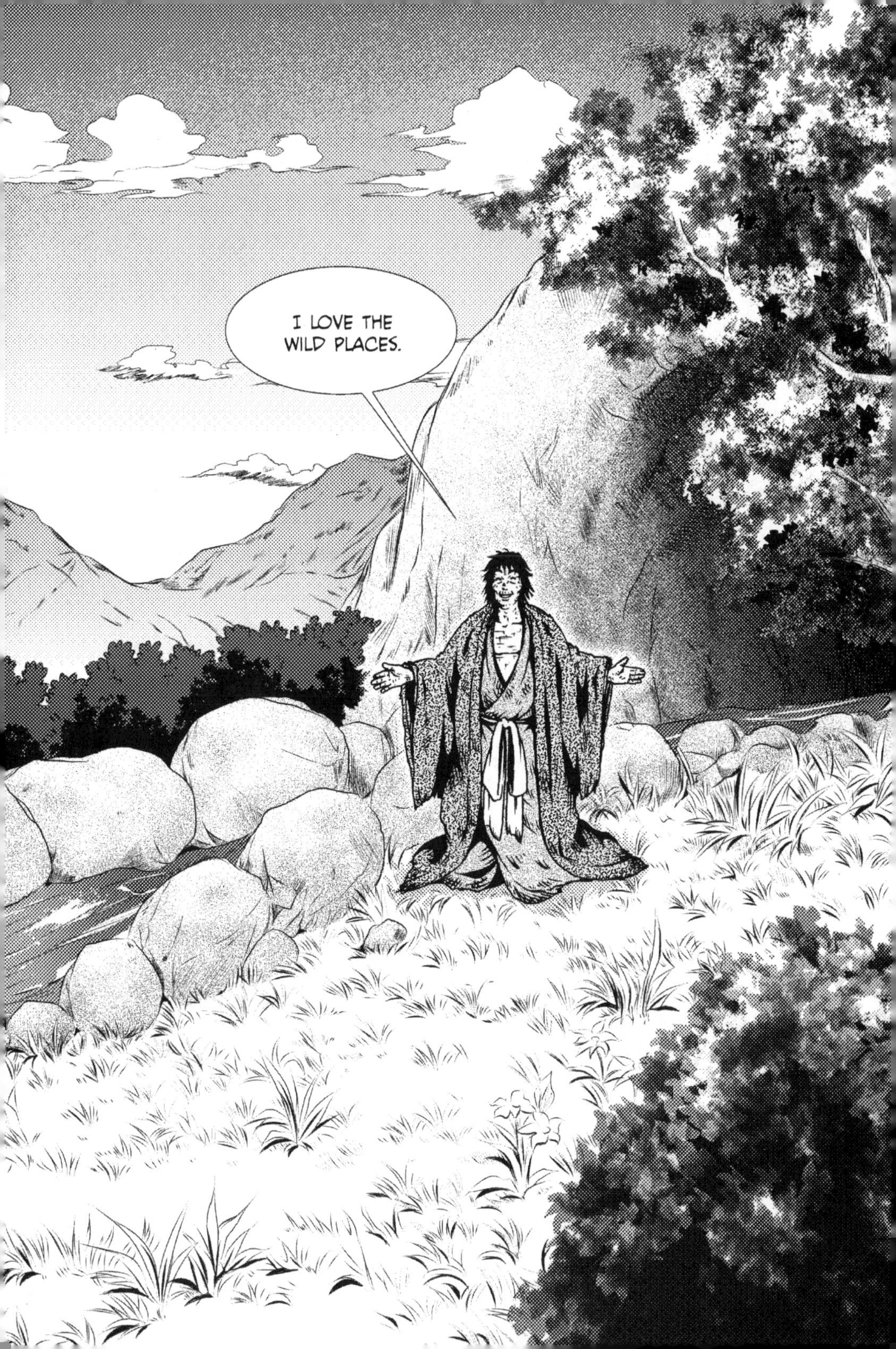
I LOVE THE
WILD PLACES.

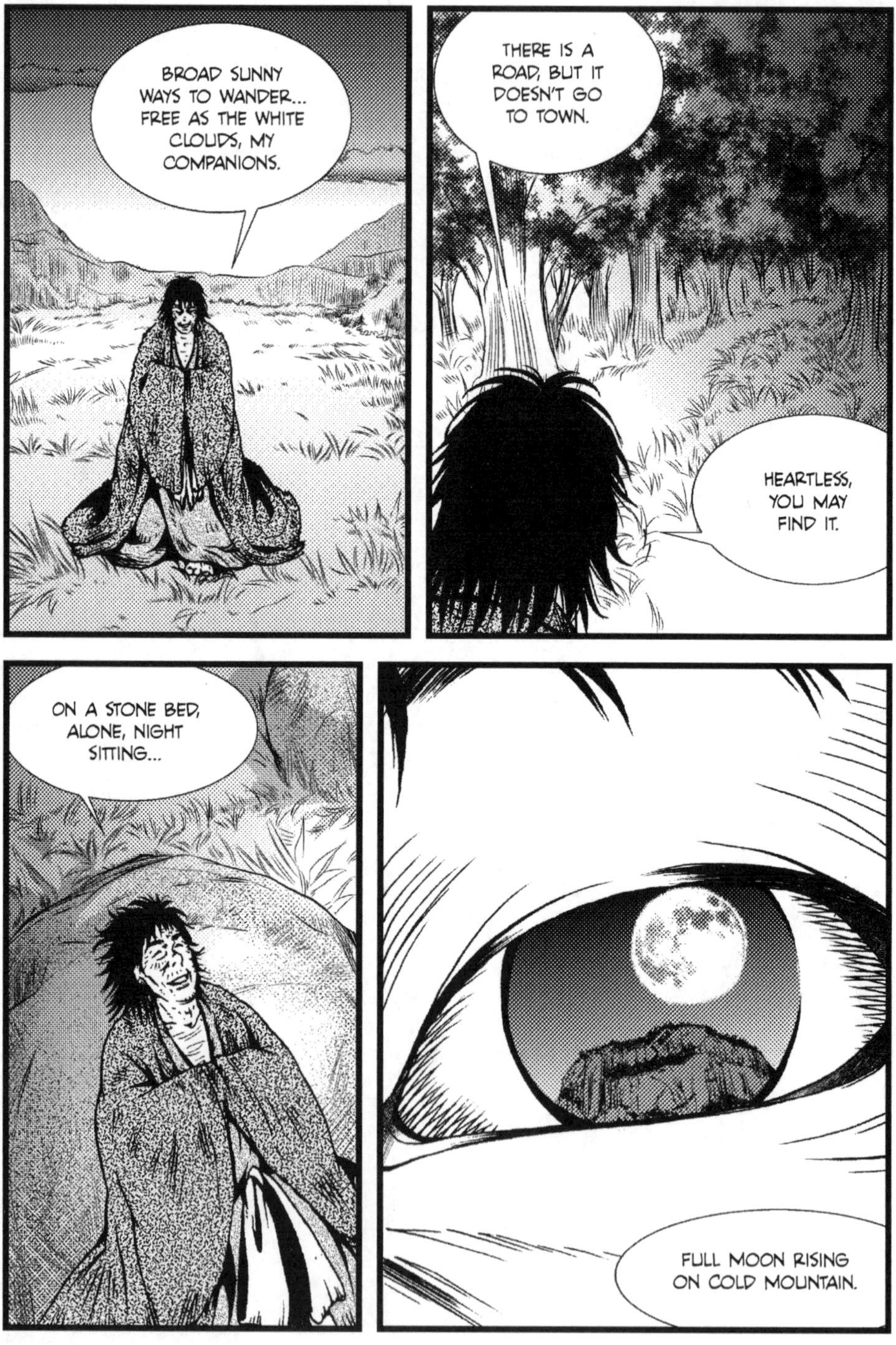
BROAD SUNNY WAYS TO WANDER... FREE AS THE WHITE CLOUDS, MY COMPANIONS.
THERE IS A ROAD, BUT IT DOESN'T GO TO TOWN.
HEARTLESS, YOU MAY FIND IT.
ON A STONE BED, ALONE, NIGHT SITTING...
FULL MOON RISING ON COLD MOUNTAIN.

SHIH TE - POEM XVII

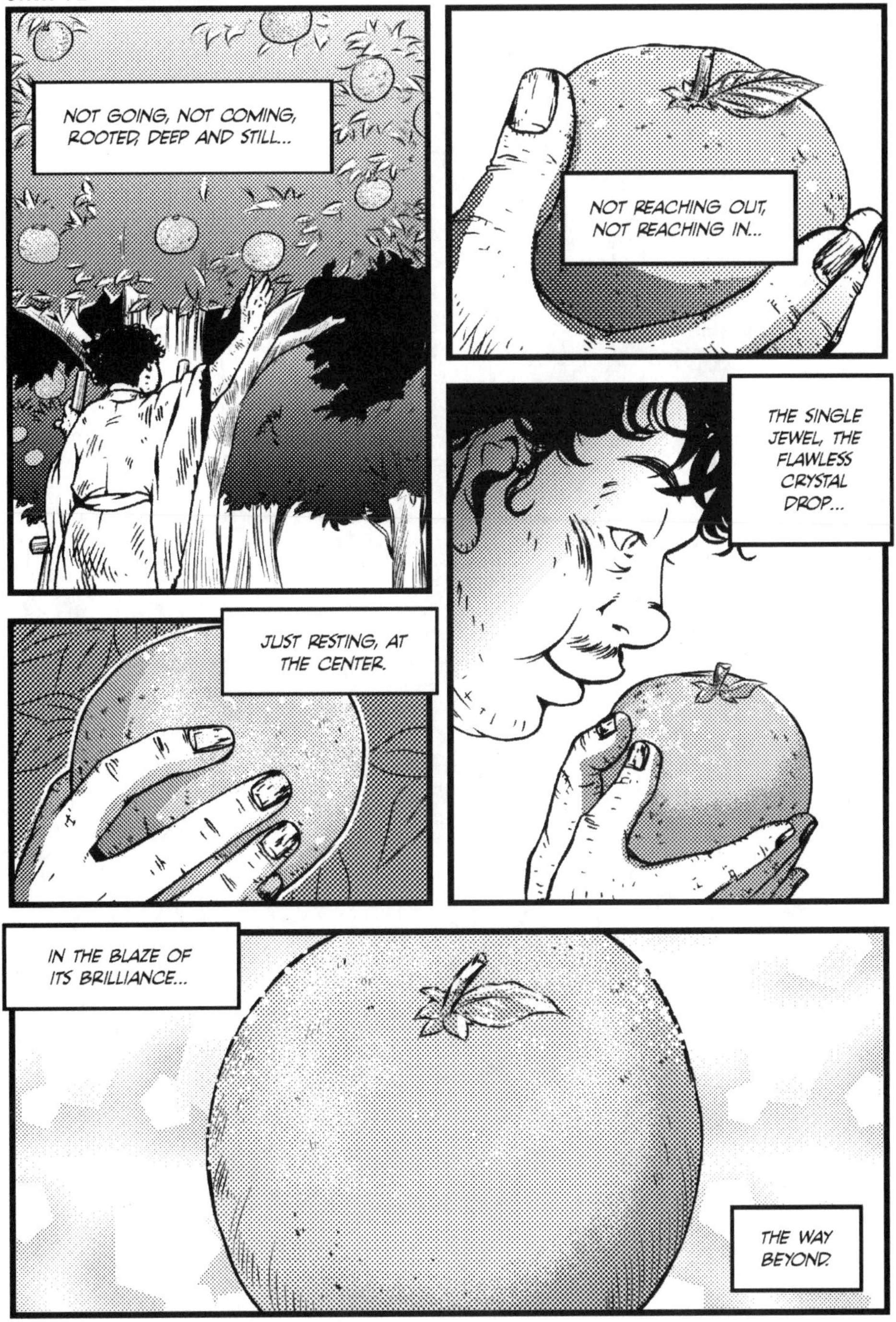
NOT GOING, NOT COMING, ROOTED, DEEP AND STILL...
NOT REACHING OUT, NOT REACHING IN...
JUST RESTING, AT THE CENTER.
THE SINGLE JEWEL, THE FLAWLESS CRYSTAL DROP...
IN THE BLAZE OF ITS BRILLIANCE...
THE WAY BEYOND.

SHIH TE - POEM XV

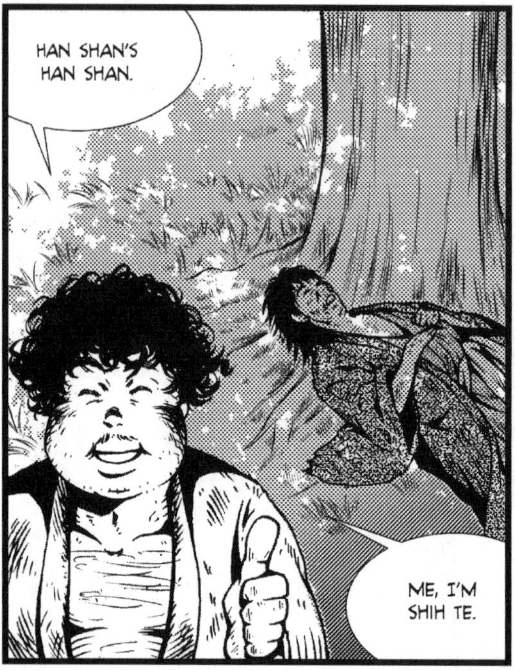
HAN SHAN'S HAN SHAN.
ME, I'M SHIH TE.

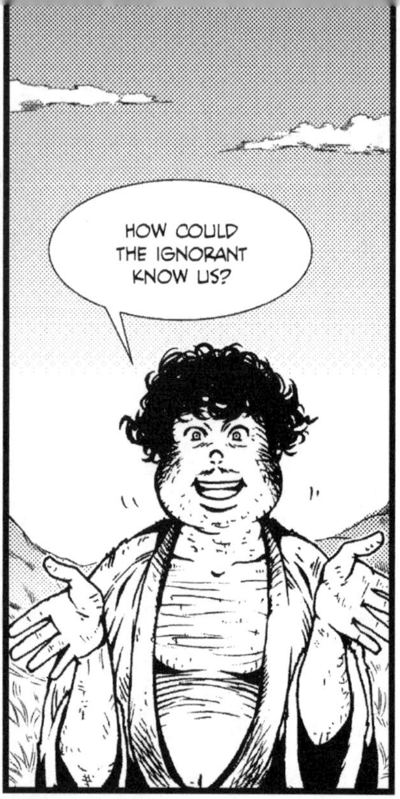
HOW COULD THE IGNORANT KNOW US?

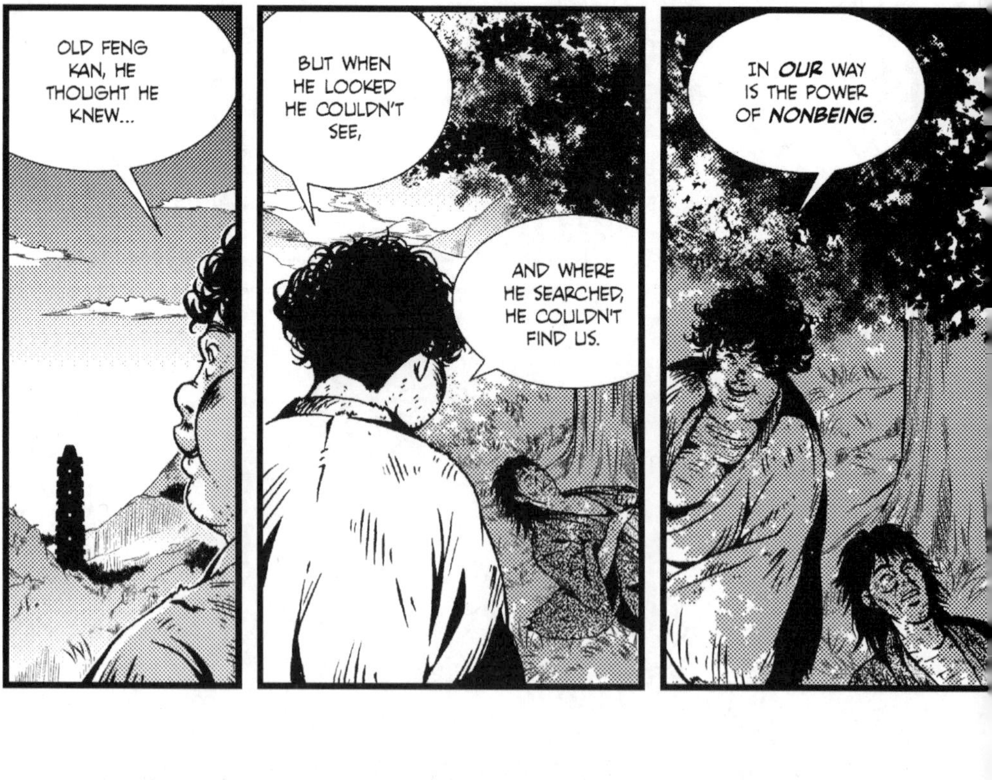
OLD FENG KAN, HE THOUGHT HE KNEW...
BUT WHEN HE LOOKED HE COULDN'T SEE,
AND WHERE HE SEARCHED, HE COULDN'T FIND US.
IN OUR WAY IS THE POWER OF NONBEING.

SHIH TE - POEM XVI

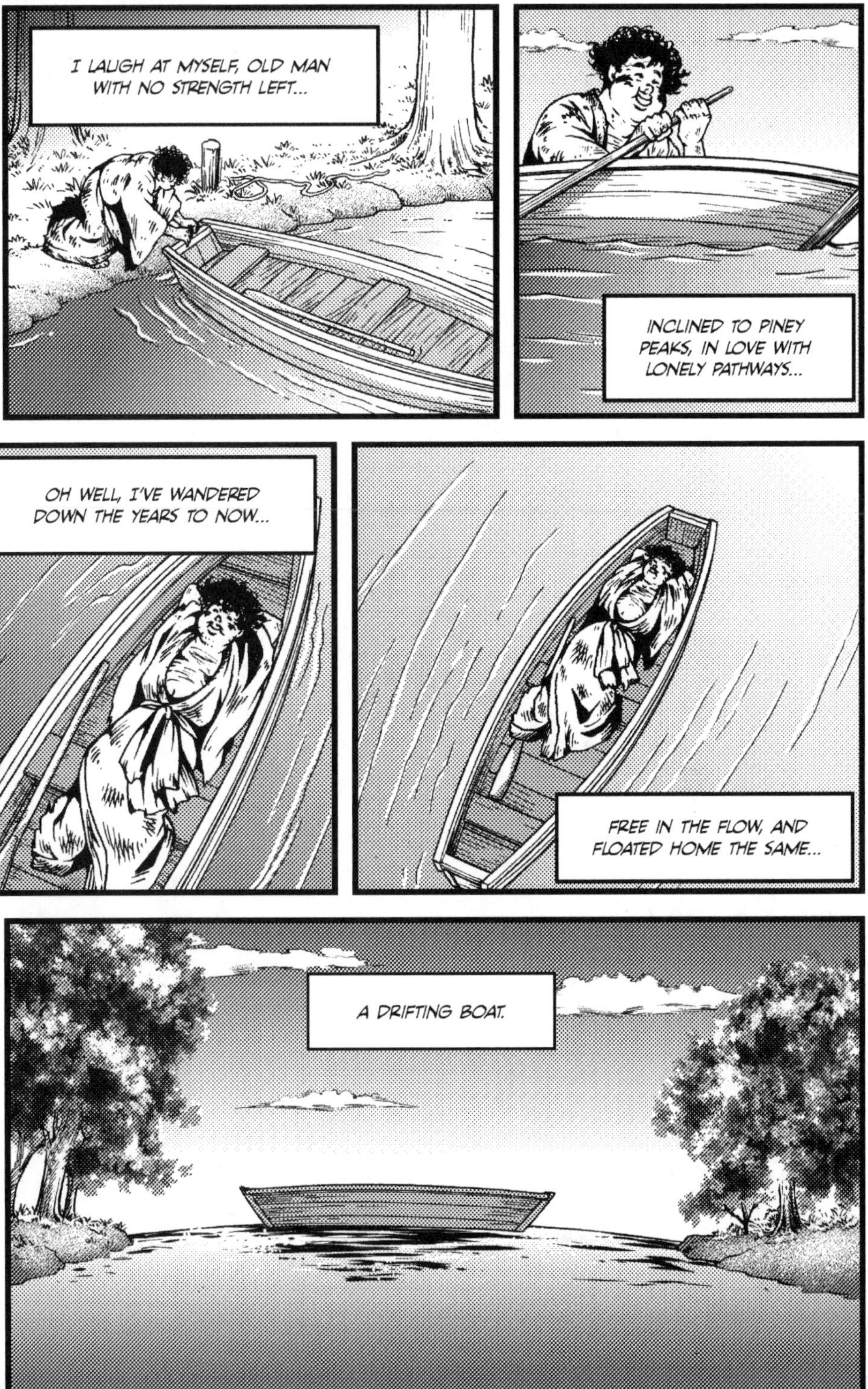
I LAUGH AT MYSELF, OLD MAN WITH NO STRENGTH LEFT...
INCLINED TO PINEY PEAKS, IN LOVE WITH LONELY PATHWAYS...
OH WELL, I'VE WANDERED DOWN THE YEARS TO NOW...
FREE IN THE FLOW, AND FLOATED HOME THE SAME...
A DRIFTING BOAT.

HAN SHAN · POEM XCV

I LIVE ON THE MOUNTAIN
NO ONE KNOWS.

AMONG WHITE CLOUDS
ETERNAL PERFECT SILENCE.

About the Author and Illustrator

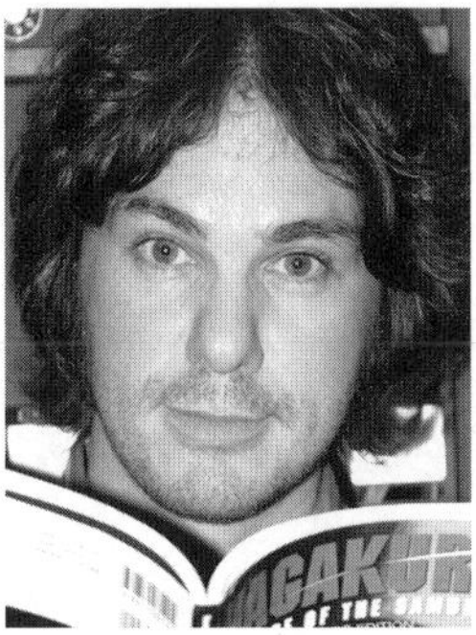
HAGAKURE

SEAN MICHAEL WILSON is a Scottish comic book writer who lives in Japan. He has published numerous comics and graphic novels with a variety of U.S., U.K., and Japanese publishers, including *Hagakure, The Book of Five Rings,* and *The 47 Ronin*. He is also the editor of the critically acclaimed *Ax: Alternative Manga*.

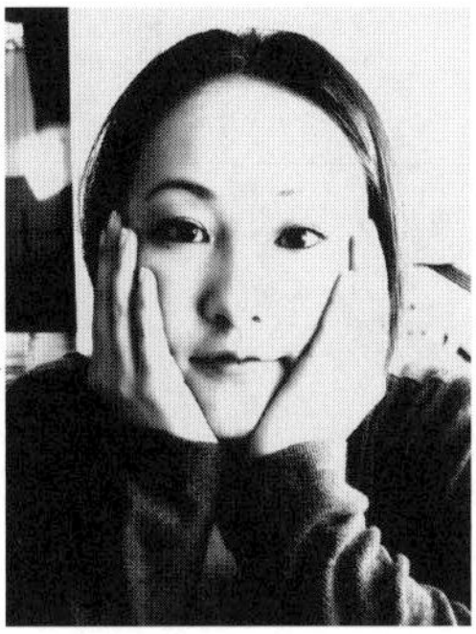

AKIKO SHIMOJIMA is a comic artist from Tokyo, Japan, who started her career as a university student in the U.S. Her comics have been published by a number of Japanese companies. In 2011, she drew two strips for charitable book projects from the U.S. and the U.K. to benefit the victims of the earthquake and tsunami disaster in Japan. She is also the illustrator of Sean Michael Wilson's *The 47 Ronin*.

Also Available from Shambhala Publications

Graphic Novels by Sean Michael Wilson

THE BOOK OF FIVE RINGS

"Truly a tribute to the original [classic]. There is a tremendous amount of depth and insight into this work, an exploration of the five elements of life (the 'five rings' of the title) that represent the cosmic Buddha. Readers get complex but eminently readable explorations of each ring and are led to see them all together as an overriding philosophy that enriches and broadens the life of any reader."
                                —Jason Sacks, *Comics Bulletin*

"This graphic adaptation of Musashi's seventeenth-century treatise on the martial arts makes careful, effective use of imagery to emphasize both the narrative and instructional aspects of the original text. . . . Musashi's lessons, in their focus on preparation and mindfulness, can easily be applied to most areas of life. Kutsuwada's art is delicate and clean, balancing the physiological dynamics of swordplay with a clear-eyed appreciation of Musashi's natural environment. An engaging, thoughtful update of what could be esoteric."
                                —*Publishers Weekly*

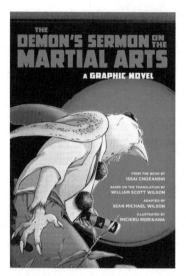

THE
DEMON'S SERMON ON THE
MARTIAL ARTS
A GRAPHIC NOVEL
FROM THE BOOK BY
ISSAI CHOZANSHI
BASED ON THE TRANSLATION BY
WILLIAM SCOTT WILSON
ADAPTED BY
SEAN MICHAEL WILSON
ILLUSTRATED BY
MICHIRU MORIKAWA

THE DEMON'S SERMON ON THE MARTIAL ARTS

"As a book of philosophy, it's fascinating; a dreamlike exploration of consciousness, life, and death. Michiru Morikawa's artwork is the perfect match for the text, her eerie, detailed illustrations—especially the lovely renderings of various animals—perfectly fitting the poetic feel. Recommended."

—Jason Thompson, *Otaku USA*

"Wilson and Morikawa capture all the wisdom and beauty of these original texts and enhance them with the visual vitality and playful charms of modern manga. Their faithful retellings of these allegorical fables and philosophical reflections prove how timeless and rewarding they truly are."

—Paul Gravett, editor of *1001 Comics You Must Read before You Die*

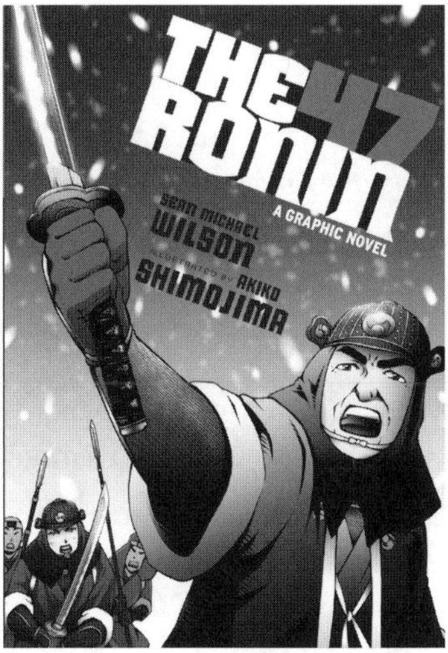
THE 47 RONIN
A GRAPHIC NOVEL
SEAN MICHAEL WILSON
AKIKO SHIMOJIMA

THE 47 RONIN

"A masterful retelling of one of the greatest stories in Japanese culture. An engrossing, engaging, emotional, and unforgettable epic."

–Jonathan Ross, BBC television presenter

"Wilson uses exactly the right scenes to tell this famous story, creating a quick, engaging read."

–Library Journal

"A dignified telling of a dignified story. It's violent when it needs to be, precise and calm when it's called for, and never once loses focus."

–BleedingCool.com

"Readers interested in accurate Japanese history rather than Hollywood embellishment will enjoy this well-done retelling of the legendary event."

–The Japan Times

宮本武蔵
MUSASHI
SEAN MICHAEL WILSON
Illustrated by
MICHIRU MORIKAWA

MUSASHI

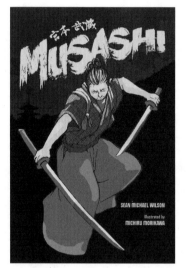

"If you are into the martial arts, this is a book that should be in your personal library—along with *The Book of Five Rings: A Graphic Novel*. A beautifully fully illustrated book. 5 Stars."

–Joseph J. Truncale, author of *The Samurai Soul*

"Based on William Scott Wilson's biography *The Lone Samurai*, this work includes much historical material. The detailed black-and-white artwork provides a strong sense of the era. Well-drawn facial expressions and body language convey emotions in the often wordless art panels. . . . Pacing is deliberate, examining milestones in Musashi's life. The man himself remains enigmatic, shown speaking in only a few panels. Readers expecting only duels and bloodshed will be surprised by Musashi's disciplined, meditative qualities. This dichotomy of developing technical skills with sword as well as an enlightened and philosophical mind will appeal to fans of Star Wars's lightsaber-wielding Jedi and their Jedi way."

–*School Library Journal*

"Morikawa's art, with its atmospheric compositions, gives the book a feeling of dignity and grace. Wilson and Morikawa also do a good job conveying Musashi's strategies even in short, two- to three-page fight scenes. . . . As a one-volume introduction to the real historical figure, this is a very fine synopsis."

–Jason Thompson, *Otaku USA*